Brent Eugene Barksdale, ΦBK, ATΩ

June 3, 1937–August 9, 1960

Class of 1959

The **BRENT EUGENE BARKSDALE
FUND** has made this book available to give
continuing force to Brent's profound concern
for the humanities. Both the unassailable good
will underlying his convictions and the tena-
cious courage to act upon them were an inspiration to the friends who support this Fund.

BRITISH DRAMA
1950 TO THE
PRESENT

TWAYNE'S
CRITICAL HISTORY
OF
BRITISH DRAMA

Kinley E. Roby
SERIES EDITOR
Northeastern University

BRITISH DRAMA
1950 TO THE PRESENT
A CRITICAL HISTORY

SUSAN RUSINKO
Bloomsburg University of Pennsylvania

TWAYNE PUBLISHERS • BOSTON
A Division of G. K. Hall & Co.

British Drama, 1950 to the Present: A Critical History
Susan Rusinko

Copyright 1989 by G. K. Hall & Co.
All rights reserved.
Published by Twayne Publishers
A Division of G. K. Hall & Co.
70 Lincoln Street
Boston, Massachusetts 02111

Copyediting supervised by Barbara Sutton
Book design and production by Gabrielle B. McDonald

Typeset in 10 point Bembo
by Huron Valley Graphics, Inc., Ann Arbor, Michigan

Printed on permanent/durable acid free paper
and bound in the United States of America

Library of Congress Cataloging-in-Publication Data

Rusinko, Susan.
  British drama, 1950 to the present : a critical history / Susan
Rusinko.
     p.   cm.—(Twayne's critical history of British drama)
  Bibliography: p.
  Includes index.
  ISBN 0-8057-8952-9 (alk. paper)
   1. English drama—20th century—History and criticism.   I. Title.
II. Series
PR736.R87   1989
822'.914'09—dc19   88-37951
                                                                        CIP

*To my family, mentors,
colleagues and students
whose friendship I value*

CONTENTS

ACKNOWLEDGMENTS

I am grateful to Bloomsburg University for several summer research grants; to Virginia Duck and Gerald Strauss for many hours of proofreading and valuable editorial help; to librarians at the Harvey A. Andruss Library, particularly Aaron Polonsky for his continual supply of information, as well as to reserve librarians Alice Getty, Monica Howell, and Alex Shiner for their practical and affable help in the use of microtexts; to Holly Hill for her efforts in locating photographs in London; and to Martin Gildea for his expertise on world events.

CHAPTER I

INTRODUCTION: NEW FREEDOMS

George Bernard Shaw's death in 1950 provides a conveniently arbitrary starting point for a discussion of post–World War II British drama. The date, however, that gave impetus to what has been called a stage revolution is 8 May 1956, when John Osborne's *Look Back in Anger* was staged by the English Stage Company at the Royal Court Theatre on Sloane Square in London. Overnight the Royal Court became the leading edge of experimentation, beginning a heady decade in which the proliferating new dramatists were provided opportunities to have their plays produced.

Labeled "annus mirabilis" by critics and historians of twentieth-century British drama, the year 1956 remains, more than thirty years later, the chief symbol of the new British drama; and Sloane Square has become a symbol for experimental drama, as Shaftesbury and the West End have been for the commercial productions in London's theater district. The symbolism of the year is contained in the title of the play; the play's antihero, Jimmy Porter; its author, Osborne; and the Royal Court Theatre with its driving force, the director-producer George Devine. From the depiction of the play's hero emerged such labels as the "angry young man," the "angry theater," and the "new wave." John Russell Taylor's book *The Angry Theatre* (1962), revised and retitled *Anger and After* (1969), confirmed the label for the new wave of dramatists that dominated the stages of England for the next decade. The new wave, as it receded and then swelled again, bifurcated into the "first wave" and the "second wave." Another book by Taylor, *The Second Wave* (1971), pointed out the directions of a second decade of new dramatists.

Unless otherwise noted, the dates of plays mentioned in the text are dates of performance.

Ironically, although *Look Back in Anger,* in its immediate effect on audiences and on younger writers like Harold Pinter and Tom Stoppard, went beyond existing boundaries for strong emotion and language on the stage, it broke no new stylistic ground. Conventional in structure and style, it suffers by comparison with later plays by Osborne and with the more daringly experimental dramas of Pinter, Joe Orton, N. F. Simpson, and Stoppard. It is important to distinguish between the literary quality of *Look Back in Anger* and the strong impact of its first production on the time, particularly on the new dramatists.

According to Arnold Hinchliffe, "what John Osborne and the Angries did . . . was to break through into conventional theater by their sheer vitality, by using language that seemed contemporary (and often provincial), by encouraging young dramatists into believing that if they wrote plays they would be produced, and by showing that the theatre was a place where contemporary problems could be discussed."[1]

Although attempts have been made to diminish the importance of the annus mirabilis, the historian Allardyce Nicoll sees no justification for them. He contends that "despite the significance of this production, a full understanding of its force depends upon an appreciation of the conditions amid which it came into being, conditions which have determined the characteristic forms of the contemporary theatre."[2] Those conditions, for Nicoll, include the popularization of television, a new spirit of freedom for younger dramatists, and the launching in 1940 of CEMA (the Council for the Encouragement of Music and the Arts), which was replaced in 1945 by the Arts Council of Great Britain. Subsidies to theatres, acting companies, and young dramatists grew annually, and the arts flourished, setting the stage literally and figuratively for the advent of Porter, Osborne, George Devine, and the Royal Court.

"Presented at court" (as John Russell Taylor aptly comments) in addition to John Osborne were the new writers Ann Jellicoe, N. F. Simpson, John Arden, and Arnold Wesker; they were among the earlier writers for whom the Royal Court functioned as the modern counterpart to the patrons of earlier times. The Arts Council served as financial patron to theaters as well as to individual writers. Even into the next decade, the Royal Court introduced dramatists like David

Storey and Edward Bond and presented the plays of major dramatists discovered elsewhere, such as Harold Pinter.

But the Royal Court, however important its influence, was only one of many private stage companies that performed the same function. One of the most famous of the early groups was the Theatre Workshop of Joan Littlewood. Many small private stage companies were formed to circumvent the censorship law in effect for several hundred years. Not until 1968 was the law finally repealed.

Adding their part to the new forces at work, provincial and university playhouses discovered and nurtured new writers. Pinter, for example, made his debut in Bristol, and Oxford's student production of *Rosencrantz and Guildenstern Are Dead* at the Edinburgh Festival in 1966 called the attention of London and the world to Tom Stoppard. The tiny Traverse Theatre in Edinburgh became one of the more important showcases for new writers.

Far from least in this brief introduction to the revitalization of drama is the slow development of England's two national companies—the creation of the National Theatre and the expansion of the Royal Shakespeare Company of Stratford-upon-Avon to a location in London, long only dreams of artists and managers. The 1970s saw the opening of a complex of three theaters for the National—the Cottesloe, the Olivier, and the Lyttelton. Then in the 1980s the Barbican Centre in the City was completed, and the Barbican Theatre, along with its tiny Pit Theatre, deep in the bowels of the complex, became the official London home of the Royal Shakespeare Company (RSC). Both national companies are heavily dependent on subsidies from the government and have periodically experienced financial problems as they have wrestled with conservative politicians who see the arts as a likely place to trim budgets. Along with their productions of traditional dramas, the National and the RSC have steadily accommodated experimental works at their small houses, the Cottesloe and the Pit.

With the new theaters battling their way in an economically strapped society, the commercial theaters—London's "Broadway," known as the West End or Shaftesbury, is located in the Picadilly area—remained stolidly in place. On occasion, experimental plays that proved successful in "off-Shaftesbury" productions were transferred to the commercial houses in the West End.

Not to be ignored as an important force in the new era is the opportunity that television and film provided to writers. Unlike their American counterparts, English writers wrote television scripts of the same quality as their stage plays. Television became not only a means to develop their writing skills but, in its artistic merits, at times an equal partner with the stage. Witness John Mortimer, Alan Plater, John Hopkins, and Frederic Raphael, whose reputations rest more comfortably on their many television adaptations and original television plays—for example, Mortimer's *Brideshead Revisited* and *Rumpole of the Bailey* and Raphael's *Glittering Prizes*—than on their stage plays.

The symbolic anger of Jimmy Porter's generation has deep roots in the mid-1950s economic, political, and cultural malaise that permeated the very character of a once proud and powerful English civilization. In fact, the pessimism regarding Western civilization that Shaw has so powerfully dramatized in his post–World War I play *Heartbreak House* seems to have become an actuality in the post–World War II decades. England's heavily taxed economy, desperately struggling to regain a decent standard of living for everyone, has made it virtually impossible for Osborne's Jimmy Porter, a college graduate, to do anything more than operate a sweets stall in the dreary Midlands. For him, there is not even any clear, identifiable object for his anger, and so he explodes with rage at those nearest him—his wife, Alison, and his friend, Cliff. Jimmy's rage moved a generation of audiences as the prevailing theater had not been able to do.

The malaise in the theater was not unlike that of the economy. According to Kenneth Tynan, it was "quite necessary—if one were to be eligible for dramatic treatment—to have an annual income of more than £3,000 net or to be murdered in the house of somebody who had."[3] The polite, middle-class drawing-room plays of J. B. Priestley, Noel Coward, and Terence Rattigan dominated the plays of the West End. There were also the poetic dramas of T. S. Eliot and Christopher Fry, who had attempted to reinvigorate the language of the stage with their poetry, but these appealed for the most part to academically elite audiences. Although small changes characterized the later dramas of both Coward and Rattigan as they adapted to changes in the times, essentially nothing had changed. It was Osborne who became the catalyst for change on the British stage for the next two generations.

Porter's lacerating expression of hatred for the entrenched class system broke the ground rules of the prevailing middle-class drama.

International events of the 1950s only fed the malaise reigning on the economic and cultural fronts. In 1956 the invasion of Hungary by the Soviet Union and, closer to home, the Suez debacle placed in sharp focus England's decline as an international power and the criticism of her colonialist history. Thus at home and abroad dissatisfactions increased and developed into the anger that Jimmy Porter unleashed that year, later to be revived in the intellectualized fury of the more outspoken politicized dramatists such as Howard Brenton and David Hare.

On the economic front, an important piece of legislation, the Local Government Act of 1948, provided sorely needed help for struggling writers. Local authorities were given power to levy a tax from which repertory theaters could be subsidized, providing an alternative to the commercial touring companies so vividly dramatized in Priestley's work *Lost Empires,* televised in the 1980s. In addition, England's frequently controversial Arts Council began to subsidize promising new playwrights. Large numbers of dramatists from the working and lower-middle classes joined the ranks of the traditional writers. They seemed at times to come in droves. In fact, much of the revolutionary drama in its rich variety of approaches attacked not only the existing class system but the very values at its base.

As the cutting edge of the new drama, the Royal Court fostered individual writers—Osborne, Wesker, and Arden among early leaders—and set the pattern for many experimental movements and theaters, labeled "the fringe." Joan Littlewood in her theater workshops developed an important tradition, the director-producer's theater, practiced in its most radical form by Peter Brook, whose daring experiments in Shakespearean productions included a spectacularly innovative *Midsummer Night's Dream* and an existentialist interpretation of *King Lear.* Littlewood was also a strong advocate of populist drama and collaborative writing and had staged Brendan Behan's *Quare Fellow* and *Hostage* and Shelagh Delaney's *Taste of Honey* on the basis of these two traditions.

Meantime the Royal Shakespeare Theatre's Peter Hall added to the larger Aldwych Theatre in London his experimental Arts Theatre Club, and the Royal Court added its own tiny Upstairs Theatre to the main performing auditorium. Even Americans such as Charles Marowitz and Ed Berman, a working colleague of Stoppard's, contributed to the people's-theater type of workshop activity.

The talents of a whole new generation of actors and actresses—Alan Bates, Kenneth Haigh, Peter O'Toole, Albert Finney, Glenda Jackson, Vanessa Redgrave, Judi Dench, Eileen Atkins, and the three Ians (Holm, McKellen, and Richardson), to name only a few among the huge number—were developed in the new plays. Established actresses and actors like Peggy Ashcroft, John Gielgud, Ralph Richardson, and Laurence Olivier integrated new roles with old.

When the energy of the new drama subsided about the middle of the 1960s, questions were asked about its noticeable decline, especially as conventional dramatists, the most traditional of whom is Robert Bolt, were being increasingly staged with commercial success. With many of the new dramatists like Osborne and Wesker also realizing success in the West End, the distinction between the experimental and the established diminished.

In 1964 George Devine, the force behind the Royal Court, commented that he didn't "want to exaggerate this famous revolution that everybody talks about." He suggested that perhaps "a period of hiatus" was at hand and talked about the desirability of "an effusion like the one of 1956" appearing "more than once every ten years." With the present blurring of distinctions "between the West End and the opposition," the energy of experimentation seemed diminished. Earlier writers "simply wrote themselves out; they became famous so quickly that they lost the impulse to break through the barrier of public indifference. And now smart magazines will print anything they care to send in. It's too easy. . . . Nowadays everybody wants to be 'with it'; there must be a place for people who don't want to be with it, because they are the people who create the 'with-its.' "[4]

As though in response to these doubts and the threat of lethargy, a second annus mirabilis occurred in 1968. First of all, it saw the repeal of the detested censorship in existence for several hundred years. No longer did theaters find it necessary to form private stage companies to circumvent the law. Writers felt free to write without fear of not having their plays staged because of frank language or scenes of nudity, violence, or homosexuality.

National and international events again conspired to encourage a second generation of agitation in drama. On the international scene, the Vietnam War was at its height, with the American widening of the war to include Cambodia. In America, following the burning of cities in 1967, the black revolution was underway. Political unrest in the United States found violent expression in the assassinations of Martin Luther King and Robert Kennedy. These assassinations were followed by the violence between police and demonstrators at the Democratic convention in Chicago. In France, the student anti–de Gaullist demonstrations evoked strong sympathy from across the English Channel. And in eastern Europe, Soviet armies marched into Czechoslovakia. Approaching its activist heights in England, the CND, the Committee for Nuclear Disarmament, was making its voice heard; it would continue into the 1980s.

The anger expressed in the first wave of postwar dramatists found new channels, this time mostly in younger playwrights who were at school or university during the earlier upheaval—at Cambridge especially, but also at less prestigious universities such as Manchester, Bradford, and East Anglia. Referring to his Manchester University days, David Edgar thinks that "the most important things that happened were nothing to do with . . . academic life at all. They were to do with being at a university in 1968—you know, bliss was it in that dawn to be alive, but to be in full-time higher education was very heaven."[5] For middle-class students like himself, the political evils of the time took clear definition.

Unlike Jimmy Porter, who has no outlet for his anger except against those he loves, the younger generation knew its targets. David Hare complained about not being allowed to wear his CND badge at his "liberal, arty public school," which was "very decadent and art-oriented."[6] Howard Brenton asserted that the fringe effort had failed in its "whole dream of an 'alternative culture.' "[7] Describing himself as "northern, working-class and puritan,"[8] Trevor Griffiths became passionately leftist, yet he feels all men are prisoners of "some sociocultural formation or other. In my case, I feel very responsible to the left, to the history of Left thought and Left action—socialist, communist, revolutionary, whatever. . . . And I've simply learned to live with the fact that that isn't going to happen, or it isn't going to happen very easily."[9] Agitational propaganda, agitprop for short, became a familiar label on both sides of the Atlantic as an expression of the new political consciousness. Edgar remains fond of what he calls his agitprop period, when he wrote plays such as *The Case of the Workers' Plane*.

In this second annus mirabilis of 1968, from which emerged a more radical, frequently anarchistic group of dramatists, an important literary event occurred: the establishment of the *Theatre Quarterly*, a journal in tune with the new writers, especially in its publication of a series of interviews with dramatists, chronicling their views on drama and politics. As an expression of the new theater voices of the seventies, it paralleled the function that had been served by *Encore*, a magazine founded in 1956 as an outlet for those of the fifties and sixties.

Ironically, one comes away from a consideration of the socially and politically committed dramatists (who outnumber by far the non-committed writers) with the realization that the three most innovative stylists have remained aloof from the ideological interests of their contemporaries. In France, Samuel Beckett made his imprint on British theater with *Waiting for Godot*. In London, Pinter, although from a working-class, north London background, still retains aesthetic distance from the controversial issues of his time. And Tom Stoppard, a naturalized Englishman, not only revels in being, as Kenneth Tynan wrote, more English than the English but also seems conservative by contrast with most of the new dramatists who criticize or condemn traditional English values and institutions.

The new drama enjoyed its share of critical support from influential voices such as Tynan's. Early on he had used a timely political reference, in accusing Terence Rattigan of being the reactionary of the modern stage. Champion of the new wave, Tynan wrote the single decidedly favorable review of *Look Back in Anger*. Later he served with Laurence Olivier as artistic director of the National Theatre. In that capacity he was involved in the first London staging of Stoppard's *Rosencrantz and Guildenstern Are Dead*. Until his death, Tynan remained an eloquent critic-chronicler of the stage revolution.

More traditional in his views of the new drama, London *Times* critic Harold Hobson listed as his great experiences in the theater Beckett's *Waiting for Godot*, Osborne's *Look Back in Anger*, Pinter's *Birthday Party*, and Peter Barnes's *Ruling Class*.

If we were to single out one influence above all others on the new drama, it would certainly be the Royal Court Theatre, which numbers among its protégés, according to John Elsom, three of the five "major dramatists of the English renaissance: Osborne, Arden and Wesker."[10] The influence of the Royal Court as a place for writers was vital, and there is little doubt that the stage revolution as it occurred would not have been possible without the Court's openness to experimental writing, so that dramatists had the necessary opportunities to fail as well as to succeed.

Although Osborne had initiated the stage revolution in 1956 by freeing the stage from the choking hold of middle-class drama, it was Pinter, Osborne's contemporary, who emerged as the leading figure among the writers of the first wave from the middle 1950s to the middle 1960s. His minimalist Beckettian style and poetic language broke with prevailing, conventional realistic modes. Ten years after Osborne's *Look Back in Anger,* the second wave can be said to have begun with the Edinburgh Festival staging of *Rosencrantz and Guildenstern Are Dead* by Stoppard. Stoppard, like Pinter, broke molds, his parodic iconoclasm consisting of dazzling reinventions of other dramatists' work and of brilliantly witty and new stage language. Osborne's importance remains historical, whereas Pinter's and Stoppard's rests on breaking new stylistic ground. All three are outsiders to the university-educated, middle-class dramatist tradition, and all started working early, Osborne and Pinter as actors and Stoppard as a news reporter.

Like Pinter, many of the new dramatists are from working or lower-middle-class backgrounds. Arnold Wesker is a son of a tailor of Russian-Jewish extraction, and Peter Terson the son of a Newcastle-upon-Tyne joiner. N. F. Simpson's father was a London glassblower and David Storey's a Yorkshire miner. Middle-class dramatists like Peter Nichols, who trained at a teacher's college—not quite as accepted as the universities—are also a part of the new wave. And from the establishmentarian backgrounds of Cambridge and Oxford came writers such as Christopher Hampton, John Mortimer, Anthony and Peter Shaffer, and David Hare.

But the infusion of the lower classes as serious subjects in plays—subjects heretofore treated pretty much in comedies and satires—came with Osborne. In places such as the Shaw Theatre, dramas of, by, and for the poor were performed, for example, Terson's *Zigger-Zagger,* set in a soccer stadium. Drama even took to the streets, as in Ed Berman's company, Dogg's Troupe. Treated up to then by writers like John Galsworthy as victims of social injustice to be pitied, the Jimmy Porters now began to fight back, articulating their ideas and emotions with impressive clarity and vehemence. This breaking down of class barriers on stage became the rallying cry of the new dramatists and of the theaters that encouraged them.

Many of the experiments entered the mainstream, gradually ushering in a time of consolidation, the hallmark of the 1980s. Even the two most spectacularly innovative dramatists (at least on the international stage scene)—Harold Pinter and Tom Stoppard—became "establishment," and some, as in the case of Pinter, have turned their energies to directing. One indication of the absence of the energetic innovativeness that characterized the previous decades is the large number of introspective plays about dramatists, such as Stoppard's *The Real Thing* (1982), which deals with the subject of the artist and his art. As though to underscore this introversion, a new play, *A Piece of My Mind* (1987) by Peter Nichols, takes a long, self-indulgent, and bitter look at what has transpired. On a time journey through the last thirty years, his main character, a dramatist, reflects on the fashionable ideas and the new critical terminology, satirizing especially the critics of the new drama.

Artificial and abused though they may be, two labels have emerged in the post-World War II era to give rough definition to the new dramas. The first, "theater of the absurd," was coined by Martin Esslin in 1961 in his book by that title. The second, the "angry theater," became common parlance through John Russell Taylor's book title *The Angry Theatre* in 1962. Philip Barnes, however, traces the "angries" to an even earlier date, 1951, when an Irish writer, Leslie Paul, published an autobiographical work, *Angry Young Man.*[11] The early angry young men included novelists such as John Braine, Kingsley Amis, John Wain, and Alan Sillitoe; the philospher Colin Wilson; producers, at whose head stands George Devine of the Royal Court; the director Lindsay Anderson; and, of course, the large number of dramatists to be discussed here.

The subject matter and style of the absurdist theater are embodied in Samuel Beckett's play *Waiting for Godot;* the subject and mood of the angry theater are the essence of Osborne's *Look Back in Anger.* Time has not dealt kindly with Osborne's play, even though its title became the catchphrase for the new drama. Beckett's play, on the other hand, has gained in critical stature in addition to being identified as the essence of the theater of the absurd. What these two plays have in common, however, is their liberation of drama from traditional restraints. An interesting, although less important, similarity is that both enjoyed productions with singular effects on their audiences.

On 19 November 1957, the San Francisco Actors' Workshop performed *Waiting for Godot* at the San Quentin penitentiary in San Francisco, holding captive an audience of hardened criminals in a prison where a live play had not been performed since the appearance of Sarah Bernhardt there in 1913. What audiences and critics in Europe and America had intellectually analyzed and debated was instantly felt by the empathic prisoners and was described as follows in the *San Quentin News:* "The trio of muscle-men, biceps overflowing, who parked all 642 lbs on the aisle and waited for the girls and funny stuff. When this didn't appear they audibly fumed and audibly decided to wait until the house lights dimmed before escaping. They made one error. They listened and stayed. Left at the end. All shook."[12]

Six months earlier and in totally different circumstances, the newly formed English Stage Company at the Royal Court Theatre opened its third play on 8 May 1956: *Look Back in Anger.* The dynamism of the raw emotions of an educated young man legitimized the stage language of a new antihero and moved audiences, among whom were many young, soon-to-be-famous playwrights, such as Harold Pinter and Tom Stoppard, and establishment dramatists like Terence Rattigan, whose *Separate Tables* was in the second year of a successful run. Rattigan stated later that thenceforth new playwrights would be judged by how unlike himself they were. Stoppard wrote that he "started writing plays not very long after being moved to tears and laughter by *Look Back in Anger.*"[13]

Like the prison reviewer of *Waiting for Godot,* Kenneth Tynan recorded the impact of the play on himself and on a potential audience. "That the play needs changes I do not deny. . . . I agree that *Look Back in Anger* is likely to remain a minority taste. What matters however is the size of the minority. I estimate it at roughly 6,733,000, which is the number of people in this country between the ages of twenty and thirty. . . . I doubt if I could love anyone who did not wish to see *Look Back in Anger*. It is the best young play of its decade."[14] Osborne's play stirred the emotions of a postwar generation. Beckett's play profoundly moved an audience of convicts to silence. Both audiences responded to the sense of alienation, one social and the other profoundly philosophical.

To group these dramas by Beckett and Osborne together is not to give them equal weight in their literary importance. *Waiting for Godot* has become the touchstone for both dramatists and critics in the new era. *Look Back in Anger,* on the other hand, seems a reworking of the marital conflicts of August Strindberg and Henrik Ibsen. Hinchliffe, while recognizing its impact as a breaker of barriers, sees its substance as being in the tradition of D. H. Lawrence and Strindberg.

Revolutionary in both its style and its themes, *Waiting for Godot* has exerted a wide influence on many dramatists, most notably on Pinter. If Osborne's Porter gave impetus to a succession of antiheroes in British drama, Godot, a character who never appears in the play, provided the age with a profound expression of itself, in a revolutionary style that has made Beckett's name to the twentieth century what Euripides in his time was to Greece. Osborne's drama shook the English stage at the time; Beckett's shook the age.

Kenneth Tynan divides the new British dramatists into two groups: the "hairy men—heated, embattled, socially committed playwrights like John Osborne, John Arden, and Arnold Wesker, who had come out fighting in the late fifties"—and the "cool, apolitical stylists," like Harold Pinter, the late Joe Orton, Christopher Hampton, Alan Ayckbourn, Simon Gray, and Stoppard. Tynan borrows his descriptions from an Old Testament passage used by Alan Bennett in a satiric stage spoof of an Anglican clergyman in *Beyond the Fringe:* "Behold, Esau my brother is an hairy man, and I am a smooth man."[15] For the hairy dramatist, the stage is a proper forum for the social, political, and moral dilemmas of the time. For the smooth dramatist, aesthetic commitment overrides or absorbs into itself matters of social conscience. The two kinds of drama have persisted since 1956, varying with the unique qualities of each dramatist.

Tynan's metaphors for the two types of playwrights translate roughly into the two broad categories of influential European drama of the modern era: Beckettian, or the theater of the absurd, and Brechtian, or the epic theater. Beckett is an expatriate Irishman who has spent his professional years in France. Bertolt Brecht, a Marxist, fled Nazi Germany during World War II, spent his exile in the United States, and returned to East Germany after the war to establish the famed Berliner Ensemble. The founders of two traditions of drama in the postwar era, one apolitical and the other firmly committed to the stage as a forum for sociopolitical change, have both exerted strong influence on other dramatists. Beckett's alienated man is the prototypical absurdist hero; Brecht's antihero, moving in a socially determined life from one episode to another, derives from the old epic traditions. Iconoclasts, both dramatists have broken old forms and, out of the shards, created new ones for their time.

Many of the new dramatists are artistic descendants of Beckett or Brecht. Hinchliffe reminds us that "at first the Angry dramatists were traditionalists and only later came to graduate through self-conscious applications of Brechtian techniques to mature plays which include dream and fantasy."[16] Those plays, for example, in which Osborne employs epic techniques are aesthetically superior to the conventionally structured *Look Back in Anger*. On the other hand, most of Tynan's "smooth" stylists have made use of absurdist techniques. Thus, although Osborne's angry young man touched off an era of dramatic experiments, the real changes in substance and style are those adaptations, conscious or unconscious, of the techniques of Beckett and Brecht.

Though discussed in subsequent chapters in specific contexts, certain terms have entered the critical vocabulary and deserve brief mention here. Important to the understanding of them are the centuries-old traditions from which they derive.

Through the Greek, Roman, Renaissance, neoclassical, romantic, and realist periods of literature, certain commonly held cultural assumptions have initiated the forms that the dramas of those times assumed. Greek tragedy and comedy sprang from the beliefs of that time, particularly in the portrayal of an individual finding himself or herself in conflict with those shared assumptions. The Romans gave to the future the

Plautine comedy and the Senecan tragedy, defining, with a precision theretofore lacking, the conventions of those two genres. Medieval drama originated in the religious impulses of the age, its form, the mystery and morality plays, growing from that religion. With the long reign of Elizabeth I, a national consciousness incorporating the past and present in unprecedented fashion could only result in large numbers of dramatists reflecting that consciousness—Thomas Kyd, Marlowe, Jonson, and Shakespeare among them.

With the advent of the Puritans, the seventeenth century teemed with Jacobean dramatists, the heroic dramas of Dryden, and the Restoration comedies influenced by the returning Stuarts. Dramatic traditions reflected the spirit of an age convulsed in political, scientific, and religious changes. These developed into the sentimental dramas and satiric comedies of the neoclassical period.

The development in France of the "well-made play," the *pièce bien faite* of the nineteenth century, a fashionable tradition practiced by Émile Augier, Augustin Scribe, and Alexandre Dumas, featured highly contrived plots. Theme and character were subordinated and the formulaic plot reigned supreme, resulting in the split between theater of entertainment and serious theater. The well-made play had become an industry by the time of Scribe in the first half of the nineteenth century, and it had taken on derogatory critical implications. Yet even Ibsen and Shaw used it as the scaffolding on which to build their dramas, although Ibsen made attempts to move away from it.

In his book *The Rise and Fall of the Well Made Play* (1967), John Russell Taylor provides a glimpse into the prevalence of the well-made play in England at the time the new waves of drama washed ashore. Tom Robertson, Henry Arthur Jones, Arthur Wing Pinero, George Bernard Shaw, Oscar Wilde, Somerset Maugham, Noel Coward, and Terence Rattigan all found structural elements of the *pièce bien faite* convenient for dramas that satisfied the taste of middle-class audiences.

In their most formulaic form, according to Stephen Stanton, the conventions of the well-made play include: (1) "a plot based on a secret known to an audience but withheld from certain characters," (2) "a pattern of increasingly intense actions and suspense prepared by exposition," (3) "a series of ups and downs in the hero's fortunes, caused by his conflict with an adversary," (4) the *scène à faire,* or obligatory scene, in which a fraudulent character is unmasked and fortune restored to the hero, (5) "a central misunderstanding," (6) "a logical and credible denouement," and (7) "the reproduction of the overall action pattern in the individual actions."[17]

When World War II shattered common cultural assumptions and completed the sense of disillusionment begun after World War I—the war that was supposed to end all wars—the sense of alienation that had set in found expression in the work of Beckett and Eugène Ionesco, leading stylists in the theater of the absurd. Alienated from his society, from the natural world, and even from himself, modern man was portrayed by Beckett in music-hall style in his four famous characters, Didi, Gogo, Lucky, and Pozzo, in *Waiting for Godot.* Aware of the indifference of society and the universe, Gogo and Didi self-consciously decide how to spend their time and what questions to ask, realizing that they are asking the same questions over and over. Their lives turn into a series of repetitive games. The existential absurdity of their condition is illustrated in their recurrent talk of going somewhere or of doing things, even as they do not move nor do anything. Beckett's absurdist techniques include non sequiturs; broken sentences; pauses and silences; a richness of allusions to the Bible, literature, religion, and history; an abundance of carefully chosen platitudes; music-hall jokes and routines; bits of narrated stories; repetitions, which create a cyclical effect; and physical gestures. The setting of a Beckett play is usually bare—an unidentified landscape, a beach, an old man's dusty room, urns—symbolic of man's isolation from his fellowman and his alienation from the comfortable beliefs of the past, which no longer pertain. Beckett's plays focus on the philosophical position of man in an absurd universe.

Brecht's, on the other hand, are essentially sociopolitical, and they contain a message. His message addresses the problems that man has created and therefore must solve. Institutional evils are at the core of his problems: war (*Mother Courage and Her Children*); poverty (*The Good Woman of Setzuan*); injustice (*The Caucasian Chalk Circle*); and capitalism and crime (*Threepenny Opera* and *In the Jungle of Cities*). Brecht's method of instruction is to involve the audience in reaching solutions to problems, rather than, as in the cathartic Aristotelian tradition, providing those solutions. Thus, the audience must think, rather than feel. If Beckett's alienation is philosophical, Brecht's is strongly sociopolitical.

Instead of abandoning traditional style and stage conventions, as does Beckett, Brecht uses them, turning them upside down, as his method of emotionally distancing the audience in order to get them to think. The German term for his stylistic alienation is *Verfremdungseffekt*. To realize this purpose, Brecht uses interruptive devices: a narrator who steps out of his role to provide the audience factual information such as history and legends, a loose episodic style rather than the tightly sequenced plot of the well-made play, songs with messages that repeat what has just been seen, signs that flash the titles of these songs, frequent paradoxes, a hero or heroine who somehow survives victimization by society. These conventions are employed to destroy the audience's expectations of the customary illusions of the theater, illusions that Brecht regards as "a branch of the bourgeois drug traffic."

Martin Esslin defines Brecht's intention. "The audience is to be confronted with a body of evidence from which it is to draw its conclusions in a critical, highly lucid state of mind. The emotions are to be involved only at a further remove; the critical analysis of the social facts, presented in the concrete form of living pictures, is to produce socially useful emotions such as indignation at injustice, hatred of oppressors, or an active desire for the overthrow of the existing social system."[18]

A rebel in the tradition of Euripides, who used popular style and themes to parody themselves, Brecht employs epic conventions and prevailing institutional evils in a self-parodic manner to advance his theories of humanistic socialism. His dramas are the source of a new critical terminology: non-Aristotelian, epic, estrangement, alienation, episodic, distantiation, and the *V-effekt* (short for *Verfremdungseffekt*).

In addition to the absurdist and epic traditions of Beckett and Brecht, a third European influence came into being: the theater of cruelty. Its theorist is the Frenchman Antonin Artaud; and its chief practitioner on the stage, his countryman Jean Genet. At the heart of this genre is the total rejection of theater as entertainment and in its place the destruction of all barriers between the spectator and the actor. No longer is the stage an illusion to be enjoyed for a few hours but a reality that changes the very being of the spectator. All are participants in or celebrants of the darker natural instincts and the subconscious and share a basic distrust of the rational and verbal processes. The theater becomes a religious experience incarnating the dark, irrational impulses of man and activated by the hope that "mankind might be diverted from the disastrous path that led toward increasing atrophy of the instincts, which amounted to the death of vitality and to eventual extinction."[19]

Layers of illusion must be peeled off, or, as in Genet's *Blacks,* layers of illusion are shown as they are slowly put on by blacks in a white society. Gradually the color white appears and then grows, until the faces have turned completely white. Actors draw the audience into the process by physical contact. In Genet's *Balcony,* a house of prostitution is the holy of holies where social institutions are sanctified. Representatives of those institutions are born here, and they come here to die—justices, clerics, generals, police. All undergo masochistic sexual rituals as one power dies and another takes its place. Sometimes called "black mass" because of its inversion of good and evil, the theater of cruelty evokes the religious origins of Western drama—both pagan and Christian.

In this drama, images, physical gestures, and sounds replace the logic and language of the illusionist drama. The experience of all participants—audience, actor, producer, director, writer, and stagehand—is intended to revitalize primitive instincts.

In the United States, the theater of cruelty found a home in the Living Theatre of Julian Beck and Judith Malina, who traveled worldwide with their company. Another famous figure in this "total theater" concept, Jerzy Grotowski of the Polish Laboratory Theater, also traveled abroad, influencing especially U. S. companies with his ideas.

Allied to this tradition are the plays of Ionesco, who draws portraits of man reduced to bestiality and to being the unfeeling creature of habit (*The Rhinoceros* and *The Bald Soprano*). In *The Lesson,* an examining professor destroys his student with the vehemence of his passion. Ionesco's theater-of-the-absurd plays merely begin what Artaud, Genet, the Becks, and Grotowski carry out to its ultimate expression. The full force of this drama is most visible in the films of Federico Fellini, whose exaggerated use of physicality illustrates ritualized revulsion at its most powerful.

In Britain, the dark farces of Joe Orton hilariously dislocate the illusions of civilized attitudes and behavior. In plays by David Rudkin and John Arden (*Afore Night Come* and *Sergeant Musgrave's Dance,* respectively), as masks drop, ritual violence begins.

In the spectrum of dramatic genres, the theater of cruelty lies at the opposite end from the theater of entertainment. One destroys illusions on stage, and the other builds them.

In addition to the terms for these three major genres of the new drama—absurdism, epic, and cruelty—other expressions have emerged from the first and second waves of postwar English experimentation. *Kitchen sink* refers to the alleged pots-and-pans realism of dramas about the lower classes, like those of Arnold Wesker, in particular his drama entitled *The Kitchen. Agitprop,* short for agitational propaganda, describes the politicized protest drama of the younger second-wave dramatists—Brenton, Hare, and Griffiths. In the United States, agitprop plays protested the Vietnam War and the injustices suffered by minorities: blacks, homosexuals, and women.

In attempting to write about the immense changes that have taken place and about the proliferation of new dramatists (most of them still living and writing) and to assign them to a historical pattern, one can only suggest a perspective that at best is arbitrary. One possibility is to arrange the dramatists in two groups: those launched at the Royal Court and those with beginnings at other experimental theaters. Another approach could be a chronological division into the first wave, roughly from 1956 to 1966, and the second wave, from 1968 to the present.

For reasons alluded to earlier, I have chosen to begin with chapters devoted to each of the three stylistically innovative British dramatists— Beckett, Pinter and Stoppard—as well as to Osborne, who launched the new era and then continued to write an impressive number of plays in various styles. Although Arden, Bond, and Wesker are generally regarded by critics as major dramatists at the Royal Court, I have included them in group chapters: Arden and Bond with the politicized writers, and Wesker with the playwrights associated generally with writing about the working classes. In the group chapters, I have organized what seems at times a motley crowd of distinctively individualistic writers into categories—social realists, proletarian writers, fantasists, left-wing polemicists, and an extremely loosely arranged group of traditional farceurs, or conventional stylists. Needless to say, at best, classification is arbitrary, for no writer rests easily in a given category.

Throughout the volume's organization and commentary, the consciousness of an American with limited access to the living stage remains the filter through which facts, opinions, and judgments are presented. Beckett, Osborne, Pinter, and Stoppard, for example, are familiar enough to the American mind, whereas dramatists such as Bond, Arden, and Edgar (except for his adaptations) have retained a certain English insulation. And there is the distinctive phenomenon of Ayckbourn, who, despite his popularity in England, has not fared well in New York and yet has enjoyed regional popularity in a long-standing relationship with the Alley Theater of Houston, Texas. During the 1987 season, in fact, Ayckbourn himself directed the premiere of his newest play, *Henceforward*.

I have omitted a large number of dramatists who have written primarily for television, who have written adaptations, who have remained minor fringe playwrights, or who have written only a few plays. Not included in the volume, for example, are single plays deserving of mention, such as Ronald Harwood's *Dresser,* Frank Marcus's *Killing of Sister George,* Charles Dyer's *Rattle of a Simple Man* and *Staircase,* Keith Waterhouse's *Billy Liar,* Charles Wood's *Cockade,* and Heathcote Williams's *AC/DC,* a play described by Ronald Hayman as "one of the few English plays to challenge comparison with the work of Beckett, Ionesco, Genet, and Handke" as "a genuine example of the Theatre of Cruelty."[20]

CHAPTER II

SAMUEL BECKETT: REDUCTIONIST

On 5 January 1953, at the Thêâtre de Babylone in Paris, *En attendant Godot,* which was to lead the audience and the world into a new era of drama, opened. The play received favorable critical notices, which kept growing even as controversies about its meanings multiplied. Dubbed a succès de scandal by Martin Esslin, the play became the leading edge of what has been called the antitheater or antiliterary movement, because of its violation of the conventions of the traditional drama to which audiences, critics, and scholars had become accustomed. The title character, who never appears in the play, immediately became the password for the new drama of the second half of the twentieth century. The audience is given no realistic details of character or action, the plot goes nowhere, the locale is unidentifiable, and the dialogues are disjointed and riddled with pauses and silences.

Yet no single drama perhaps in the history of the West has so influenced its own time and succeeding generations of writers or has been responsible single-handedly for the financial well-being and the popular reputation of its author.

Translated into English by Beckett and produced in 1955 at the Arts Theatre in London, *Waiting for Godot* won the *Evening Standard* Drama Award and is part of the body of work for which Beckett received the Nobel Prize in 1969, work that, "in new forms of fiction and the theatre, has transformed the destitution of modern man into his exaltation."[1]

Productions of this play have continued in theaters, university campuses, and amateur groups. Eventually it outsold the entire output of Beckett's other writing and, according to its author, enabled him to buy the home outside Paris in which he lives even today. For Beckett it is the house that Godot built. Although Beckett considers himself a novelist and prefers his play *Endgame* to *Waiting for Godot,* the manuscript for the latter is the only one that he refuses to let out of his hands.

Born in Dublin to affluent professional parents of Huguenot stock on Good Friday, 13 April 1906, Beckett enjoyed the advantages of a privileged upbringing and attended Trinity College in Dublin. Graduation was followed by an exchange lectureship at the Ecole normale superieure in Paris and frequent visits with a family of cousins in Germany, whose interests were the arts and writing. It was through his predecessor as lecturer at the school, Thomas McGreevy, also a graduate of Trinity College, that Beckett met Joyce and that the future course of his life took shape. At the request of Joyce, Beckett published an essay entitled "Dante . . . Bruno. Vico . . . Joyce." This publication was followed by another entitled "Proust," on *Remembrance of Things Past. Whoroscope* (1930) was his first published book. Short stories and novels followed, as did periods of depression and sessions with analysts. Work on his first major novel, *Murphy* (1938), and its poor sales contributed to Beckett's depression, and it was the activity in the theater that provided him with some relief. His trilogy of novels (*Murphy, Molloy,* and *Malone Dies*) was published before his dramatic activity began with any seriousness. In fact, he turned to writing his unpublished and unperformed drama, "Eleutheria," for relief from the fatigue of finishing his novel *Mercier et Camier.* Written in fewer than four months, *Waiting for Godot* was also a "marvellous liberating diversion"[2] from the exertion of novel writing and, shortly, from the financial worries brought on by the lack of success of his novels.

An early play about Samuel Johnson and his relationship with Mrs. Thrale, "Johnson Fantasy," as he called it, remains unfinished. His first completed drama, "Eleutheria," concerns a young man named Victor Krap (a name returned to in *Krapp's Last Tape* in 1958), who, much like Beckett himself, attempts to exercise his freedom from a middle-class family.

Things changed remarkably for Beckett in 1953, when *Waiting for Godot,* written four years earlier, was finally produced. The director of the production was Roger Blin, with whom Beckett formed a close association in France, just as later George Devine in England and Alan Schneider in America became trusted friends and professional colleagues of Beckett's. The change in Beckett's fortunes, financially, critically, and academically, was phenomenal as the theatrical and scholarly worlds began paying tribute not only to *Waiting for Godot* but also to all of Beckett's work. Nearly thirty years of writing suddenly caught the attention of the world at large. Rarely during his own lifetime has any writer been accorded such meticulous scholarly investigation. Beckett in this respect follows in the footsteps of his master, Joyce.

Waiting for Godot establishes patterns that are readily visible in his succeeding dramas. The drama consists of two acts, of which the second seems repetitious of the first. Two tramplike characters in an arid landscape (the cosmos or one's mind) with the unusual names Estragon and Vladimir, Gogo and Didi for short, keep wondering whether a person by the enigmatic name of Godot will appear. While they wait for him two other characters arrive, one leading the other by the rope (or one pulling the other), with the similarly unlikely names Lucky and Pozzo. Godot never does make his appearance, but in his place a young boy, a messenger, appears in each act, informing Gogo and Didi that Godot will come tomorrow. While they wait for that appearance Gogo and Didi entertain each other and are entertained by Lucky and Pozzo, who provide both pain and diversion for the first duo. The two couples, on the most obvious level, are symbolic of the highly personal man (Gogo and Didi) and the impersonal socialized man, characterized by the master-slave relationship (Pozzo and Lucky). Gogo and Didi, in addition, can be seen as a composite character, one of whom (Gogo) concerns himself with matters of bodily comfort and the other (Didi) with troubling questions of the mind. Linked symbiotically, Pozzo and Lucky in their act 1 appearance clearly illustrate their social roles. But when they appear in act 2, Pozzo is blind and as abject as was Lucky earlier.

What Beckett insists on from the outset is the idea of a paradoxical duality for which there is no explanation but that does exist as long as individuals and the society they establish exist. The unexplainable and "unnameable" contradiction is illustrated by the play's dominant unanswered question, which is their topic of conversation: In the scene of Christ's crucifixion, why was one thief hanged and the other saved? There is no explanation. Ruby Cohn states that the two thieves are

Didi and Gogo, that the two thieves are you and I.[3] She sees this identification as a reflection of the "fearful symmetry" of Beckett's style, pointing out even such minute symmetrical details as the fact that Vladimir's and Estragon's names have eight letters and that their shortened names deliberately contain four letters. The major paradox of duality, however, is found at the end of each act: As one asks, "Well, shall we go?" the other responds, "Yes, let's go," but *neither moves.*" At the end of act 1 it is Estragon who asks and Vladimir who responds, and in act 2 the order is reversed. Even the boy who returns with the message that Godot will come tomorrow insists that he is not the messenger who appeared yesterday. He does, however, mention that he has a brother and that Godot beats his brother, who minds the sheep, but that he does not beat him, the current messenger, who minds the goats. He provides no reasons. In each act, when the boy leaves, Gogo and Didi decide that they will go but remain where they are, faithful in their commitment to waiting for Godot. Uncertain, they remain in a state of stasis.

In the French title, the idea of waiting rather than that of Godot is important. For it is what Didi and Gogo do while they wait that is the essence of the drama. The person of Godot, who never appears, has been most frequently identified as God or as the illusory hopes that life eternally dangles before the individual. He has also been seen as a diminution of the idea of God, as death, as de Gaulle, as future time, and as a cyclist, among other identifications. Linguistically, the name has been associated with *boot, god, lout,* and *bumpkin.* But whatever the association with the name, Godot is a force that keeps Gogo and Didi conscious of killing time until he arrives, even in the face of the uncertainty of his coming.

The context of their lives is obviously Christian, as constant allusions to the Bible are the means by which they attempt to gain some certainty about themselves and about Godot while they wait. The phrase "nothing to be done," with which the drama opens, suggests Christ's final words, "It is finished." The phrase is repeated, and its repetition leads Didi to ask Gogo if he has ever read the Bible, and the latter to reply about remembering the colored maps of the Holy Land, where they will go for their honeymoon and swim and be happy. After noticing Gogo's visibly swelling foot (shades of Oedipus!), Didi launches into the story of Christ and the two thieves, one of whom was saved and the other damned. The story will pass the time, but more importantly it contains the dilemma of unanswered questions about life that haunt the couple and that have haunted the most brilliant of philosophers throughout time. Didi and Gogo experience the pain of the dilemma immediately. Further on in act 1, Didi notices a barren tree where they were told to wait for Godot. In act 2 the tree does have leaves, and the occurrence recalls the biblical event in which Christ curses the tree that does not bear fruit. But in Beckett's play the barrenness and leaves pose a contradiction. These are but the most obvious references to the two-thousand-year-old Christian dilemma, in which the hope of Godot's appearance is repeatedly reduced to despair, only to be once more revived, buoying and teasing man.

The alternation between metaphysical despair and hope is even more poignant on the immediate level of physical and emotional experiences. They talk from time to time of separating. During one of these periods, Gogo tells a story Didi already knows, about an Englishman in the brothel who is asked if he wants a fair-, dark-, or red-haired woman. Teased by the possibility, Didi cries to Gogo to stop his (Gogo's) narration. More silences ensue, and Gogo, thinking Didi is angry, embraces him. Didi recoils at the embrace because Gogo stinks of garlic, an odor the latter justifies on the basis that garlic is good for the kidneys. The need of one for the other in this incident, one of many such in the drama, is contradicted and temporarily negated. They talk of what to do next while waiting for Godot, of even whether to hang themselves from the tree. They become sexually excited by the thought of the resulting erections but then decide against suicide, since the bough could break, killing one and leaving the other alone and bereft of his only friend. Estragon, the one with physical appetites, is hungry and asks for a carrot, but disappointingly he is given a turnip. The carrot is finally produced by Didi. Didi, the thinking half of the couple, constantly removes and replaces a hat, while Gogo complains about a boot that is painfully tight. And so they fill the frightening silence in the cosmic void by telling stories and playing verbal and physical games of separation and reunion.

Onto the scene in each of the two acts walk the visitors, Pozzo and Lucky, the latter on a leash held by Pozzo. On orders from his master,

Lucky takes the food for Pozzo's lunch from the basket he carries, as Didi and Gogo observe and comment in the stichomythic dialogue that has become one of the hallmarks of absurdist dramatic dialogue.

ESTRAGON:	Oh I say!
VLADIMIR:	A running sore.
ESTRAGON:	It's the rope.
VLADIMIR:	It's the rubbing.
ESTRAGON:	It's inevitable.
VLADIMIR:	It's the knot.
ESTRAGON:	It's the chafing.[4]

Pozzo informs Didi and Gogo that he must be on his way to the fair to sell Lucky in the hope of getting a good price. Lucky weeps, and Pozzo balances the negative and affirmative actions of life in his comment that "for each one who begins to weep somewhere else another stops. The same is true of the laugh. . . . Let us not then speak ill of our generation, it is not any unhappier than its predecessors. (*Pause.*) Let us not speak well of it either. (*Pause*) Let us not speak of it at all. (*Pause. Judiciously.*) It is true the population has increased" (*WG*, 24–25).

Lucky has been quiet throughout, except for his sobbing. Pozzo continues his conversation with the uneasy Didi and Gogo, who fidget with hat and boot, respectively. Then, after a short scene in which the three simultaneously take off their hats Chaplinesque style and press their hands to their foreheads in order to concentrate, they decide that Lucky has finally put his bags down in order to dance but needs his hat in order to think. On orders from Pozzo to stop and think, Lucky then begins a long monologue, the central one in the drama, in which stream-of-consciousness utterances flow in eloquently Joycean language and express the "unknown" and the "uncertain" (recurring motifs throughout). Punctuated by the phrases "for reasons unknown" and "labors unfinished," the active rhythms of living are blurted out by Lucky in metaphors of movement: "Tennis football running cycling swimming flying floating riding gliding conating camogie skating tennis of all kinds." The monologue concludes with repeated references to "the skull the skull in Connemara in spite of the tennis the labors abandoned left unfinished graver still abode of stones in a word I resume alas abandoned unfinished the skull the skull in Connemara in spite of the tennis . . . the stones . . . so calm . . . Cunard . . . unfinished . . ." (*WG*, 34).

The reduction of man to the essential joys and pains of life amid all the haunting metaphysical dilemmas, and the diminishment of life itself, are the essence of Beckett's work, and Lucky's speech epitomizes the human situation in which Didi and Gogo and Pozzo and Lucky discover their need for each other. Didi seizes Lucky's hat, whereupon Lucky falls back into his customary silence, the silence that Didi and Gogo fear when they are alone. They help Lucky, who has fallen, to his feet, but he falls again and is reactivated only on the sharp command of Pozzo. "Up! Pig! . . . Adieu! Pig! Yip! Adieu!" (*WG*, 38). Act 1 ends with the appearance of the small boy, who arrives with the strange message that Godot will come tomorrow.

With slight variations, most of the events of act 1 are repeated in act 2, even the consideration of hanging oneself from the tree and the decision against it. When Pozzo and Lucky reappear on their return trip, the former has gone blind. In an attempt to help the two rise after a fall, both Didi and Gogo fall with them, and all four have difficulty getting up. When the boy reappears he brings news that his brother is sick and, in answer to Vladimir's question, assures him that Mr. Godot has a beard and that it is white. In response to his information, there is a silence, and then Didi exclaims, "Christ have mercy on us!" He begs the boy not to say on the morrow that he (the boy) has never seen Didi. He insists on this certainty in order to keep some fine line between illusion and reality. The final paradoxical duality remains: "Yes, let's go. (*They do not move.*)" (WG, 83).

As thieves of time, the two tramps retain the uncertainty about why one of the two biblical thieves will be saved. All they know is that for the present they have each other. Like Oedipus of old, they confront the unanswerable question. The solution by Oedipus to the riddle of the sphinx is that man crawls on all fours in the morning, stands erect on two feet at noon, and walks with the help of a cane in the evening. The three Oedipal stages of life, man's only certainty—clearly defined in *Endgame*—are the essence of Beckett's poetry, fiction, and plays. Their lineaments, however, are most visible in the plays.

Beckett began an era of static, or interior, drama. It is the opposite of Ibsenian drama, in which large quantities of realistic details from the pasts of characters are carefully selected and organized into patterned explanations of their lives. Although deceptive with its occasional use of naturalistic details, the static drama of Beckett synthesizes realistic and metaphysical experiences of man. The result is absurdist man, with his yearnings for the infinite and his despair that accompanies the uncertainty, indeed the impossibility, of realizing those yearnings. There remains for man, as long as he breathes, only life with its joy and its equal component of despair. Like those two thieves mentioned only in the Gospel of Luke and not in the remaining Gospels of the New Testament; like the boy who minds the goats and is not beaten by Godot, and the shepherd, his brother, who is; like Lucky, the slave who is beaten, and Pozzo, the master who beats—there are Gogo, who is concerned with his stomach and his aching feet, and Didi, who thinks and questions. The physical appetites of food and sex are enjoyed and recalled with relish, the intellectual appetites are teased forever, in a universe in which the contest between body and mind, life and death, and questions and answers ends at best in a draw and at worst in despair.

With dilemmas akin to those of Sophocles' *Oedipus Rex* and Shakespeare's *King Lear,* Beckett has discovered the modern voice for the human condition, labeled "absurdism" by Esslin. The voice is heard in the varied settings of Beckett's plays, in which the human mind is symbolized by an arid plain (*Waiting for Godot*), a room with two windows and two ashbins (*Endgame*), a beach in which the sand slowly rises nearly to engulf the main character (*Happy Days*), three urns containing the speakers' heads (*Play*), or an illuminated mouth (*Not I*). The insistence on life, even if only in memory, is there to the end, along with the pain of the unanswered questions about thieves who were saved or lost, or about the distinctions between shepherds and goatherds.

Unlike *Waiting for Godot, Endgame,* his second produced play, is a drama that Beckett wrote deliberately and seriously. And unlike *Waiting for Godot,* which was first produced in Paris, *Endgame* (*Fin de partie*) was given its premiere, on 3 April 1957, in French at the Royal Court. Because of the brevity of the play, the mime *Act Without Words I* filled out the evening's program. Displeased with the combination, Beckett later wrote another short play, *Krapp's Last Tape,* to replace *Act Without Words I* as a companion piece. The compact structure of *Endgame* began a trend that has increasingly characterized Beckett's dramas, so that even a short evening in the theater in the 1980s might easily consist of three pieces in which silences far outweigh the words. In addition, evidence of Beckett's seriousness as a dramatist is seen in the lengthy set of stage directions that *Endgame* contains, in strong contrast to the almost nonexistent directions in *Waiting for Godot.* Beckett has remained adamant about the precise staging of his plays, entering into controversy with directors who wish to take liberties even in the slightest ways.

Like *Waiting for Godot, Endgame* dramatizes the situation of two couples: Hamm, a wheelchair victim who can only sit, and Clov, possibly his son, who can only stand and carry out the demands made on him by Hamm; and Nell and Nagg, parents of Hamm, who reside in two ashbins and occasionally lift the lids in order to converse with Hamm. The setting is a room with two windows, which Clov can reach only by means of a ladder. The father-son duo suggests at times the master-slave relationship of Pozzo and Lucky in the earlier play, but instead of the rope and whip, Hamm uses a whistle to summon Clov whenever he needs him. Three generations provide the familial context for this highly concentrated drama of human relationships.

The structure of the play contains the ritual formality of the Japanese No drama. At the beginning Hamm sits in his wheelchair, face covered by a large, blood-stained handkerchief that he removes and then carefully folds and puts in the breast pocket of his dressing gown. Additional ritual details include the whistle on which Hamm depends for communication with Clov, his gaff (cane), by means of which he pushes his wheelchair, and his three-legged dog, which cannot stand upright (a symbol of the Trinity?). Hamm throws away all three real and symbolic objects as part of his final moves in the chess game of life.

As in *Waiting for Godot,* the Christian context is established in Clov's opening lines: "Finished, it's finished, nearly finished, it must be nearly finished." After a pause, Clov launches into the metaphor of a grain heap, from the ancient philosopher Zeno. "Grain upon grain, one by one, and one day, suddenly, there's a heap, a little heap, the impossible heap. (*Pause.*) I can't be punished any more. (*Pause.*) I'll go now to my kitchen ten feet by ten feet by ten feet, and wait for him to whistle me."[5] In his highly concentrated allusions to Christian and pagan philosophy, Beckett blends Hamm's personal dilemma with the metaphysical questioning of centuries.

The title of the play is obviously taken from the game of chess. Beckett has said that "Hamm is a king in this chess game lost from the start. From the start, he knows he is making loud senseless moves. That he will make no progress at all with the gaff. Now at the last he makes a few senseless moves as only a bad player would. A good one would have given up long ago. He is only trying to delay the inevitable end. Each of his gestures is one of the last useless moves which puts off the end. He's a bad player."[6] These final gestures constitute Hamm's elegiac farewell to life. Important to that farewell are his parents and Clov, with whom he enjoys his last human communication and to whom he leaves the legacy of Western civilization, even as he savors his last, losing moves in the chess game of life, played by a loser. Conversations with his parents consist mostly of their demands for food and Hamm's acquiescence to, or denial of, those demands, in a more complex version of the carrot-turnip incident in *Godot*.

NAGG:	Me pap!
HAMM:	Accursed progenitor!
NAGG:	Me pap!
HAMM:	The old folks at home! No decency left! Guzzle, guzzle, that's all they think of. (*E,* 15)

When Nell and Nagg lift the lids just high enough to show heads and hands in order to ask for food, their diminution is obvious. The slow process of dying grinds to a halt, not only in their demands for food and in Hamm's request for a painkiller, but in the hopes of Western culture, symbolized by a toy dog that cannot be made to stand on its three legs. References to eyesight, blindness, twilight, and darkness abound, and Nell and Nagg stop emerging from the ashbins.

Yet even in the process of dying, memories take on an energy of their own as illusions refuse to die. Like Gogo and Didi, Hamm and

Clov argue passionately and tell stories. Some of the stories are cosmic jokes, such as Nagg's rendition of the tailor who could not in three months make him a pair of pants that fit in the "crutch," although God made the world in six days. When Hamm finds out that Clov hasn't finished making the toy dog, he informs Clov that he has forgotten the sex. Clov retorts that the sex goes on at the end. Hamm recalls that his mother, Pegg, now dead, "extinguished," was "bonny—once like a flower of the field. (*With a reminiscent leer.*) And a great one for the men" (*E*, 31).

When asked by Clov what keeps him here, Hamm replies: "The dialogue. (*Pause.*) I've got on with my story. (*Pause.*) I've got on with it well. (*Pause. Irritably.*) Ask me where I've got to" (*E*, 39). Before the final silence, he has one more long story to tell Nagg, his progenitor, promising him a sugarplum afterwards. Demanding silence, Hamm narrates a long Christmas Eve story of a man who "came crawling towards me, on his belly. Pale, wonderfully pale and thin." He asked for corn to take back to his child. In the end he requested Hamm to take the child. Hamm, nearing the end of his story, states that he cannot finish it unless he brings in other characters: "But where would I find them?" (*E*, 37). Although his life is finishing, his story, one of his last chess moves, remains unfinished. Discarding the no-longer-necessary objects—whistle, gaff and dog—Hamm unfolds the handkerchief over his face and utters, "Me to play. . . . Old endgame lost of old, play and lose, and have done with losing" (*E*, 51). Hamm gives directions to the end and asserts a relish of the little control that remains. Just as physical and verbal activity fills the "waiting" time of Didi and Gogo, so the emotional and intellectual mobility fill to the brim the "ending" time of Hamm.

Allusions to Christianity are thick in this play, the most prominent being the Christmas Eve story in which Hamm rejects the child the stranger offers him. To these allusions are added references to Zeno, the old philosopher whose allegory of the heap of grain demonstrates the "less is more" theory, to Shakespeare in lines such as "Our revels are ended," and to T. S. Eliot in Hamm's "Then let it end. . . . With a bang!" (*E*, 49). Scattered among the bits of the Christmas Eve story are allusions to the weather and to the scientific instruments that measure the weather: thermometer, heliometer, anemometer, and hygrometer. Even as man's attempts at measurement and explanation prove illusory, they energize the mind of Hamm.

Beckett's plays after *Waiting for Godot* and *Endgame* grow smaller and more compact, sparse and silence-ridden. *Krapp's Last Tape (Le Derniere Bande)* is yet another experiment for Beckett, as his first play written in English and then translated into French. Like *Endgame,* it was first performed in London at the Royal Court, on 28 October 1958. The tape that the main character plays in a dusty room contains favorite memories of his youth. In this work, the four characters of *Waiting for Godot* and *Endgame* are reduced to one.

The reduction of characters and play is continued in *Happy Days* (1961), consisting of one long interior monologue by its main character, Winnie. The setting is a beach. Behind a mound, her husband is hidden, only his hat visible above it. Winnie is visible from her waist up. In place of the recording to which Krapp listens in the earlier play, Winnie has her parasol and her purse, whose contents she extracts, in one prolonged action, as poignant memories insistently assert themselves even as the sand heap around her rises, leaving only her head visible at the end.

In Beckett's next play, *Play* (1963), three urns occupy the stage, and the heads of mistress, husband, and wife conduct dialogues and monologues in the Beckettian patterns developed in the preceding dramas. His remaining plays undergo even more condensation, as titles such as *Breath* (1970), *Footfalls* (1976), and *Texts for Nothing* (1981) suggest. Remaining stage dramas include *Come and Go* (1966), *Not I* (1972), *The Lost Ones* (1975), *That Time* (1976), *A Piece of Monologue* (1979), *Rockabye* (1981), and *Ohio Impromptu* (1981).

Characteristics of Beckett's style include: the use of allusions to the history and literature of Western civilization as well as to biblical stories; story narrations by various characters; long passages of stichomythic lines in which suspense rises and falls; non sequiturs; repetitions, not only of images and symbols but sometimes of a whole scene or act, with only slight variations; a few scattered monologues that contain the central idea(s) of the play; language jokes and inventively Joycean language; personal and philosophical debates; and, perhaps above all, the language of gesture, motion, and silence. His minimalist style is characterized by silences, pauses, unfinished sentences, sentences reduced to phrases, phrases to words, words to syllables, and syllables to silences.

What the Beckettian style eschews is the tightly patterned conventions of the Scribean well-made play, which moves logically from a heavily expositional beginning, through the ensuing complication, to a clearcut climax in which the fortunes of the hero are decided one way or another, and then to the denouement and conclusion, in which the loose ends of the drama are tied together. The linear direction of the traditional drama is not characteristic of Beckett. His direction is circular, symbolized in the novels by bicycles and in the dramas by vehicles, such as the wheelchair (*Endgame*), or by the mobility of his characters—riding, walking, or running.

The silences are the voids that may hold answers to questions if those answers exist. They are the voids that man fills with his games of the mind and the body while he waits for Godot. Perhaps the silences are Godot, the *Not I* or the nonbeing into which all life flows and that man both awaits and fears. "There is no lack of void," Gogo realizes in moments when he feels most threatened by it.

As a dramatist who has written increasingly minimalist plays and whose "unintentional" *Waiting for Godot* provided a totally new direction in dramatic style and content, Beckett remains the major influence for change in the twentieth century, not only on the British stage but on that of the world at large. His reputation among writers, critics, and scholars has solidified in the decades since the early 1950s.

The influence of Beckett extends in a direct line to the new drama of postwar England. First of all, it was George Devine of the Royal Court to whom Beckett submitted his second play, *Fin de partie* (*Endgame*), for its premiere, causing a minor furor in Paris. Secondly, a friendship between Beckett and Harold Pinter developed, a tie that is important, since the latter is England's dramatist most closely allied to the tradition of Beckett. A third tribute to Beckett's influence is Tom Stoppard's *Rosencrantz and Guildenstern Are Dead,* a play that, in its appearance more than ten years after *Waiting for Godot,* reinvents two of Shakespeare's most undistinguished characters in the mold of Beckett's most famous characters, Gogo and Didi.

Beckett's links, however, are not just to the new dramatists. He has roots in the Irish literary revolutionaries who preceded him—

Yeats, Shaw, and Joyce. An expatriate in the tradition of Shaw, O'Casey, and Joyce, Beckett enjoyed a close personal and literary association with Joyce in Paris during the 1920s. As secretary to Joyce when the latter's eyesight was failing, Beckett took dictation, conducted research for Joyce, and served as errand boy in personal matters of the Joyce family.

As the longest of his produced and published plays, *Waiting for Godot* is the first of a lengthy series of dramas that are characterized by increasing brevity until, it has been said, one day the curtain may just rise and fall without a word spoken. This reductionist style is illustrated in *Act Without Words* (I and II), two wordless plays that incorporate Chaplinesque action as their characters wordlessly act out a typical Beckettian situation, aptly expressed in the title of another work, *More Pricks than Kicks. Not I* with startling theatricality focuses on the mouth of the speaker even as the rest of the stage and the speaker remain in darkness throughout. These are but a few examples of the directions a new age of drama took with *Waiting for Godot*. Single-handedly the drama provided dramatists with the freedom to be totally new. Although Beckett has been writing since the 1920s and has written voluminously in fiction, it was not until the production of *Waiting for Godot* in 1953 that his literary importance began a whole industry in academic scholarship. *Waiting for Godot* is to twentieth-century drama what Eliot's *Wasteland* is to poetry and Joyce's *Ulysses* is to fiction.

In *Beckett at Sixty,* a festschrift that Beckett has already survived by more than twenty years, scholars, playwrights, actors, and directors pay their tributes. Martin Esslin concludes his with a question.

Can there be a more memorable summing up of that basic image of all of Beckett's oeuvre, the final equation of *Birth* into a world unfathomable to the frightened being on the threshold of life, and *Death,* that terrified emergence into another unfathomable, unknowable state of being, than the final poem composed by the voice called Words in *Words and Music?*

> Then down a little way
> Through the trash
> Towards where
> All dark no begging
> No giving no words

No sense no need
Through the scum
Down a little way
to whence one glimpse
Of that wellhead.[7]

And Harold Pinter states: "The farther he [Beckett] goes the more good it does me. I don't want philosophies, tracts, dogmas, creeds, way outs, truths, answers, *nothing from the bargain basement.* . . . He leaves no stone unturned and no maggot lonely. He brings forth a body of beauty. His work is beautiful. I can't, now, use any 'words' about his work at all, except to say that he seems to me far and away the finest writer writing."[8]

Spanish playwright Fernandal Arrabal is "always fascinated by the magic mirror of this work [*Waiting for Godot*] whose voice continues to call to me like giant days. . . . In the everyday presence of the fantastic, Beckett, jumping out from behind the tombstones, brings to us the initiation, the hope and the despair. YES."[9] Alan Schneider, American director and friend of Beckett's, "hopes that in whatever language, he will go on writing for the theatre because one knows that he will go on extending its boundaries and its dimensions. Not because he plans it that way, but because that is where his taste and imagination and talent lead him. I shall be content to follow."[10]

Beckett's own statement best describes his art, simple in its minimalism and profound in the thoughts it teases. "I take no sides. I am interested in the shape of ideas. There is a wonderful sentence in Augustine: 'Do not despair; one of the thieves was saved. Do not presume; one of the thieves was damned.' That sentence has a wonderful shape. It is the shape that matters."[11]

CHAPTER III

JOHN OSBORNE: AN ANGRY YOUNG MAN

Thirty years after the explosion of anger by Jimmy Porter on the stage of the Royal Court Theatre on 8 May 1956, an *Observer* columnist wrote that "London is traveling backwards through time towards a relationship between wealth and labor that is almost pre-capitalist." In his apocalyptic statement, the writer, Neal Ascherson, goes on to say that this social decline means a return to "a huge service and craft population, making clothes and cutlery, furniture and designer rugs for the rich, mending their electronics and guarding their homes . . . not unlike the pattern of 18th-century Paris, where almost all employment depended on the needs of the Court and the thousands of privileged royal functionaries around it."[1] The dire prediction stems from the increasingly divided society that England has become, with the rich living in the south of England and the poor, growing poorer daily, in the north. Ascherson's description of England's decline eerily recalls the bleakness against which Porter unleashed his fury in 1956.

To the younger members of John Osborne's post–World War II generation, the angry vulnerability of a young man, helpless to effect any change in his own life and overwhelmed with bitterness at the British class system, became a rallying point for a general sense of frustration. For Porter, who has graduated from a red-brick university (although according to him it wasn't even red brick but rather white tile), even language such as "coming down," used by Oxford and Cambridge graduates, remains an insurmountable barrier between the privileged and their social subordinates. Jimmy's wife, Alison, makes it clear to her friend Helena that Jimmy "left" rather than "came down."

Jimmy Porter became a byword among the new critics when Kenneth Tynan, foremost among them, was alone in giving the play an unreservedly favorable review, even as traditional critics objected to the self-laceration of the main character. In the past, the class system of England had come under fire in the satires and farces of Wilde and Shaw and even in the naturalistic dramas of Galsworthy, but never quite in the intimate, highly personalized argument of an articulate, intellectual owner of a sweets stall in the dreary Midlands, who had nothing to look forward to and, indeed, no one against whom to vent his anger, except those who were closest to him. It is these feelings with which Osborne intended his audience to identify, "to see life through my mirror, to feel my image. . . . What they do with those feelings afterwords is somebody else's business. Politicians, Journalists. Those sort of people."[2] Osborne told Robert Muller that the middle class to whom the theater belongs must be made to feel and to care, and he, therefore, prefers to treat social inequities in terms of personal relationships.

Osborne began the so-called dramatic revolution in subject matter in 1956 and served as the cutting edge of Brechtian dramatists of all styles, a major grouping whose purpose is to use the stage as a vehicle for social change. His technique is not to attack a particular system directly but to change the way people feel and, therefore, think.

Born John James Osborne on 12 December 1929, the only son of a commercial artist and copywriter, Thomas Godfrey Osborne, and a barmaid, Nellie Beatrice Grove Osborne, the dramatist spent his early years in near poverty in London's Fulham district after his father's death in 1941. Educated at day schools and St. Michael's College, referred to by Osborne as a "rather cheap boarding school," he worked on trade journals, tutored, taught school, and eventually acted. Drifting into playwriting, he wrote a number of unproduced plays and two plays produced at provincial theaters. These two were written in collaboration, *The Devil Inside Him* (produced in 1950) with Stella Linden and *Personal Enemy* (produced in 1955) with Anthony Creighton. After *Look Back in Anger* in 1956, the plays flowed: *Epitaph for George Dillon* (written with Anthony Creighton in 1954 but not produced in London until 1958); *The Entertainer* (1957); *The World of Paul Slickey* (1959); *Luther* (1961); *Plays for England: The Blood of the Bambergs* and *Under Plain Cover* (1962); *Inadmissible Evidence* (1964); *A Patriot for Me* (1965); *Time Present* (1968); *The Hotel in Amsterdam*

(1968); *West of Suez* (1971); *A Sense of Detachment* (1972); *The End of Me Old Cigar* (1975); and *Watch It Come Down* (1976). There were adaptations: *A Bond Honoured* from Lope de Vega's *La fianza satisfecha* (1966), *Hedda Gabler* from Henrik Ibsen's play (1972), and *The Picture of Dorian Gray* from Oscar Wilde's novel (1975). With a few exceptions the plays were first performed at the Royal Court and helped establish that theater's reputation as London's foremost experimental stage. As resident playwright, Osborne is one of the earliest of the new dramatists to have a close working relationship with a particular theater and director. Artistic director George Devine and director Tony Richardson began a long relationship with Osborne when he was hired as an out-of-work actor. He played in a number of dramas, including Brecht's *Good Woman of Setzuan.*

Later George Devine described *Look Back in Anger* as the "bomb that would blow a hole in the old theatre and leave a nice-sized gap too big to be patched up."[3] If any one date stands out from all the others in the history of British drama since 1950, hardly anyone would disagree it is that of 8 May 1956. It is almost equally agreed, however, that the literary quality of *Look Back in Anger* is secondary to the impact that it had on audiences, critics, and future dramatists and to the critical controversy that it stirred. It was the shot heard around the British stage world.

Osborne's earlier drama, *Epitaph for George Dillon,* is interesting as a forerunner of *Look Back in Anger.* The main character, George Dillon, is a rough version of Osborne's more famous Jimmy Porter. As a young and poor actor-playwright, Dillon accepts the generosity and hospitality of a suburban London family, whom he takes advantage of even as he ridicules them behind their backs. Spurned by Ruth Gray, a sister of Mrs. Elliot, a surrogate mother, he eventually marries young and pregnant Josie Elliot to save the family reputation. At the same time, Dillon's play, whose flaws he is only too aware of, has become a commercial success. Unlike his successor, Jimmy Porter, however, George Dillon possesses a mediocrity that dooms him, and one pities rather than identifies with him.

The drama remains in the canon of Osborne an apprentice play containing the uneven outlines of future characters and situations. For example, Jimmy Porter is close to the mother of a friend, and she is suggestive of a surrogate mother. Jimmy, like George, resents needing others, in his case Alison and Helena. An important difference, on the other hand, should be noted. When Alison describes her love-hate relationship with Jimmy, she mentions being attracted to him for his going "into battle with his axe swinging around his head—frail, and so full of fire." George Dillon, however, lacks the energy and intellectual quality of a Jimmy; and Josie, the sensitivity of an Alison. Without these qualities, there is no impact like that of Jimmy's vitriolic anger.

Look Back in Anger, in structure and style, is conventional enough. Structured in three acts, like Ibsen's *Ghosts,* it is most Ibsen-like in its central theme: the importance of the past on the present. Ghosts, both personal and political, haunt the tortured Jimmy throughout. Just as characters in *Ghosts* exorcise the past, Jimmy and Alison Porter must rid themselves of their demons.

Jimmy and Alison live in a tiny flat in the Midlands of England with a close friend, Cliff Lewis. It is the 1950s, and Jimmy and Cliff run a sweets stall; Jimmy's background is lower middle class. He has been educated and is well read and extremely articulate. Alison's background is upper middle class. Generous, affectionate, loyal, ingenuous, Cliff is one of life's givers, and as such he tolerates, as does Alison, much of Jimmy's verbal abuse. The two men playfully wrestle, their wrestling sometimes turning serious. Jimmy's relationship with Alison is similar, at one point unintentionally involving physical harm to Alison in the form of a burn while she is ironing Jimmy's shirt. Throughout the play Cliff serves as a buffer between Jimmy and Alison in their domestic strife, which to an American audience is very much like that of George and Martha in Albee's *Who's Afraid of Virginia Woolf?*

At the end of act 1, in the style of the well-made play, the catalyst for the play's dilemma is introduced in the form of a phone call from Helena, an actress friend of Alison's, who is playing at London's Hippodrome and needs a place to stay. The stalemated dreariness of their lives continues in act 2 as Helena becomes a part of the domestic situation, encouraging and sympathizing with Alison. Finally, Alison, having had enough, leaves Jimmy and returns to her family, also leaving Helena to become involved in a brief affair with Jimmy. Only after Alison leaves does Jimmy find out from Helena that Alison is pregnant. Helena replaces Alison not only at the ironing board but also in bed. Eventually Cliff, who has told Helena that things between Jimmy and Alison would have been over long ago were it not for his presence, leaves, and soon after, Helena announces her departure. Alison returns, weak and exhausted after losing the baby. She and Jimmy huddle together at the conclusion, and in a final short monologue Jimmy, with "tender irony," recalls their pet names for each other—his was the bear and hers the squirrel. "We'll be together in our bear's cave, and our squirrel's dray, and we'll live on honey, and nuts—lots and lots of nuts. And we'll sing songs about ourselves."[4] The exorcism has left both exhausted, arms around each other as the play ends. The buffers have gone, and now they have only each other, with Jimmy's anger having drained them of all illusions.

With its conventional structure—even the conventional use of animals evokes Ibsen's *Doll's House*—the play is also traditional in its naturalistic handling of a dramatic conflict, the battle of the sexes, in which one character psychologically devours another. Ibsen, Strindberg, Williams, and Albee deal with similar situations in their plays.

What is so different about Jimmy's anger, and what has made his name a synonym for the new drama, is the raw, highly articulate unleashing of the anger, for which his own stifling present and the Edwardian past of Alison's family (and Alison herself) are but convenient objects. His anger indiscriminately hits those who cannot share his pain or his real feelings, especially those whom he loves. At one point Jimmy accuses everybody else of wanting "to escape from the pain of being alive." His pain is deep-rooted, going back to a father who came back from the war in Spain when Jimmy was only ten and whom Jimmy watched die for twelve months. It includes a mother who "was all for being associated with minorities, provided they were smart, fashionable ones. . . . You see, I learnt at an early age what it was to be angry—angry and helpless. And I can never forget it. . . . I knew more about—love . . . betrayal . . . and death, when I was ten years old than you will probably ever know all your life" (*LBA*, 69).

Even Alison's name and that of her brother, Nigel, Alison claims, sound weak and pusillanimous to Jimmy. At the beginning of the play he attacks Alison's Mummy and Daddy and their marquess of Queensberry manners, which are her heritage. Throughout the play Jimmy verbalizes his way through the societal ills of class-conscious England, summing up not only his personal frustration at being an educated sweets-stall owner but also the futility of his generation. "I suppose people of our generation aren't able to die for good causes any longer. We had all that done for us, in the thirties and the forties, when we were still kids. . . . There aren't any good, grave causes left. If the big bang does come, and we all get killed off, it won't be in aid of the old-fashioned grand design. It'll just be for the Brave New-nothing-very-much-thank-you. There is no brave new world to look forward to" (*LBA,* 104–5). Jimmy scrapes his own emotions to their very essence when he talks, perhaps for the first time ever, about his early child-hood. It is this deepest layer of the psyche to which Jimmy's journey takes him and his generation and to which he has given the name angry in a long succession of antiheroes. In Jimmy, Osborne has made a stage success of a failure in real life, a failure that some critics see as a metaphor for the failure of an entire civilization.

A year later, Osborne's *Entertainer* (1957), structured in thirteen short scenes, continued the antiheroic tradition in the character of Archie Rice, who to the British is almost as well-known a name as Jimmy Porter, as he has been made even more famous by Laurence Olivier's playing of the role. Archie, a seedy music-hall performer, is developed through a series of loosely organized episodes, including musical-revue numbers. His disintegration as a performer represents that of the vaudeville art (one of England's oldest traditions) and, by extension, of England itself. Archie is an older, more cynical version of Jimmy Porter. He tours in fifth-rate places, indulges in women and alcohol, and lacks any idealism whatsoever. John Raymond sees *The Entertainer* as a "genuine place of twentieth-century folk-art, a gro-tesque cry of rage and pain at the bad hand history is dealing out to what was once the largest and most prosperous empire in the world."[5]

There is a distinction in style between *Look Back In Anger* and *The Entertainer*. Gone is the conventional structure of the former, and in its place is a Brechtian epic-theater technique that by its very looseness precludes total emotional identification with the events. Even though the skits and songs of the performer are familiar to the English audi-ence and could evoke sympathy and nostalgia, this nostalgia is ironi-cally undercut by the performer's deterioration.

The same technique is employed in Osborne's next play, about an "angry" hero whom he created in Jack Oakham, alias Paul Slickey, in *The World of Paul Slickey* (1959), another play with music. This time the journalism profession is the target of his anger. "I dedicate this play to the liars and self-deceivers; to those who daily deal out treachery; to those who handle their professions as instruments of debasement; to those who, for a salary cheque and less, successfully betray my country; and those who will do it for no inducement at all."[6] Again, the words of Osborne suggest the nation's decline and Jimmy Porter's absence of idealism. Including theater critics in his assault on the mass media, Osborne suffered the worst notices, according to him, since Judas Iscariot.

The public setback of *The World of Paul Slickey* was more than compensated for in *Luther* (1961), a play that was accorded considerable international accolades, including the New York Drama Critics Circle Award for 1963–64 and the Tony Award in 1964. Drawn from *Young Man Luther* by the American psychoanalyst Erik H. Erikson, the drama about the young Martin Luther traces his development from an idealistic monk to a religious revolutionary. Relying almost exclusively on this source, Osborne writes a drama of long monologues and sharply written dialogues, sprinkled liberally with anal and bowel images. The drama consists of twelve scenes, one linked to the next by a knight who announces the time and place of each. This historical-narrative technique is, perhaps, Osborne's closest following of the loose Brechtian epic style.

On 18 August 1961, a month after the production of *Luther* at the Royal Court, Osborne wrote a letter to the *Tribune* from Germany and unleashed his own anger at the lack of effective political leadership in England. The responses to his attack were angry. At best, Osborne has received mixed reviews for his statement, and the letter only served to confirm his reputation as a self-pitying and self-lacerating dramatist.

In his next drama, *Plays for England* (1962), consisting of two one-act plays, one titled *The Blood of the Bambergs* and the other *Under Plain Cover,* Osborne experiments with satire and with intimate marital experience, respectively. The plays are a brief hiatus between *Luther* and a major play, *Inadmissible Evidence. The Blood of the Bambergs* satirically reworks the story of an 1894 play by Anthony Hope Hawkins, *The Prisoner of Zenda,* about royal weddings. *Under Plain Cover* returns partly to *The World of Paul Slickey* in its attack on shoddy journalism but, more importantly, treats marital intimacy with a new seriousness. Tim and Jenny are a variation of the usual sadomasochistic marital relationship, dealt with here in tenderly sexual terms. A news reporter reveals that they are, unknowingly, brother and sister; this causes a temporary separation that ends eventually in a reunion. Their sexual abnormalities involving a clothes fetish create for them a fantasy world that is temporarily destroyed by the reporter. In the end they are united, heedless of the knocking on the door by the reporter, who still insists on invading their private world. The title, *Plays for England,* carries out Osborne's intent once again to lash out at the social conformities that force individuals to realize their independence in intimate rituals denied them by prevailing social patterns. Critics have called attention to the absence, in this second play, of the "thrashing about" and the presence of "a genuine mutual tenderness," so that Tim and Jenny "come out as nice, sensible, moral people."[7]

In *Inadmissible Evidence* (1964), Osborne returns to the English world of Jimmy Porter, Archie Rice, and Paul Slickey in still another disintegrating hero, Bill Maitland, a lawyer. Combining surrealism with his usual naturalism, Osborne has written a drama that has the stark inevitability and compactness of a classical tragedy. There are no extraneous events, plots, and characters to distract from a total concentration on what is happening in the mind of his central character. We see Maitland at first in a surrealistic court scene strongly evocative of Franz Kafka. He is on trial, yet is simultaneously the accuser and the accused. The evidence that is inadmissible in this self-trial is his own life: "a wicked, scandalous and bawdy object." Like Joseph K. of Kafka's famous novel, *The Trial,* he attempts unsuccessfully to get in touch with colleagues and friends who might help him, until at the end all have deserted him.

After the initial nightmare scene, the happenings of the play occur in his law office over two days, during which the mental confusion of that first scene is realistically dramatized as his nervous collapse is completed. He desperately attempts, like Jimmy Porter, to make some personal contact with his staff, secretaries, clients, wife, daughter, and mistress. His collapse is total when Liz, his mistress, walks out on him.

What happens is seen, in long interior monologues, through the mind of Maitland; it is reminiscent of scenes in Arthur Miller's *Death of a Salesman*. As a dramatic achievement, the play is one of Osborne's finest. It is relentless in its psychological and moral concentration. Maitland's personal dilemma has been described by Wilfred Sheed as "all the rottenness and stagnation and aimlessness of a whole society"[8] locked up in one skull. More than in any other of his dramas, Osborne's voice is controlled, and his style is at its best. What is most distinctive, perhaps, is that there is no longer need for an Alison, or a music-hall audience, or a Pope, against whom the disillusionment is directed and exorcised; Maitland himself, his own conscience, is both antagonist and judge. Ego and alter ego represent man and society, respectively, one creating the other and in the process making each the victim of the other.

One remaining play of Osborne's will be discussed. It is yet another successful attempt to chronicle the life of a famous historical character, in the process dramatizing also the decline of an era, in this case that of the Austro-Hungarian empire. As with *Luther, A Patriot for Me* (1965) is drawn at least partially from a biography, Robert B. Asprey's *Panther's Feast*. Captain Alfred Victor Redl, of humble working-class origins, worked his way into the elitist Austro-Hungarian Imperial and Royal Army, the War College of the General Staff, and finally the Intelligence Bureau. Living two lives, one as a highly respected and decorated officer and the other as a homosexual blackmailed into spying for czarist Russia, Redl was eventually caught and permitted to commit suicide. Combining the complex history of the time with spy intrigue and with a socially forbidden sexual preference, Osborne writes another successful play about a failure, managing to secure audience sympathy for a character whose personal and professional actions violate societal and moral codes of conduct. As with Jimmy Porter, Archie Rice, Bill Maitland, Luther, and other antiheroes of Osborne, Redl is brilliantly conceived so as to encourage audience understanding of the reasons for his failure. Nearly ten years after Porter, he demonstrates Osborne's sustaining power to teach an audience to feel, not on sentimental terms, but on the basis of understanding, through deeply intimate experience in the context of an impersonal and destructive societal structure. Like no other dramatist, Osborne once more raises the level of passionate diatribe to an art. Redl joins a long list of Osborne's heroes with this verbal gift.

A Patriot for Me is a part of the history of British censorship. Produced three years before censorship was abolished, the drama was scheduled for major cuts by the lord chamberlain. In particular, a homosexual ball staged in full dress offended the censorship office. To avoid the requested cuts, the Royal Court formed a private stage club.

Although Osborne has written six additional plays, one of which, *Watch It Come Down* (1976), was performed at the National Theatre, none has had the critical and popular reactions of those discussed in this chapter. The concerns of the later plays are localized and, also, repetitive of situations that had already been so powerfully dramatized in his earlier dramas.

Stylistically, the passionate tirades, which to some critics are self-indulgent sadomasochism and to others honest outbursts of genuine and deep feeling articulately vented, are the unique hallmark of Osborne. His works represent a striking variety of modern dramatic modes: the well-made Ibsenian play, the Brechtian epic drama, the social satire, the historical chronicle, the courtroom drama, and even the music-hall revue. Effective where audiences are concerned, his plays, which are substantial in quality, quantity, and variety, have had minimal influence on the styles of other dramatists.

The reviews of *Look Back in Anger* were mixed at best. Cecil Wilson of the *Daily Mail* writes that the "repetitiousness cries out for a knife."[9] Milton Shulman of the *Evening Standard* decries the promising start of the play and the "sickening melodramatic thud"[10] with which the audience is let down. Philip Hope-Wallace of the *Guardian* describes it as "a strongly felt but rather muddled first drama"[11]; Patrick Gibbs of the *Telegraph,* as a "work of some power, uncertainly directed"[12]; and the *Times* reviewer, as a first play which "has passages of good violent writing, but its total gesture is altogether inadequate."[13] These are but a few of the negative comments that are a part of the immediate reviews of *Look Back in Anger*. The same reviews grudgingly note these weaknesses as those of a first play or even more reluctantly note some strengths. Cecil Wilson writes, "The English

Stage Company have not discovered a masterpiece but they *have* discovered a dramatist of outstanding promise; a man who can write with a searing passion, but happens in this case to have lavished it on the wrong play."[14] Milton Shuman comments: "But underneath the rasping negative whine of this play one can distinguish the considerable promise of its author. Mr. John Osborne has a dazzling aptitude for provoking and stimulating dialogue, and he draws character with firm convincing strokes. When he stops being angry—or when he lets us in on what he is angry about—he may write a very good play."[15]

Of the Sunday reviews, the *Times*'s Harold Hobson's was partly favorable and the *Observer*'s Kenneth Tynan's was overwhelmingly approving. Calling brief attention to the play's two weaknesses—the lengthiness and the final reconciliation scene—Tynan hails Porter as a new dramatic hero who totally contradicts Mr. Maugham's famous verdict on the "class of State-aided university students," that "they are scum."[16] Tynan admires Porter for his "flair for introspection, his gift for ribald parody, his excoriating candor, his contempt for phoniness," his weakness for soliloquy, and his desperate conviction that the time is out of joint. In fact, "Jimmy Porter is the completest young pup in our literature since Hamlet, Prince of Denmark." Tynan accuses many critics of falling "into the trap of supposing that Mr. Osborne's sympathies are wholly with Jimmy. Nothing could be more false. Jimmy is simply and abundantly alive; that rarest of dramatic phenomena, the act of original creation, has taken place; and those who carp were better silent." Tynan then responds to the main criticism of the character of Porter: Why doesn't he do something, rather than just excoriate and complain? "Why," Tynan responds, "don't Chekhov's people *do* something?" Tynan concludes that *Look Back in Anger* "is the best young play of its decade." With this review, Tynan established himself as a leading critic of the new wave of dramatists.

John Elsom (in 1976) also sees Porter as the "exact opposite" of "all those heroes of the time [T. S. Eliot's Becket] who could afford to disdain political power from a stance of natural superiority," whereas "Jimmy hungers for power from the position of social inferiority."[17] He notes, "Failing any other outlet for his energy, Jimmy's frustrations turn into self-loathing and are then redirected outward, into aggression against Alison."[18] Elsom sees Porter's alienation, and his view of the State as rotten, to be Osborne's major strength and limitation. Osborne's contribution to the theater, Elsom asserts, is not simply that of his plays but that of a pervasive, though indirect, influence during the 1950s and 1960s. First, the theater no longer needed to be genteel; second, audiences no longer needed "nice" people with which to identify; third, writers did not need to "be so overawed by the complexity of writing plays" or "deterred by the hopeless impracticability of finding managements to produce their works"; and fourth, "it was possible to write vivid and powerful speeches without making them sound verbally narcissistic."[19] Osborne's general theme of social alienation is dominant in many of the new playwrights: in the "wry comedies of Mortimer, Cooper and Orton, in the sense of 'losing roots' (a subject tackled by Mercer and Storey); in the fear-ridden world of Pinter; in the Marxist interpretations of 'alienation' expressed by Arden, Bond, Brenton and Griffiths: in many disguises and forms."[20]

The themes of social alienation and of the destructive nature of political systems, especially England's, pervade his plays and make them allegories for the times. The criticism of Osborne's later dramas has been fairly consistent with that of his first professionally produced play. In all his dramas, the anger remains, muted in some and dissipated in others by wryness, satire, or even tenderness (as in *Under Plain Cover*).

Events, as they are wont to do, provide interesting speculation in a historical survey. The year of *Look Back in Anger,* 1956, was marked also by the death of Bertolt Brecht, some of whose techniques Osborne employs in his historical plays and whose general didacticism regarding the inhumanity of systems toward man are given a unique, if limiting, voice in the plays of Osborne.

An indication of critical and academic views on Osborne is the relatively small number of short monographs or book-length studies published about his writing. Among them are monographs by Simon Trussler (1969), Harold Ferrar (1973), and Wilfred Owen and Dominic Hibberd (1975), and two book-length studies by Ronald Hayman (1972) and Arnold Hinchliffe (1984).

CHAPTER IV

HAROLD PINTER: MINIMALIST

If Osborne represents the dramatists with a social conscience, Harold
Pinter epitomizes the cool, apolitical nonpolemicists among the new
writers. With Beckett as a friend and major influence, Pinter, according
to Arnold Hinchliffe, who wrote the first of a prolific number of book-
length studies of the dramatist, is responsible for "the assimilation of the
Absurd Drama into the British way of life."[1] Hinchliffe writes: "This
ability to fuse European Absurdity with the English way of life, the
foreign with the native, the timeless and universal with the immediate
and local, gives Pinter's plays a lasting quality. He will remain one of
Britain's most important twentieth-century dramatists—in my opinion, the most important."[2]

Yet, even with the readily identifiable Beckettian influence, Pinter
has assimilated and shaped absurdist techniques into a style that remains distinctively his. Unlike Beckett, he does not have a philosophical ax to grind. Where ideas do exist, they are only a very small part of
a dramatic corpus that is sufficiently its own to have earned for its
author's name adjectival status in the English language. The "Pinteresque" label immediately evokes specific stylistic and situational
characteristics, in much the same way that Osborne's name calls to
mind the anger of a rebel without a cause. Like Beckett, Pinter has
influenced other writers and is also discussed in other chapters of this
book, as in the treatment of David Storey's *Home*.

If Beckett's dramas have invited aesthetic and philosophical analyses
and Osborne's social (and some psychological) commentary, Pinter's
plays have evoked stylistic, or linguistic, and psychological scrutiny.

Lois Gordon's monograph, *Stratagems to Uncover Nakedness* (Pinter's
own phrase), psychoanalyzes Pinter's characters. James Hollis's *Poetics
of Silence* views Pinter's plays in light of his aesthetic deployment of
language. Martin Esslin's *Harold Pinter: The Peopled Wound* traces the

development of Pinter's plays on the theme of "man's existential fear, not as an abstraction, not as a surreal phantasmagoria, but as something real, ordinary and acceptable as an everyday occurrence—here we have the core of Pinter's work as a dramatist."[3] Esslin notes that in one of Pinter's earliest writings, "A Note on Shakespeare," there is reference to a wound that is open, contained, and peopled. The wound is the world, and man, trapped in it, can "rely on a 'few well-chosen words' to bring him through any doubtful patch. He belongs, of course, ultimately to a secret society, a conspiracy of which there is only one member: himself."[4] Ambiguities, uncertainties, unverifiability, the constantly changing nature of truth and reality as these are perceived from one day to the next, fears of dislocation, menaces and threats to security: all these dictate the substance and style of Pinter's plays. Of the writers Pinter read at an early age—Joyce, Dostoyevski, Henry Miller, Kafka, and Beckett—the last two impressed him the most strongly. Assuming a hauntingly Kafkaesque basis for interpreting Pinter's plays, Esslin mentions the "political battlefield" in which the Mosley fascists of East London, where Pinter grew up, frequently "clashed with left-wing Jewish militants."[5]

The three approaches—psychological, linguistic, and archetypal—characterize in combination the many articles and books written about Pinter's dramas. Analyses of his use of silences and pauses point to his distinctive innovations of stage language, in which Beckett's influence is most visible. Attempts by critics to solve "Pinter's puzzles" provide the basis for the generally held view that his language and silences are not merely vehicles of expression but weapons in the enigmatic battles for dominance and security, the very substance of the dramas. Characters consciously or unconsciously use, or refrain from using, language in sparring with their threatening antagonists. According to Andrew Kennedy in *Six Dramatists in Search of a Language,* "Pinter has, then, invented a drama of 'human relations at the level of language itself.' "[6]

Born to Hyman Jack Pinter and Frances Mann Pinter on 10 October 1930, Harold attended Hackney Downs Grammar School, which, like the shabby section of London in which his family lived (his father was a tailor of Hungarian-Jewish extraction), was educationally poor, except for one English master, Joseph Brearley, whom Pinter describes as brilliant. During World War II, Pinter was evacuated to the country along with other youths. In 1948 he was fined thirty pounds for his conscientious objection when he was called up for military service. After acting on radio and television and attending the Central School of Speech and Drama, he toured Ireland for eighteen months with the company of Anew McMaster, about whom Pinter wrote a brief memoir entitled *Mac* (1968). He then acted at Hammersmith's King's Theatre during Donald Wolfit's 1953 season, and he met there Vivien Merchant, who later became his wife, the mother of their son David, and the leading actress in many of his plays. Pinter acted under the stage name David Baron.

In 1975, while Pinter directed Simon Gray's *Otherwise Engaged,* news of his affair with Antonia Fraser, a highly respected biographer and the wife of Sir Hugh Fraser, M.P., made headlines in London papers, a cause célèbre made even more sensational by Vivien Merchant's publicly expressed bitterness. In 1980 Pinter and Fraser were married.

Pinter's activities on the stage were increasingly directorial, and for a time he served as an artistic director at the National Theatre. His fierce insistence on privacy, one of the hallmarks of a Pinteresque character, eventually caused a split with the National Theatre's director, Peter Hall, when the latter published his diary (1985), in which he invaded Pinter's privacy. Pinter has continued directing plays, including Simon Gray's *Common Pursuit* in 1985 and Tennessee Williams's *Glass Menagerie* in 1986.

When, at the request of a friend, he wrote *The Room* (1957) for production at Bristol University, Pinter launched his playwriting career. Up to this time he had written poems, a few of which contain situations and characters that appear in his plays. Later that same year, *The Room* was entered in the *Sunday Times* drama festival and received a favorable review from Harold Hobson.

In a program note for the London production of *The Room* and *The Dumb Waiter* in 1960, Pinter wrote a simple statement that serves as basis for all the plays he has written and comes as near to explaining (something he is loath to do) what his characters and plays are about as anything he has said:

The desire for verification is understandable but cannot always be satisfied. There are no hard distinctions between what is true and what is false. The thing is not necessarily either true or false; the assumption that to verify what has happened and what is happening presents few problems I take to be inaccurate. A character on the stage who can present no convincing argument or information as to his past experience, his present behavior or his aspirations, nor give a comprehensive analysis of his motives is as legitimate and as worthy of attention as one who, alarmingly, can do all these things. The more acute the experience the less articulate its expression.[7]

What fascinated yet puzzled audiences of Pinter's early plays is the amount of information he withheld about his characters, and the explanations he refused to provide about them. The above program note very simply explains why he did so. In one stroke, it seemed, Pinter dismissed, at least for himself as a dramatist, the detail-laden plays of Ibsen, the highly articulate idea debates of Shaw, and, yes, the naturalistically detailed style of Osborne's *Look Back in Anger,* a play that Pinter had seen and been moved by. Following Pinter's major plays—*The Caretaker* (1960) and *The Homecoming* (1965)—audiences became accustomed to Pinter's puzzles and, consequently, came to expect what they saw in *Old Times* (1971), *No Man's Land* (1975), and *Betrayal* (1978).

In yet another rare explanation of his plays, in a speech delivered at Bristol University's Seventh National Students Drama Festival, reprinted under the title "Between the Lines" in the *Sunday Times* on 4 March 1962, Pinter provided the bases for the minimalist style for which he has become so famous. The comments on style lock into those quoted earlier about the information that his characters refuse to divulge to him and that, consequently, he cannot truthfully provide for audiences. Pinter's speech at Bristol begins with a reaction to a recent article by Robert Bolt in *New Theatre Magazine*. In that article Bolt suggests that the new plays (of Beckett, Ionesco, Simpson, Pinter) will be short-lived.

Rejecting the traditional notion of definitive statements and of definitive language usage in drama, Pinter explains:

Such a weight of words confronts us today, words spoken in a context such as this, words written by me and by others, the bulk of it a stale dead terminology; ideas endlessly repeated and permutated, become platitudinous and trite, meaningless. Given this nausea, back into, paralysis. I imagine most writers know something of this paralysis. But if it is possible to confront this nausea, to follow it to its hilt, to move through it and out of it, then it is possible to say that something has occurred, that something has even been achieved.[8]

Relating his comments on language to his creation of characters, Pinter goes on:

You and I, the characters which grow on a page, most of the time we're inexpressive, giving little away, unreliable, elusive, evasive, obstructive, unwilling. But it's out of these attributes that a language arises. A language, I repeat, where under what is said, another thing is being said. Given characters who possess a momentum of their own, my job is not to impose upon them, not to subject them to a false articulation, by which I mean forcing a character to speak where he could not speak, of making him speak of what he could never speak.

Explaining that he does not regard his characters as uncontrolled or anarchic, Pinter admits in the article to careful selection and arrangement of his characters' action and words, but also that "a double thing happens. . . . Sometimes a balance is found, where image can freely engender image and where at the same time you were able to keep your sights on the place where the characters are silent and in hiding. It is in the silence that they are most evident to me."

Narrowing his focus, Pinter mentions "two silences. One when no word is spoken. The other when perhaps a torrent of language is being employed. This speech is speaking of a language locked beneath it. That is its continual reference. The speech we hear is an indication of that which we don't hear. . . . One way of looking at speech is to say that it is a constant stratagem to cover nakedness." In a kind of "continual evasion" and in "desperate rear guard attempts to keep ourselves to ourselves," indeed, "to disclose to others the poverty within us," communication is alarming and fearsome. Yet there is a time when a character can say what he means. "And where this happens, what he says is irrevocable, and can never be taken back."[8]

Pinter's three language levels, then—the silence when no word is spoken, the silence in which a torrent of words occurs, and then the irrevocable spoken word that does express what a character means— become both the arena in which his dramatic conflicts are fought and the substance of those conflicts, rather than mere vehicles for thought. It is in this respect that Pinter's major contribution to the new drama is made.

The reliability of a character at a given moment in a play is constantly subject to change. Pinter states in the *Sunday Times* article, "A categorical statement . . . will immediately be subject to modification by the other twenty-three possibilities of it." This protean nature of truth invades the characters of Pinter's dramas and dictates that today's definitive statement may not be such tomorrow.

The silences—and they are dominant—in the dramas of Pinter can be likened to those voids of uncertainty in which Beckett's characters exist, and the constant contradictions in his characters evoke the fluidity and the psychological realities with which Luigi Pirandello endowed his characters. But the naturalistic patterns of speech are Pinter's. They constitute both the structure of his plays and a return to the stage of a poetry that the plays of T. S. Eliot and Christopher Fry may have realized, but only for the educated elite. Pinter's early inarticulate characters are the inhabitants of shabby tenements in the poverty-ridden sections of London.

Pinter's dramas of withheld details begin with a short play entitled *The Room* (1957). Important for images that reappear in his remaining plays, *The Room* features a married couple, Rose and Bert Hudd, whose day begins with a Ionesco-like conversation at breakfast before Bert sets off for his job as a lorry (truck) driver. Concern about the cold outdoors and the warmth of their small room in an old, dark apartment building dominates Rose's comments. Her nervous chatter slowly changes from concern about the weather to questions about who lives in the basement, her continual comments and questions being interrupted only by her pauses and her nervous movements from table to window to the rocking chair. The tension is increased by the appearance of Mr. Kidd, their landlord, whose comments about the weather are a prelude to his questions regarding household help, the rocking chair, and the room itself, which was once his bedroom "a good while back."

MR. KIDD: Best room in the house.

ROSE: It must get a bit damp downstairs.

MR. KIDD:	Not as bad as upstairs.
ROSE:	What about downstairs?
MR. KIDD:	Eh?
ROSE:	What about downstairs?
MR. KIDD:	What about it?
ROSE:	It must get a bit damp.
MR. KIDD:	A bit. Not as bad as upstairs though.
ROSE:	Why's that.
MR. KIDD:	The rain comes in.
	Pause
ROSE:	Anyone live up there?⁹

After divulging information about himself, including his "old mum," who he thinks "was a Jewess," he is asked by Rose where his bedroom is now. He gives her no definite answer except to say that he can take his pick of rooms. Bert, who has not spoken, leaves.

Lengthy stage notes describe Rose's anxious movements within the room, which precede her opening the door to find a young couple, Mr. and Mrs. Sands, on the landing, looking for the landlord. A conversation similar to the earlier one ensues, with a heated argument between Mr. and Mrs. Sands about whether Mr. Sands was sitting down or just perching, and with a similar linguistic quibble between Rose and the couple about whether they had said they were coming up or coming down. They leave, and Mr. Kidd reappears, raising questions in Rose's mind about whether her room is to be rented and whether or not he really is the landlord. He informs her that a man has been waiting to see her. The man, a blind black named Riley, appears, and her anxiety is raised even more in a strange conversation that moves the earlier realistic conversations into new linguistic territory. Riley has a message from her father, who wants her to come home.

ROSE:	Home?
RILEY:	Yes.
ROSE:	Home? Go now. Come on. It's late. It's late.
RILEY:	To come home.
ROSE:	Stop it. I can't take it. What do you want?

RILEY: Come home, Sal.

. . . .

ROSE: Don't call me that." (*R*, 114)

Bert eventually returns home and, for the first time, speaks. "I got back all right." It is obvious, from his narration about edging another driver off the road so that he could have it all to himself, that he is angry. He strikes the blind Riley with a chair, whereupon the play closes with Rose's "Can't see. I can't see. I can't see" (*R*, 116).

The images of the play are Pinteresque: 1) a room with two people in it, one standing and the other sitting; 2) the menacing entrance of an intruder whose presence creates a threat to the security of the inhabitants; 3) a reversal of positions of superiority. Rose seems to have handled the intrusions of the landlord, the young couple, and even Riley, until Bert returns to find Rose touching Riley's eyes, back of the head, and temples with her hands. In the play's brief and theatrically sudden ending, in which for the first time Bert speaks and, also, acts, a displacement has occurred. The warmth and security of their room are gone. The intruders, particularly Riley, give little of themselves away and serve only to create uncertainties. Riley, awakening in Rose some deeply buried note from a real or imagined past, represents the culmination of the many intrusions on her security.

Pinter's rooms are metaphors for the psychological rooms that his characters have built for themselves. In protecting their rooms from intruders, the characters create the conflict in which what they say and what they don't say build the tension in the drama. When the spoken and unspoken silences collide, the irrevocable word is spoken and the displacement occurs. Bert refers to his van as "she," and the references of his short speech are overtly sexual: "I kept on the straight. There was no mixing it. Not with her. She was good. She went with me. She don't mix it with me. I use my hand. Like that. I get hold of her. I go where I go. She took me there. She brought me back." Riley's last words are "Mr. Hudd, your wife—" and Bert's response is "Lice!" as he strikes Riley (*R*, 116).

The conflicts of Pinter's dramas are internal, and the only evidence of them is what each character chooses to withhold about himself or herself. Inner uncertainties take the form of external threats such as the landlord and the young couple, but the realism soon changes to surreal menace in the person of the enigmatic Riley, who emerges from the dark basement that Rose fears. He gives the audience and Rose no comfortably realistic details about himself. His vagueness and unexplainability dislocate the comfortable room Rose has created for herself. Riley's hauntingly oedipal influence on Rose and Bert's virile self-assertion at the conclusion complete her inner dislocation. At the end of the play, in a reversal of the initial positions in the room, Bert is vocal, active and dominant.

The situation of *The Room* is extended in *The Birthday Party* (1958), Pinter's first full-length play. The setting is a shabby seaside boarding house run by Meg and Petey Boles. Petey rents out chairs on the beach, and Meg runs the boarding house. Her only boarder at the time is Stanley, a failed musician, whose fantasy speeches include a catalog of exotic places where he has performed. Two men, Goldberg (a Jew) and McCann (an Irishman) arrive, ostensibly as guests, although it is soon evident that their intentions are hostile. They arrive on the eve of a birthday party Meg plans for Stanley in honor of his first anniversary as guest. When they leave, taking Stanley with them, they have sanitized him from the human derelict that he was, into a kind of humanoid whom they will deliver to a "Monty" for treatment.

The birthday party ends theatrically with the lights going out and Lulu, a local seductress, on a table, spread-eagled, with Stanley bent over her. Goldberg and McCann take him upstairs. The next morning they promise him rehabilitation.

GOLDBERG: You need a long convalescence.

MCCANN: A change of air.

GOLDBERG: Somewhere over the rainbow.

MCCANN: Where angels fear to tread.

GOLDBERG: Exactly.

MCCANN: You're in a rut.

GOLDBERG: You look anaemic.

MCCANN: Rheumatic.

GOLDBERG: Myopic.

MCCANN: Epileptic.

GOLDBERG: You're on the verge.

MCCANN: You're a dead duck.

GOLDBERG: But we can save you.

MCCANN: From a worse fate. (*BP,* 82)

Who are Goldberg and McCann? Their platitudes in the long, stichomythically written diagnosis of Stanley's condition suggest cultural pressures of the Western world, symbolized by Goldberg, a Jew, and McCann, a Christian. Their Kafkaesque charges against Stanley remain as vague and troublesome to audiences and critics as does Riley's appearance in *The Room.* Meg's mothering of Stanley suggests the oedipal theme that is present in the Riley–Rose episode. The comfortable pattern of life for Petey, Meg, and Stanley has been disrupted by the surreal menace over which they have no control.

The Dumbwaiter (1959), frequently compared with Hemingway's "Killers," again is about a room in a basement, in what used to be a restaurant; it is occupied by two men, evidently hired to kill someone. While they wait for the victim to come, they receive strange messages from someone via the dumbwaiter. They fill the time by telling stories, reading newspapers, and arguing about whether one "lights the stove" or "lights the kettle" for tea. In their language games they reveal increasing tensions. Gus leaves the room briefly. When he returns, he faces Ben with his gun in hand. The initially realistic situation develops into a psychological and surreal battle, in which Gus beomes Ben's victim.

In *A Slight Ache* (1959), a play first produced by BBC Radio Third Programme and then later (1961) staged, Pinter changes his setting to an upper-middle-class country house occupied by a middle-aged couple, Edward and Flora. Their comfortable life-style is disrupted by a dirty old match seller at their gate. As they watch him and eventually invite him into the house, layer after external layer of their comfortable existence peels off, and the play ends with Flora embracing the old man and placing his tray of matches, which are useless, around Edward's neck.

The first of Pinter's several major dramas, however, did not appear until 1960: *The Caretaker.* The couple here consists of two brothers, one of whom, Aston, has had a lobotomy and is the caretaker of an apartment building that his brother, Mick, owns. Aston brings home a tramp, Davies, who takes advantage of him and attempts, when Mick arrives on the scene, to ingratiate himself with the latter by derogating Aston. The friendliness soon turns hostile, climaxing in a duel between Davies and Mick.

Interpretations of the play range from Esslin's view of the brothers' actions as a classical struggle between sons and a father figure, and of the brothers as a Beckettian Didi and Gogo duo,[10] to Simon Trussler's view that Pinter has mythicized Aston into Everyman and Mick into Mercy, thus creating an allegory for our time. According to Trussler, Everyman Aston represents thwarted creativity, symbolized by the cluttered junk shop of an attic in which Aston resides, always planning to build a shed and working with "good wood."[11]

The linguistic exchanges between Aston and Davies grow threatening as the latter asserts a hold on Aston. Davies's threat against Aston, however, boomerangs and ends in his own eviction from the building. He continues to search for identity papers that, he keeps repeating, he has left in Sidcup.

Much more detail about the characters is provided in this play than in the preceding ones. Aston explains his lobotomy in a long monologue, and Mick and Davies have realistically hostile arguments about Davies's intentions. The theatrical climaxes of *The Room, The Birthday Party,* and *A Slight Ache* have been replaced by naturalistic scenes that contribute to the audience's increased understanding of the play.

We know from Mick's first appearance that he is the man of action who will tolerate no threats to his brother's security, even though in a fantasy-joke speech he suggests exotic improvements Davies could effect in the apartment. "You could have an off-white pile linen rug, a table in . . . in afromosia teak veneer, sideboard with matt black drawers, curved chairs with cushioned seats, armchairs in oatmeal tweed, a beech frame settee with a woven sea-grass seat, white-topped heat-resistant coffee table, white tile surround. Yes."[12] He seems to have convinced even himself of the improvements, carried away by the images he projects. Fantasy speeches regarding furniture and food are hallmarks of Pinter's plays. Ben and Gus in *The Dumbwaiter* occupy their time with small talk of food; in *A Slight Ache* the imagery is floral, a contrast with the animal appeal of the match seller. The poetic images increase with every play, replacing the histrionics of the early ones.

If Mick's identity is safely assured, those of Aston and of Davies are less so. Aston's elliptical sentences, silences, nonsequiturs, and vague confusion about what "they" did to him in the hospital build into a poetry, as do Davies's more instinctive fears about the possibility of being taken in for not having the right number of stamps on his identity card. He has changed his name, revealing his real name to Aston but using the assumed name with Mick. Aston and Davies perhaps have more in common than do the two brothers. Both have identity problems, one mental and the other physical. The clutter of functionless objects in Aston's attic resembles his basic inability to build the shed; he can only talk about building it. Davies, like Stanley in *The Birthday Party,* who loses what identity he has, will go on looking for his Sidcup papers, in order to have a proper identification card.

In the second of his major dramas, *The Homecoming* (1965), the information provided by Pinter and the sophistication of his stylistic techniques increase. Even so, verification remains elusive. Pinter's room this time is a shabby old house in north London in which reside a father (Max), his two sons (Lenny and Joey), and his brother (Sam). Returning to his ancestral home, Teddy, another son, who teaches philosophy at an American university, brings with him his wife, Ruth, who causes an upheaval with her influence on her husband's entire family. Max, the father and a retired butcher, calls her a whore and yet makes arrangements at the end for her to remain in London while her husband returns to America. Sam, Teddy's uncle and a cab driver, serves as an object for Max's hostility, because Jessie, Max's late wife, had enjoyed a sexual intimacy in the back seat of his cab. Lenny, a homosexual, has plans for Ruth's work as a prostitute. After all, she had been a "model" before she and Teddy married. Both Lenny and Joey enjoy Ruth's favors, although Lenny accuses her of being a "tease." At the end, Teddy leaves for his campus and his three children, admonishing Ruth not to become a stranger.

Pinter has described *The Homecoming,* in an interview granted a year or so after it opened, as "the only play which gets remotely near to a structural entity which satisfies me. . . . *The Birthday Party* and *The Caretaker* have too much writing."[13] Integral to the structure of *The Homecoming* is the development of one main character, Ruth, whose appearance in her husband's home is the means by which Pinter is able to unify what in earlier plays may seem like the wandering of each character into his own labyrinthine psychological and linguistic paths. Ruth serves as a mover of the play's action. In the course of her confrontations with members of her husband's family, she catalyzes each into revealing enough about himself to create tensions, tensions that are finally resolved by her decision not to return to America.

Like the sale of the cherry orchard that Chekhov, in his play of that title, uses as a means to evoke his characters' innermost states of being, the homecoming of Ruth disrupts the conscious surfaces of life in her husband's family home. She and Teddy arrive at night while the family are supposedly asleep. Unable to sleep, Ruth goes out for a walk and upon her return faces Lenny, who also is unable to sleep. Immediately, the first of a series of psychological negotiations occurs in which her intrusion, resented at first, eventually results in her domination of those who would dominate her.

Max's attempted domination of the household is clearly established in the first scene. He demands to know where Lenny has put the scissors, and Lenny tells him to "shut up, you daft prat?" They argue about which horse will win a race. When Sam comes home from his cab driving, Max teases him about banging away at his lady customers on the back seat. Sexual references dominate his language, whether he is speaking of fillies with Lenny or of customers with Sam. Sam resents the constant sexual innuendos and finally asks to be left alone, explaining that when he had taken Jessie out in the cab, he had merely been taking care of her for Max. Max's domination extends to Joey, his youngest son, who has just returned from boxing lessons. Unlike his brother and uncle, Joey does not engage his father in verbal play, but merely goes off to bed.

It is into this male household that Teddy and Ruth arrive. In her first meeting with Lenny, Ruth puts him on the defensive as he launches boastfully into a long speech about his sexual conquest of an "insistent lady" who took liberties with him under an arch. To a quietly listening Ruth, he relates at length another story, of an old woman who approached him about helping her move her iron mangle. His stories of exploits of women contrast sharply with his nature as an impotent pimp. He later accuses Ruth of being only a tease when he discovers that she has not "gone the whole hog" in a sexual episode upstairs with Joey. Pinter's technique in dramatizing a psychological battle is illustrated in the incident of the water glass. When she first arrives, Ruth accepts Lenny's offer of a glass of water. When he offers to relieve her of the glass, she refuses, saying she hasn't quite finished. He says she has had quite enough, in his opinion. "Not in mine, Leonard," she responds. His offense at her calling him a name his mother used is followed by her suggestive and very direct comment that if he takes the glass, she'll take him. He responds by questioning whether her final draining of the glass was some kind of proposal. The extended argument about the trivial glass of water externalizes a deep psychological conflict.

The play consists of a series of these psychosexual duels until Ruth has asserted herself as the mistress of them all, including Max, whose early, strongly worded hostility to Ruth ends with his crawling on his knees before her. Teddy emerges as the sterile intellectual of the family, whose living of the American dream is insufficient for Ruth. Lenny articulates his resentment of his brother's life after Teddy has eaten a cheese roll Lenny had put in the cabinet. "We're in the land of no holds barred now."

It's funny, because I'd have thought that in the United States of America, I mean with the sun and all that, the open spaces, on the old campus, in your position, lecturing, in the center of all the intellectual life out there, on the old campus, all the social whirl, all the stimulation of it all, all your kids and all that, to have fun with, down by the pool, the Greyhound buses and all that, tons of iced water, all the comfort of those Bermuda shorts and all that, on the old campus, no time of the day or night you can't get a cup of coffee or a Dutch gin, I'd have thought you'd have grown more forthcoming, not less.[14]

Meantime, Joey and Max have joined Lenny in planning an elaborate apartment for Ruth so that she can support herself and them sexually and financially. Lenny even suggests that Teddy encourage his American professor friends who visit England to patronize Ruth's establishment. Failing to persuade Ruth to return to America with him, Teddy leaves.

However shocking the actions of the play, *The Homecoming* is generally regarded as Pinter's major play. In the United States especially, its critical reception was strong. It received the Tony Award, the New York Drama Critics Circle Award and the Whitbread Anglo-American Award. Controversies, however, remain. In England, Simon Trussler, nearly ten years later, writes that the play "is sick, and each thing melts in mere, unmotivated oppugnancy."[15] At the other end of the critical spectrum, Esslin comments that "the universality of the archetypal situation in *The Homecoming* . . . and its immense, if perhaps subconscious, relevance to theatre audiences everywhere, seems to me another explanation for the powerful impact of the play in spite of an initial reaction of incomprehension and puzzlement over its apparent surface 'implausibility.' However much audiences may reject *The Homecoming* on the rational level, they ultimately respond to it in the depth of their subconscious. Hence the abundance of the discussion and probing about *The Homecoming*."[16] Esslin explores the oedipal theme in earlier Pinter plays, concluding that in *The Homecoming* the theme "had gradually risen to the surface as Pinter gained the self-confidence and formal skill that enabled him to meet it head on rather than merely obliquely."[17]

After *The Birthday Party* and *The Homecoming,* Pinter wrote three more full-length plays: *Old Times* (1971), *No Man's Land* (1975), and *Betrayal* (1978). All three are characterized by their middle- or upper-middle-class characters, in a Proustian treatment of the effect of their pasts on the present.

In *Old Times,* Anna remarks that "there are some things one remembers even though they may never have happened. There are things I remember which may never have happened but as I recall them so they take place."[18] In this play a husband (Deeley) and wife (Kate) are visited by a mutual friend (Anna) whom they haven't seen for twenty years. During her visit, Anna vies with Deeley for Kate's attention, making the play a teeter-totter of psychological games. Kate remains silently enigmatic in her reactions to recollections of the past that Anna and Deeley use in their wittily genteel battle for possession of Kate. At the end, Deeley sits slumped in an armchair, Anna lies on the divan, and Kate, dominant, sits up on the divan. These final positions reflect the relative winner and losers of the psychosexual battle. Throughout the play, the constantly changing positions of the characters indicate temporary dominance by one character or another.

In Pirandellian fashion, the past proves to be a strange, uncharted country that continually dislocates the familiar present, as all three remember the same situation quite differently. The most lyrically poetic of Pinter's dramas up to this point, *Old Times* marks a decided shift by Pinter into the introspective play, in which the unverifiability of any one of the twenty-four possibilities of a given situation, discussed in his Bristol speech quoted above, is the glue that holds together the puzzling actions and verbal exchanges.

No Man's Land, a compendium of Pinter's earlier characters and themes, is about a successful writer (Hirst) who takes into his home a shabby stranger (Spooner), and the action is generated from Spooner's attempt to take the place of one of Hirst's two servants while pretending to be Hirst's friend. It is the servants, however, who close ranks with their master, and Spooner finds himself eventually expelled.

Betrayal, a play about marital betrayals, stands out with its structure, in which Pinter reverses the chronology of events. Each scene moves backward in time in the affair between Emma and Jerry, who was best man at Emma's wedding to Robert. The conspicuous absence of the puzzles of earlier plays and the mechanical structure of the drama brought accusations of stylistic betrayal from some critics. Pinter's own marital situation involving Lady Antonia Fraser had only recently been a cause célèbre, and much of the criticism focused on the autobiographical parallels.

Of Pinter's three later full-length stage plays, only *Old Times* demonstrates the inventive quality evident in *The Caretaker* and *The Homecoming. No Man's Land* was enhanced by Sir John Gielgud and Sir Ralph Richardson, who played the leading roles. Spooner and Hirst seem elaborate, upper-middle-class versions of Davies and Aston.

Pinter's dramatic influence, however, is not limited to the six full-length dramas. He wrote sketches for radio and television, film scripts for his own plays, and film adaptations of novels, and he has continued to write short stage plays. Among his film scripts is *Proust,* a remarkable adaptation of the seven novels of *Remembrance of Things Past.* The script was not produced because of financial difficulties, but it has been published. A master of the short play, in which one or more voices speak, Pinter has received strong acclaim for two: *Landscape* and *Silence.* These "sketches" recall Beckettian characters like Winnie of *Happy Days* or Krapp of *Krapp's Last Tape. Triptych* (1984) is a trio of short dramas: *Victoria Station, One for the Road,* and *A Kind of Alaska.* The last, about a woman awakening from a long coma, is a fascinating variation of one of Pinter's favorite themes, that of the "no man's land" that people inhabit. Conscious or unconscious of this habitation, Pinter's people play games of language and silence, dominance and subservience, truth and lies, knowing and being known, and hostility and friendship, and, perhaps most importantly, the largest games of all, those warding off the threatening menaces to their security.

In addition to the short plays discussed, Pinter's early sketches include *Trouble is in the Works* and *The Black and White* for *One to Another,* a revue (1959), and *Request Stop, Last to Go, Special Offer,* and *Getting Acquainted* in another revue, *Pieces of Eight* (1959).

His radio scripts include *A Slight Ache* (1959); *A Night Out* and *The Dwarfs* (1960); *That's Your Trouble, That's All, Applicant,* and *Interview* (1964); *Dialogue for Three* and *Landscape* (1968); and *Family Voices* (1981). For television, Pinter wrote *Night School* (1960), *The Collection* (1961), *The Lover* (1963), *Tea Party* (1965), *The Basement* (1967), and *Monologue* (1973).

To those familiar with the novels listed below, it is obvious that their subjects would hold interest for Pinter. Most of them contain the identifiably Pinteresque themes. In addition to writing scripts for his own plays—*The Caretaker,* with the film title *The Guest,* (1964), *The Birthday Party* (1968), and *The Homecoming* (1971)—Pinter has written film adaptations: *The Servant* (1963), from Robin Maugham's novel; *The Pumpkin Eater* (1964), from Penelope Mortimer's novel; *The Quiller Memorandum* (1967), from Adam Hall's *Berlin Memorandum;* *Accident* (1967), from Nicolas Mosley's novel; *The Go-between* (1971), from L.P. Hartley's novel; *The Last Tycoon* (1975), from Scott Fitzgerald's novel; *The French Lieutenant's Woman* (1981), from John Fowles's novel; and *The Turtle Diary* (1985), from Russell Hoban's novel. Pinter's screenplay for Proust's *Remembrance of Things Past* is published in a separate edition. *The Servant, The Pumpkin Eater, The Quiller Memorandum, Accident,* and *The Go-between* are available in a published collection. Whether for radio, television, or film, Pinter's writing contains the thematic and stylistic concerns that have made his stage plays distinctive.

Walter Kerr, likening Pinter's influence in his time to that of Euripides in Greek drama, writes that "Pinter might be called 'traditional' in the sense that he has begun to restore, under the fresh questioning of a twentieth-century philosophical method, an old and neglected urge to enter the arena naked, without the support of tried-and-true tricks or proved propositions but with a firm determination to move as much as a man may move against whatever can be made to yield to him."[19] Thus, Pinter breaks current dramatic patterns even as he adheres to a much larger literary tradition—that of the iconoclast. William Baker and Stephen Tabachnik conclude their book on Pinter with the comment that "through his art, the Hackney Jew [Pinter] like the French half-Jew, Marcel Proust—attempts to capture the movement and set it above the uncertainties that time brings."[20]

Simon Trussler sees Pinter as an actor's playwright, who writes "around a hard kernel of situation, enwrapping this in arbitrary layers of attitude, ambivalence, distortion and doubt that is the individual's attempt to bring reality within the bounds of personality and so to make it bearable."[21] Latent violence at the beginning of a play slowly simmers into its externalization, a private concern on stage that mirrors the public condition of the world at large in the twentieth century.

With regard to techniques of language and silence, James Hollis contends that Pinter's tradition "is not so much that of Stanislavski with his 'sub-texts' as the ancient silences of the Kabuki and mime. The silences of his plays are not programmatic; they are dramatic."[22] Lois Gordon sees Teddy in *The Homecoming* as returning to the rituals of civilization, and Ruth as remaining "to provoke the ancient antagonisms between generations. Ironically, Eden is not innocent, nor civilization corrupt; the latter is an endless round of banal responsibilities, the former—to use Freud's phrase—'a seething cauldron' of sexual intrigues. Things are not what we suppose; but then, if they were, we would have no need for Pinter and his stratagems."[23] In his revised study (1981), Arnold Hinchliffe asserts that Pinter will survive, since "of all contemporary British dramatists he alone manages to be topical, local, and universal—to give a shape to unconscious impulses and record ordinary behavior." He is the "*miglior fabbro*" (master craftsman).[24]

Like his characters in their rooms, guarding their territory against the twenty-four possibilities in a given statement or situation, Pinter guards his territory against the many interpretations of his plays. In response to an inquiry about the meaning of his plays, he said, "The weasel under the cocktail cabinet." To a woman who wrote a letter about *The Birthday Party,* asking who the two men are, where Stanley comes from, and whether all the characters are supposed to be normal, Pinter replied: "I would be obliged if you would kindly explain to me the meaning of your letter. These are the points which I do not understand. 1. Who are you? 2. Where do you come from? 3. Are you supposed to be normal? You will appreciate that without the answers to my questions I cannot fully understand your letter."[25]

However many the interpretations and whatever the adjectival coinages that Pinter dislikes (Pinteresque, Pinter pauses, Pinter puzzles, Pinter's people, Pintermania), all verify the uniqueness and importance of Pinter. Ultimately, all demonstrate Pinter's own major dramatic thesis, the unverifiability of experience and truth.

Without identifying his characteristics as influenced by other writers, one can hardly avoid noting Pinter's kinship with them: the psychological flux of Pirandello, the concern of Proust with the past and with tricks of memory, the conversational techniques of Ionesco, and the voids of uncertainty that pain Beckett's Didi and Gogo. Pinter's drama is that of the cool, clean-shaven, apolitical new English dramatists, whose characters survive, however they will, in a Kafkaesque world created by politicians.

CHAPTER V

TOM STOPPARD: PARODIC STYLIST

Collaborative dramatist, creative plagiarist, inventive parodist—these are but a few descriptions of Tom Stoppard, who startled the dramatic world in 1966 with his drama *Rosencrantz and Guildenstern Are Dead*. In this play, two of Shakespeare's most insignificant characters assume center stage, relegating Hamlet, Claudius, and Gertrude to peripheral status. Similarly in *Travesties* (1974), a minor British consular official stationed in Zurich, Henry Carr, who existed historically, becomes the consciousness through which revolutionary characters and events in literature, art, and politics are filtered. Those characters include James Joyce, Tristan Tzara, and Lenin from real life, and Gwendolen and Cecily, two fictional characters from Oscar Wilde's *Importance of Being Earnest*. In yet another drama, *Dogg's Hamlet, Cahoot's Macbeth* (1979), Stoppard combines a school performance of *Hamlet* with a farcical and deadly serious "living room" production of *Macbeth* by Pavel Kohout, a Czechoslovakian dramatist, living in the restrictive milieu of his native Czechoslovakia.

In addition to reinventing plots and characters from other dramatists, Stoppard has a sizable list of traditional adaptations to his credit. Some of these are fairly standard: Slawomir Mrozek's *Tango*, Federico Lorca's *House of Bernarda Alba*, and Arthur Schnitzler's *Das Weite Land* and *Leibelei*. Others—Johann Nestroy's *Einen Jux will er sich machen*, as Stoppard's *On the Razzle*, and Ferenc Molnár's *Play at the Castle*, as his *Rough Crossing*—undergo the kind of reinvention that characterizes Stoppard's major dramas.

Stoppard's literary raids, however, are only half the reason for his success on the stage. The other half consists of the unabashedly theatrical verbal gymnastics through which he directs his characters, and the brilliantly incongruous situations that make up his plots. Rich with literary allusions, puns, paradoxes, parodies, verbal and intellectual games, and strong visual images, his language has been likened to Joyce's, and his high comedies of ideas to those of Wilde and Shaw.

Stoppard's freewheeling plots and his linguistic exuberance contrast with the severity and stark minimalism of Pinter's dramatic speech and Pinter's style of withheld information. Yet both dramatists share an aloofness from the social, political, and moral polemics of the new waves of dramatists in England.

Both writers, having created stylistic revolutions of a sort, wrote plays in the late 1970s (Pinter's *Betrayal* and Stoppard's *Night and Day*) that are toned-down imitations of their early plays. And both have commented on their awareness of having cast themselves in dramatic molds they need to break. Pinter is tired of writing about people in rooms, and Stoppard is "sick of flashy mind projections peaking in long, articulate witty sentences about the great abstractions."[1] As a result, Pinter's most recent plays have been short ones or, more accurately, long sketches; Stoppard's have increasingly been "committed" dramas about political freedoms in eastern Europe or, as in *The Real Thing,* attempts to provide credibly emotional dimensions to his characters, both characteristics missing in the flashy earlier dramas.

The brilliant linguistic and visual tapestry of Stoppard's dramas has tested the descriptive vocabulary of the critics. *Travesties* is a "tinderbox of a play blazing with wit, paradox, parody, and yes, ideas. It is exhilarating, diabolically clever. The bloodline of Wilde and Shaw is not extinct while Tom Stoppard lives."[2] If an enthusiastic critic's plaudits sound extravagant, those of Richard Ellmann, noted Joycean scholar, are similar, if more subdued. He refers to "a stoppardism or a tomism, as when Tzara is accused of being 'Kant-struck,' and Wilde disparaged as 'coxcomb and bugbear of the Home Rule Sodality.' These laundered obscenities perhaps convey some sense of the flagrant high spirits of this admirable play."[3]

In an article on Stoppard's earlier play *Jumpers* (1972), Sir Alfred Ayer, Wyckham Professor of Logic at Oxford University, writes that "Tom is the only living dramatist whose work I would go to see just because he wrote it."[4] Ayer, a logical positivist, is parodied in *Jumpers* in the character of Sir Archibald Jumper. Clive Barnes, the *New York Times* critic, describes *Jumpers* as a "zany, theatrical invention with cerebration" that at its best "suggests the Shaw of *Man and Superman,* the Wilder of *The Skin of Our Teeth.*" Barnes "cannot really think of any English writer since John Donne who has been able to joke in such amusing philosophical terms. Mr. Stoppard is not a philosopher—he is very definitely a playwright. But he uses the world and that world's thought that he finds around him in something of the wild, dizzy and exhilarating manner of a metaphysical poet."[5]

Other critics have found the debates in plays such as *The Real Thing* and the Beckettian conundrums of Rosencrantz and Guildenstern to be shallow attempts at being clever. Irving Wardle describes the former as "cleverness with its back to the wall."[6] Martin Gottfried, acknowledging the literacy of *Rosencrantz and Guildenstern Are Dead,* regards the play as hammering "at a philosophical point of view that is never developed beyond the basic statement. Its existentialism is shallow and its debt to Samuel Beckett extreme. Mr. Stoppard is clever but his play is not profound."[7] C. W. E. Bigsby agrees with Gottfried that the play is not complex, but that "its strength lies precisely in the skill with which he [Stoppard] has blended humour with metaphysical inquiry, the success with which he has made the play's theatricality an essential element of its thematic concern. It is, indeed, a kind of *Waiting for Godot* in which Vladimir and Estragon become university wits."[8]

Like Pinter, Stoppard is the subject of many book-length studies, most of them investigations of the prolific allusions in, and sources of, the plays.

Born the younger of two sons to Dr. and Mrs. Eugene Straussler on 3 July 1937 in Zlin, Czechoslovakia, he was only two years old when, on the eve of Hitler's move into that country, his father, a company doctor at Bata, an international shoe company, was transferred to Singapore.[9] Prior to the Japanese invasion of Singapore, Mrs. Straussler and her two sons were again moved, this time to India. In Darjeeling, Stoppard's mother managed a Bata shoe shop, and the boys attended a multinational American school. Dr. Straussler was killed during the Japanese invasion. His widow later married Major Kenneth Stoppard, who moved the family to England in 1946. Tom Stoppard's education continued at the Dolphin School in Nottinghamshire and at Pocklington School in Yorkshire. Saying he was "thoroughly bored by the idea of anything intellectual," gladly selling "all my Greek and Latin classics to George's Bookshop in Park Street," and "totally bored and alienated by everyone from Shakespeare to Dickens besides,"[10] he describes the influence of his education as chiefly negative.

His stepfather, who was in the machine-tool industry, moved the family from place to place, finally arriving in Bristol, where at seventeen Tom Stoppard joined the *Western Daily Press.* His journalistic experience there consisted of news reporting and feature writing. After four years, he went to write for the *Evening World,* where his interest in the theater began. Moving to London and to *Scene,* a short-lived magazine, he wrote theater reviews. Within seven months he reviewed 132 plays, under the pseudonym William Boot, a character from Waugh's novel *Scoop.* The name Boot recurs in a number of Stoppard's plays.

Meantime, Stoppard published three short stories ("Life, Times: A Fragment," "Reunion," and "The Story") and wrote two radio plays ("*M" Is for Moon among Other Things,* about Marilyn Monroe's death, and *The Dissolution of Dominic Boot*). An option on his play *A Walk on the Water* was purchased by a commercial television company. These efforts he describes as the "transition to living off playwriting."

About the time that *Scene* magazine folded, Stoppard was granted a Ford Foundation grant to attend a Berlin colloquium for promising young playwrights. Between May and October 1964, he wrote a Shakespearean pastiche, *Rosencrantz and Guildenstern Meet King Lear.* Two years later the piece, which had grown into a full-length play, was produced at the Edinburgh Festival. The next year, on the stage of the National Theatre at the Old Vic, Stoppard's career as dramatist was convincingly launched with the play with whose title characters Stoppard still remains strongly identified: *Rosencrantz and Guildenstern Are Dead.* In addition to the auspicious Edinburgh debut of the play, 1966 is important as the release date of his only novel, *Lord Malquist and Mr. Moon,* commissioned by Anthony Blond. Having expected a favorable review, Stoppard was surprised when it was the play, and not the novel, that garnered positive notices.

Stoppard's writing in 1965 included seventy episodes of *A Student's Diary,* a serial about an Arab in London, translated into Arabic and

Figure 1. Samuel Beckett
Photograph by Jerry Bauer

Figure 2. Peter Woodthorpe, Peter Butt, and Paul Daneman in a scene from *Waiting for Godot*
Photograph courtesy of the Theatre Museum, London

Figure 3. John Osborne
Photograph by Mark Gerson

Figure 4. Kenneth Haigh, Vivienne Drummond, and Tam Bassett in a scene from *Look Back in Anger*
Photograph courtesy of the Theatre Museum, London

Figure 5. Harold Pinter
Photograph by Mark Gerson

Figure 6. Tom Stoppard
Photograph by Dr. Miriam Stoppard

Figure 7. Royal Court Theatre
Photograph by Mark Gerson

Figure 8. National Theatre
Photograph by Mark Gerson

broadcast on BBC Radio. In addition, *A Walk on the Water* and *If You're Glad I'll Be Frank* were broadcast on BBC Radio, *A Separate Peace* on BBC Television.

The awards began coming. He received the John Whiting Award (jointly with David Storey) from the Arts Council and the *Evening Standard* award as the most promising playwright in 1967. In America he won both the Tony Award and the New York Drama Critics Circle Award for *Rosencrantz and Guildenstern Are Dead.* In addition, *Teeth* and *Another Moon Called Earth* were broadcast on BBC Television, and *Albert's Bridge* (BBC Radio) won the Prix Italia.

Play followed play on stage, radio, and television, as *Enter A Free Man* (revised from *A Walk on the Water*) and *The Real Inspector Hound* opened on the London stage in 1968, *After Magritte* opened in 1969, and additional short plays—*Where Are They Now?* and *The Engagement*—were aired on BBC Radio and Television, respectively.

Stoppard's second major play, *Jumpers,* produced by the National Theatre at the Old Vic in 1972, received the *Evening Standard* award and the *Plays and Players* award as the best play of the year. *Jumpers* was followed two years later by *Travesties,* the third of his major dramas. Both enjoyed successful productions in London and New York, and Stoppard's reputation for dazzling images and linguistic pyrotechnics reached new heights. *Dirty Linen and New-Found-Land,* two plays in one, is Stoppard's tribute to America's bicentennial in 1976.

Up to this time, Stoppard had rejected the notion of social commitment in his writing. Like Harold Pinter, he insisted on the primacy of theater as an event in and of itself and not as a forum for ideas or causes. Although ideas and political causes may grow from that event, they are neither the beginning nor the end of the play. Later, however, political protests became a part of his personal and professional life. As a member of the Committee Against Psychiatric Abuse, he spoke in 1975 at a rally in Trafalgar Square and marched to the Soviet embassy to petition for the rights of Soviet citizens. In 1977 he visited Moscow, Leningrad, and Prague with an Amnesty International official. He wrote long newspaper articles and letters on behalf of political freedom. In Czechoslovakia he met dissident playwrights Vaclav Havel and Pavel Kohout.

That same year, 1977, *Every Good Boy Deserves Favour,* about eastern European political prisoners, with music composed by André Previn, was performed at the Royal Festival Hall in London and at the Metropolitan Opera House in New York. Also in 1977 *Professional Foul,* about English academics at a Czechoslovakian philosophical congress, was aired in England, and the next year in America.

Although not advocating any particular political cause, *Night and Day* (1978) is a play about newspapermen involved in an African revolution. It received attention as a naturalistic drama about various journalistic types, rather than as political commentary. The generally mixed reviews emphasized Stoppard's seeming change of stylistic direction from the imaginatively innovative techniques of his earlier plays to a more naturalistic and, consequently, lesser mode. *The Real Thing* (1982) opened to similar critical reception in London.

Scattered among his full-length stage plays, five of which stand out sharply as his major work, and his many radio, television, and shorter stage plays are his stage adaptations mentioned earlier. His screen adaptations include Thomas Wiseman's *Romantic Englishwoman,* Vladimir Nabokov's *Le Meprise,* Graham Greene's *Human Factor,* and P. D. James's *Innocent Blood.* He also rewrote the film script for *Brazil.*

Degrees have been conferred on Stoppard by Brunel University (1979), the Universities of Leeds and Sussex (1980), and the University of Warwick (1981). He is the recipient of the Shakespeare Prize of the FVS Foundation, Hamburg (1979), and was named a Commander of the Order of the British Empire (1978).

Stoppard prefers, above all, the quiet life in Iver Heath, a London suburb, where his family and his writing constitute his life.

Kenneth Tynan's description of Stoppard is as appropriate a conclusion as any for a biographical sketch of the dramatist.

[It is] essential to remember that Stoppard is an émigré. A director who has staged several of his plays told me the other day, "You have to be foreign to write English with that kind of hypnotized brilliance." . . . Stoppard loves all forms of wordplay, especially puns, and frequently describes himself as a "bounced Czech." . . . Nowadays, he is *plus anglais que les anglais*—a phrase that would please him, as a student of linguistic caprice, since it implies that his English can best be defined in French.[11]

Each of Stoppard's five major dramas is characterized by a debate carried on between antagonists: about the nature of fate and free will

(*Rosencrantz and Guildenstern Are Dead*), moral philosophy (*Jumpers*), art (*Travesties*), love (*The Real Thing*), and science (*Hapgood*). The debates are carried on with a linguistic brilliance that invites comparisons with Shaw and Wilde, as already mentioned. In the first play, Shakespeare's two insignificant characters debate with the Player, a member of a troupe of itinerant players who perform the Gonzaga play in *Hamlet,* regarding the reason they find themselves in the court at Denmark and the question whether or not they can outwit destiny. In Pirandellian terms, the debate is about role playing as reality and about the protean nature of life, which denies man absoluteness or fixity. In *Jumpers* Stoppard takes on modern logical positivists in the person of Sir Archibald Jumper, who practices philosophical jumperism as George Moore, a traditionalist, prepares throughout the play for his competition with Duncan McFee, a logical positivist, for the chair of logic at a university. Debating the nature of revolutionary art in yet another high comedy of ideas, *Travesties,* Stoppard dramatizes ideas in the persons of Lenin, to whom art is a vehicle for political reform, Tristan Tzara, to whom art is dadaism (the extreme opposite of Lenin's position), and Joyce, for whom art is its own excuse for being.

In *The Real Thing* Stoppard conducts a debate on the nature of love, orchestrating an ex-wife, a precocious teenage daughter, and the current wife's lovers, an actor and a writer, into a play-long debate between Henry, the playwright-husband, and Annie, the actress-wife–political activist. In near unanimity, critics called attention to Stoppard's attempt to create, at last, characters in their full human dimensions. Henry and Annie are witty, articulate protagonists, as are characters in his other plays, but here their debates are rounded out with the pains and joys of human needs, Henry learning the painful truth about his wife, whose sexual and activist needs are not entirely fulfilled or approved of by him. Stoppard had been criticized for creating characters with intellectual and linguistic brilliance but without credible emotional dimensions, and it is these qualities that he has combined with wit and intelligence in *The Real Thing.*

Other stage plays, *Every Good Boy Deserves Favour* and *Dogg's Hamlet, Cahoot's Macbeth,* and television plays, *Professional Foul* and *Squaring the Circle,* are Stoppard's response to the critics who complained about the absence of social commitment in his early dramas. Political conscience, conservatively attuned, is present in Stoppard's plays since the late 1970s. In *Night and Day,* about a revolution in Africa, two journalists—one a seasoned liberal unionist and the other a young nonunionist—argue their respective positions, and it is the latter who is portrayed sympathetically and the former cynically. Similarly, Brodie, a coarse political activist in *The Real Thing,* for whom the stage is the vehicle for his ideas, is a caricature, rather than a fully realized character like the nonactivist playwright Henry.

As a writer of high comedies of ideas, then, Stoppard belongs to a long-standing tradition. The wildly extravagant, farcical plots and vivid images around which he builds the debates constitute the basis for his distinction. Rosencrantz and Guildenstern are wrenched from their positions of insignificance to those of metaphysical pretensions. The opening scene of *Rosencrantz and Guildenstern Are Dead*—with its Beckettian characters, Ros and Guil, tossing coins endlessly and repetitiously—is the image that dominates the drama. In what is perhaps the most extravagant of Stoppard's plot concoctions, *Jumpers* opens with a party scene, hosted by Dotty, wife of a moral philosophy professor, George Moore. Her party celebrates a radical-liberal election victory. A pyramid of gymnasts, clothed in yellow uniforms, performs, and Dotty, a retired but still young popular songstress, attempts to sing, although with little success. A shot is fired, one of the jumpers is killed (he turns out to be Duncan McFee, George's rival for the university chair), and an Agatha Christie–like investigation of the murder follows. George, heedless of the goings-on in his home, prepares his lecture with the help of a pet hare and a tortoise, which he uses to demonstrate his theories. Tortoise and hare are killed accidentally by George, and his theories undergo a similar fate.

Travesties is yet another creatively plagiarized plot, this time from Oscar Wilde's *Importance of Being Earnest.* Wilde's characters Gwen and Cecily are transformed by Stoppard into a secretary and a librarian who mishandle the briefcases of their respective employers and/or heroes. The opening scene is a library in Zurich in which three revolutionaries—Lenin, Joyce, and a dadaist painter, Tristan Tzara—work. Stoppard conjectures that since all three were in Zurich in 1917, they may have used the library at the same time. Acknowledging his debt to Richard Ellmann's *James Joyce,* Stoppard, using the library scene as setting, incorporates an actual event from Ellmann's biography into a reworking of Wilde's play. The event is a production of *The Importance of Being Earnest* by Joyce, with a lawsuit stemming from an argument with a young consular official, Henry Carr, over payment for clothes Carr has bought to wear in his role as Algernon. The debates on art by the revolutionaries, political, literary, and artistic, and the minor theatrical event are held together in the plot by the confusion of briefcases. Joyce's notes for a chapter of his *Ulysses* (the famous Homeric episode of the "Oxen of the Sun") mistakenly find their way into Tzara's possession, and Lenin's political treatise into Joyce's. Identity confusions abound when, as in Wilde's play, Tzara takes a pseudonym in order to further his romantic interest with Gwen; Carr's interest in Cecily is romantically concluded when the mistaken identities are finally cleared up.

The plotting of *The Real Thing* seems toned down after the extravaganzas that the three earlier dramas presented. Yet even this play has its own distinctive "ambush for the audience" (a phrase used by Stoppard in connection with his plots). Unknown as such to the audience until the second scene, the first scene in this drama is that of an onstage performance of a play by Henry, whose main character is Henry, an architect. The architect's role is played by Max, whose unfaithful wife, Charlotte, played by playwright Henry's wife, Charlotte, returns from a "business" trip. His house of cards, in the form of a hotel, collapses with her slamming of the door; she brings him a present from her supposed trip to Switzerland, a bowl with a snowstorm activated upon shaking. In the next scene, a real-life one, Henry and Charlotte are visited by Max and Annie, and it is obvious that Henry and Annie are enjoying an affair. Swiftly the play focuses on Henry and Annie's married life after their respective divorces. For Annie, their honeymoon is soon over, and she finds her sexual and emotional fulfillments with a fellow actor and with Brodie, a playwright inferior to Henry but competition for Henry in his marital life. In the tradition of Noel Coward's *Private Lives* and, sometimes, Edward Albee's *Who's Afraid of Virginia Woolf,* the plot develops into an intellectual sparring between Annie and Henry. Henry is eventually educated into an understanding of his wife's needs, which include her social activism, her acting, and her sexual-emotional nature. His former wife, Charlotte, and his young daughter, Debbie, contribute to his education. And so the marital situation of Henry the architect in the play-within-a-play in act 1 is played out in the real life of Henry the dramatist.

One more example will be mentioned here to illustrate the inventive plotting of Stoppard. In *Dogg's Hamlet, Cahoot's Macbeth,* the construction of a stage for a schoolboys' performance of *Hamlet* turns, in the second half of the play, into a truncated *Macbeth,* acted in the living room of Cahoot; the incident is borrowed from a real-life experience of Pavel Kohout. Professor Dogg is the bond between the two parts as he introduces schoolboy doggerel from act 1 into the Czech portion in act 2 to confuse the inspector (censor) there. But ingeniousness here overwhelms substance; cleverness obtrudes on aesthetic quality. Stoppard has frequently spoken of his difficulty with the "nuts and bolts," or plotting, of his plays. He has described, for instance, *After Magritte* and *The Real Inspector Hound* as attempts "to bring off a sort of comic coup in pure mechanistic terms."[12] At its best, however, his wedding of plots with ideas results in a high comedy of ideas that is unique in twentieth-century British drama.

If the imaginative reinvention of other writers' plots is a hallmark of Stoppard's plays, even more so are the intellectual sparkle and the sheer poetic joie de vivre provided by his linguistic exuberance. The ideas of the comedies seem merely a vehicle for the exotic, frequently parodic, wordplay and word images. He has described the idea debates in his dramas as "a series of conflicting statements made by conflicting characters, and they tend to play a sort of infinite leap-frog. You know, an argument, a refutation, then a rebuttal of the refutation, then a counter-rebuttal, so that there is never any point in this intellectual leap-frog at which I feel *that* is the speech to stop it on, *that* is the last word."[13] In a variation of this statement, Stoppard pays tribute to Beckett, describing in the process his own frequent adaptations of Beckettian technique. "Beckett qualifies as he goes along. He picks up a proposition and then dismantles and qualifies each part of its structure as he goes along, until he nullifies what he started out with. Beckett gives me more pleasure than I can express because he always ends up with a man surrounded by the wreckage of a proposition he had made in confidence only two minutes before."[14]

Stoppard's only novel, *Lord Malquist and Mr. Moon,* Kenneth Tynan asserts, contains Stoppard's philosophy, if it can be called such, at its purest. Two types of characters embody the philosophical stances to be found in the people of his plays. These are the Boots and the Moons: those who do things and those to whom things are done. In the novel, Lord Malquist rides his eighteenth-century carriage through the labyrinthine streets in the heart of modern London on the day of the funeral of Britain's last heroic man of action, presumably Winston Churchill. He pronounces the death of the old hero and the emergence of the new one: one to whom style is all. Lord Malquist is a Boot character, even as Moon, whom he hires to record his pronouncements for posterity, is the character to whom things are done. Moon himself intends to write a history of the world, but he has difficulty with the meanings of events and finds it impossible even to begin his monumental work. He eventually loses himself in those meanings, his loss symbolized by the explosion of the ticking bomb he carries with him throughout his Boswellian journey with Lord Malquist. Boot survives as a stylist; Moon dies as a failed philosopher-historian.

George Moore, the leading character in *Jumpers,* is one of Stoppard's Moon characters from real life, this one the G. E. Moore whose philosophical work *Principia Ethica* is sympathetically parodied in the character of George Moore. In rehearsing for his lecture (on good and evil) in the academic competition, George synthesizes the traditional philosophies of the Western world in a brilliant confusion of references that include Plato's "fire at the mouth of our cave." Illustrating the nature of causality, in this case why his socks exist, he expounds: "Because a sock maker made it, in one sense; because, in another, at some point previously, the conception of a sock arrived in the human brain; to keep my foot warm in a third, to make a profit in the fourth. There is reason and there is cause and there is the question, who made the sockmaker's maker? etcetera, very well, next. . . ."[15] Causality is the link among actions, as Aquinas, Zeno, Bertrand Russell and his theory of descriptions, and others join Plato and Aristotle in George's philosophical romp through time. George's lecture occurs in a nightmarishly surreal coda to the drama, in which he calls as witness to his arguments Zeno Evil, St. Thomas Augustine, and Jesus Moore—all of them dead—and the late Herr Thumper, the hare he had intended to use in demonstration of his thesis about good and evil. George collapses under the weight of his confused arguments, just as Moon in the novel dies in the explosion. Archie Jumper survives. George's verbalized intellectual propositions are wrecked by the life-style and logical positivism of Archie, who can explain away even the murder of George's academic rival, McFee, shot dead out of the pyramid of gymnasts performing at the outset of the play.

The ultimate stylist in Stoppard's dramas is James Joyce in *Travesties*. The parodic style of Stoppard is at its peak in his use of Wilde's plot and his use of scenes from Joyce's *Ulysses*. The Ithaca episode in *Ulysses* is jokingly imitated in a debate between Joyce and Tzara, the dadaist.

JOYCE: What is the meaning of this?

TZARA: It has no meaning. It is without meaning as nature is. It is Dada.

. . . .

JOYCE: Are you the inventor of this sport or pastime?

TZARA: I am not.

JOYCE: What is the name of this inventor?

TZARA: Arp.

JOYCE: Is he your sworn enemy, pet aversion, bete noir, or otherwise persona non grata?

TZARA: He is not.

JOYCE: Is he your friend, comrade-in-arms, trusted confident or otherwise pal, mate or crony?

TZARA: He is.[16]

The surrogate father–son relationship between Leopold Bloom and Stephen Dedalus in *Ulysses* is transformed by Stoppard into the quarrel between Joyce and Tzara on the nature of art. Stoppard's own definition of the artist, in response to Tzara's statements that "making poetry should be as natural as making water" and that traditional forms should be smashed, is that he is "put among men to gratify—capriciously—their urge for immortality. . . . If there is any meaning in any [of history], it is in what survives as art, yes even in the celebration of tyrants, yes even in the celebration of nonentities." It is the broken pots of history, "enriched by a tale of heroes . . . above all, of

Ulysses, the wanderer, the most human, the most complete of all heroes—husband, father, son, lover, farmer, soldier, pacifist, politician, inventor and adventurer . . . by God *there's* a corpse that will dance for some time yet and *leave the world precisely as it finds it*" (*T,* 62–63).

Stoppard parodies Joyce's use of limericks.

> A Rumanian rhymer [Tzara] I met
> used a system he based on roulette
> His reliance on chance
> was a def'nite advance
> and yet . . . and yet . . . and yet . . .
>
> . . . .
> When I want to leave things in the air
> I say, "Excuse me, I've got to repair
> to my book about Bloom." (*T,* 35)

Stoppard's parody of Joyce's language reaches its heights in a long monologue by Carr, the minor consular official, who speaks of being "released into folds of snow-white feather beds, pacific civilian heaven! the mystical swissticality of it, the entente cordiality of it! the Jesus Christ I'm out of it!—into the valley of the invalided—Carr of the Consulate!" (*T,* 41). Stoppard's parodies of language, style, and plot in *Travesties* are, indeed, "caviar for the general public," a phrase from *Hamlet* used by Stoppard to describe Joyce's *Ulysses.* In Shakespeare's play, Hamlet remembers that the Gonzaga play he asked the players to perform "pleased not the million; 'twas caviar to the general."[17] If any drama of Stoppard's can lay claim to being caviar to the general public, it certainly is *Travesties,* with its enormous leapfrogging of parodic allusions to literary and historical events and characters.

Stoppard has fun playing with what critics have called the "cognomen syndrome." A character is given a variety of names. For example, there is the play on Joyce's feminine-sounding name as Carr, angry at Joyce for the latter's stinginess, unleashes epithets: Irish lout, Deirdre, Bridget, Joyce, Sponger.

One final example of Stoppard's ingenious word play is seen in the fantasy monologue of *Every Good Boy Deserves Favour,* in which two Ivanovs (the cognomen syndrome here provides fascinating confusion in identities) are incarcerated, one a political prisoner and the other a "mental patient." One of them launches into a personal anecdote, evocative of Stanley's fantasy narrative of his concert performances in Pinter's *Birthday Party*.

You can speak frankly. You will find I am without prejudice. I have invited musicians into my own house. . . . Listen, I've had clarinet players eating *at my own table.* I've had French whores and gigolos speak to me in the *public street,* I mean horns, I mean piccolos, so don't worry about me, maestro, I've sat down with them, *drummers* even sharing a plate of tagliatelle Verdi and stuffed Puccini—why I know people who make the orchestra eat in the kitchen, off scraps, the way you'd throw a trombone to a dog, I mean a second violinist, I mean to the lions."[18]

The variety and the freshness of Stoppard's language, highly entertaining in his high comedies of ideas, turns somber in the political plays, where the parodies are of language manipulated for repressive purposes. As Stoppard becomes tired of "flashy mind projections," his later dramas, such as *Night and Day* and *The Real Thing,* lose the linguistic scintillation of the earlier dramas.

An important part of Stoppard's success, both critical and commercial, is the recognition factor as characters appear from fictional sources and from real life. In *Jumpers,* the philosopher, G. E. Moore, and the singer, Dorothy Moore, are named for real people, and Sir Alfred Ayer, the prominent logical positivist and an acquaintance of Stoppard, is indirectly parodied. The reinventions of characters from *Hamlet* and from *Beckett* in *Rosencrantz and Guildenstern Are Dead* are obvious. The mythical characters from Sophocles' *Philoctetes* are recognizable in *Neutral Ground.* Characters from Robert Bolt's *Flowering Cherry* and Arthur Miller's *Death of a Salesman* are easily spotted in *Enter a Free Man.* And, in fact, Stoppard reinvents even his own plays. An early television play, *Another Moon Called Earth,* is re-created in *Jumpers,* and a radio play, *Artist Descending a Staircase,* is expanded and sophisticated into *Travesties.*

In a retrospective view of his work, Stoppard comments that although *The Real Thing* "seemed to come closer to people's experience than anything else I'd written," he is "not sure that the kind of play I'm here to write isn't closer to *Jumpers* and *Travesties*—intellectual extravaganzas."[19] The brilliant structuring and then dismantling of philosophical propositions in *Jumpers* and the equally brilliant display of linguistic fireworks in *Travesties,* pointed out in review after review of these dramas, support Stoppard's own view of his writing to date.

In demonstration of his comment about "intellectual extravaganzas" as the type of play he is here to write, Stoppard definitely returns to the high comedy of ideas in *Hapgood* (1988), a spy thriller, whose real thrills consist of what seem like an orgy of intellectual constructions built to dislocate audience assumptions. He creates ambushes for the audience in a series of dizzyingly intricate scientific propositions that become a metaphor for arguments on the nature of truth.

Set in the murky world of M.1.6, M.1.7, or M.1.8 (British CIA), the play focuses on an English female operative, Hapgood, who ranks high on the intelligence scale. Her code name is Mother, and she is working with German-born Kerner in an attempt to find out if secrets have been passed on to the Russians. There is a proliferation of possibilities of double, triple, quadruple, etc., spying, not only by the major characters but by several lesser spies. The confusion of identities is complicated by a liaison between Hapgood and Kerner. Their child, now a boy in a public school, adds an important personal dimension to the actions. Questions grow as identities and counter-identities are revealed. Is Kerner a "sleeper" placed in England by the Russians? Has Hapgood turned him into a defector? Is she herself a double agent? Or is one of several minor characters, Ridley, the guilty one? Or, finally, have secrets been passed at all?

Stoppard's metaphor for the determination of what is reality and what is illusion—light particles that may become waves and that may simultaneously pass through two holes—is brilliantly argued by Kerner. At one point, Kerner states that "the particle world is the dream world of the intelligence officer."[20] Thus, truth in the spy world is as random and as confusingly elusive as particles.

Kerner joins a growing galaxy of characters in Stoppard's plays, particularly Archibald Jumper (*Jumpers*) and James Joyce (*Travesties*), who explore the nature of truth from the perspectives of moral philosophy and art, respectively. In Hapgood, that perspective is science carried to a philosophical end. In his review of the play, Benedict Nightingale declares that it would help a viewer "to be familiar with quantum theory, Heisenberg's uncertainty principle, Kant's philosophy, and the novels of John Le Carré."[21] Nightingale adds, however, that such knowledge is not necessary to enjoy the play simply as a "*Tinker, Tailor, Soldier, Spy,* as it might have been written by Einstein in collaboration with Groucho Marx."[22]

CHAPTER VI

FANTASISTS: ABSURD, FARCICAL, AND PRIMAL

N. F. SIMPSON, JOE ORTON, DAVID RUDKIN

The plays of N. F. Simpson, Joe Orton, and David Rudkin would seem to have little in common, except that all three dramatists possess a striking originality in dealing with subjects and styles that have been the concern of their contemporaries of the new waves of British drama. Simpson's dramatic vision enlarges the absurdity of societal behavior even beyond the treatment given it by Rumanian-born Ionesco, to whom Simpson demonstrates obvious affinities. So outlandish that they are beyond any expectation of explanation, his situations remain unrivaled in their lack of reason. In fact, they contradict every law of cause-and-effect logic and do so in the most acceptable modes of proper behavior and articulate speech. This paradox is obvious in the names of Mr. and Mrs. Paradock, the married couple of his first play, *A Resounding Tinkle*. Like the title of his first play, that of his widely recognized play, *One Way Pendulum,* unabashedly declares the paradoxes that are the beginning, middle, and end of a Simpson play. Likened to Lewis Carroll by his admirers and to popular British television writers by others, Simpson is a memorable voice of the new drama, the master of non sequitur situations that proceed in rational modes.

Another equally distinctive voice, but one whose relentless logic is the means by which his characters pervert conventional attitudes into the most outlandish conclusions, is that of Joe Orton, whose farcically grotesque humor excludes no sacred cow from its attack. To Americans, the closest approximation to the farces of Simpson and Orton, the one situational and the other verbal, would be the British Monty Python television series. Both Simpson and Orton are so British in their high-style farces that to Americans, who possess little homogeneity of manners or culture, the deadpan seriousness with which the farces are played sometimes creates only confusion or misunderstanding. Yet it is this genius to dramatize the ludicrous and outlandish situation in the guise of ordinary speech and logic that is the uniqueness of both dramatists. It is also the genius of Pinter, who uses the ordinary, not for farcical effects, but for the surreal transference of the banal speech and actions of daily life to a psychological dimension beyond themselves.

A third dramatist to claim uniqueness is David Rudkin, who begins with a realistically ordinary situation, such as workers on a farm in rural England, and by the end of the play transforms that deceptively familiar situation into a ritual of human cruelty that has critics identifying him with the theatre of cruelty of the French playwright Antonin Artaud. Civilized veneers are slowly penetrated in the gradual enactment of ancient, primitive rituals of Orpheus-like dismemberment.

All three dramatists have written relatively few stage plays, and each is especially famous for one play that critics have lauded as his best: Simpson's *One Way Pendulum,* Orton's *What the Butler Saw,* and Rudkin's *Afore Night Come.* All three writers are very much a part of the new waves. Simpson began his association with the Royal Court Theatre in 1956. Orton and Rudkin both enjoyed the admiration and encouragement of Pinter, who recognized in them a kinship with his own dramatic voice and view of life.

In what may seem a strange coincidence, Terence Rattigan, whose well-made and conventionally structured popular dramas felt the impact of the new forces on the stage, also paid homage to both Orton and Rudkin. He "fell wildly in love" with *Entertaining Mr. Sloane,* comparing it with Restoration comedies, particularly Congreve, and seeing it in some ways "better than Wilde because it had more bite."[1] Rattigan wrote Orton that if the play were not a masterpiece, Orton would "write a masterpiece before the decade is out."[2] And when Rudkin, after seeing a production of Rattigan's *The Browning Version* in 1975, wrote that the play held its audience of blue-denimed young people rapt by its depiction of a "deep personal, surely sexual pain, which he [Rattigan] manages at the same time to express and disguise,"[3] Rattigan said that Rudkin was quite right but that he, Rattigan, "never thought my slip showed as much as that, [nor] if it did, [that] the author of *Afore Night Come* would be the one to spot it."[4]

In the use of the ordinary both to express and to disguise the extraordinary (Orton and Rudkin) and in the use of the extraordinary to point out the banality of the ordinary (Simpson), all three dramatists, despite the small number of their stage plays, have earned an important place in the history of British drama since 1950.

N. F. SIMPSON

Born in London on 29 January 1919 to George Frederick and Elizabeth Rossiter Simpson, Norman Frederick Simpson served in the Royal Artillery in World War II, took an honors degree from the University of London (Birkbeck College), and taught in an adult education program at the City of Westminster College, London. A latecomer to playwriting, he gave up teaching to write plays full-time in 1963. Simpson served as literary manager at the Royal Court from 1976 to 1978. His first play, *A Resounding Tinkle,* shared third-prize honors with plays by Ann Jellicoe and Richard Beynon in 1956 in the *Observer* play competition.

In its literal and very obvious form, the theater of the absurd takes command in a Simpson play. Ionesco-like, the strangest of happenings occur and are treated as usual and ordinary events. In *A Resounding Tinkle,* a visitor arrives at the home of suburbanites Bro and Middle Paradock to announce that he wishes Bro to form a government. Then comedians arrive to entertain the couple and to propound theories of comedy. Both events are regarded for the most part as normal, with the explanation for the first event that it is a joke played on them by an uncle. Act 2 focuses on a pet elephant of the Paradocks, particularly in regard to the appropriateness of its size for their prefab dwelling. They solve the problem by deciding to exchange it for a boa constrictor, which can fit into a pencil box. The comedians reappear. In the same act there is a sudden shift to a meeting of author and critics. The conversations among husband, wife, and their sex-changed son who visits them, and the discussions of the visiting players and the author-critics, are carried off in the most usual of fashions.

Having lost some of its effect by its length, the play was shortened and performed with greater effect as part of a double bill with *The Hole* (1958). In the latter play, a crowd gathers around an excavation in a street. As the curious onlookers grow in number—dividing into two groups, men and women—they offer various explanations for the purpose of the hole. Meantime, their hostility toward a tramp camped near the hole increases, even as their explanations become more arbitrary: the hole is a tennis court, an aquarium, a prison, a voodoo rite. The electric cables with which the crew is working become the subject of lengthy discussion, in repetitive Ionesco style. At one point Soma describes the cables as "two inches across," and Cerebro replies that "they'll be for telephones in all probability," to which Mrs. Meso responds that "if they're two inches thick they're going to eat up the conversation." The tramp who has been the target of the women's hostility (Mrs. Meso has the last line in the play: "He should be put away") waits nevertheless to see the unveiling of a stained-glass window in the south transept of a church. Characters have names like Endo, Soma, Cerebro, Mrs. Meso, Mrs. Ecto. The tramp, named Visionary, tells a woman in the group that he is "forming the nucleus of a queue" and later that his "ambition once was to have a queue stretching away from me in every direction known to the compass. I meant in those days, God willing, to have a queue radiating out from me like the spikes from a prison railing. Like nodules endlessly attenuated. . . . What a consummation of my hopes and ambitions that would have been! To be first in an infinity of queues! Cosmically first! Omniprimal!"[5] The absence of thinking in the attempted rationales, arrived at with relentlessly mechanical logic, seems like pure Ionesco. In fact, to dramatize absurdity in terms of a British institution, the queue, for which England is famous, returns Ionesco's sense of the absurd back to its home base, since his *Bald Soprano* is based on his attempt to teach himself the English language from an English primer.

Simpson's major play, *One Way Pendulum,* once again tackles ludicrously improbable behavior. People act and talk like machines as each member of this family eventually realizes the obsession of his life. Mabel Groomkirby is so highly regulated as a housewife that she must hire someone to eat her leftovers. Arthur Groomkirby builds a model of the Old Bailey, and he is obsessed with parking meters. Kirby

Groomkirby, their son, has his own obsessive project: to get 500 speak-your-weight machines to sing Handel's "Hallelujah Chorus." Meantime, their daughter Sylvia complains about the ridiculous length of her arms. Important to the plot is Kirby's habit of wearing black, for which he must find a reason. Consequently, he commits forty-three murders; and when his weight machines can act as sirens to lure many people to the North Pole so that they jump off simultaneously, he will have reason to wear black forever. Arthur's Old Bailey is finally completed. Kirby is tried for murder and set free; the reason for the judge's discharge of the case is that "in sentencing a man for one crime, we may be putting him beyond the reach of the law in respect of those other crimes of which he might otherwise have become guilty. The law, however, is not to be cheated in this way."[6] *One Way Pendulum* remains Simpson's most structurally satisfying full-length play in bringing together its disjointed and ludicrous happenings and in its thematic development of the obsessive ends to which man goes in justifying his behavior and in then making that justification the basis for further actions.

George Wellwarth describes Simpson's style as "showing up what he considers the ridiculousness of the world . . . to create a special world in which reality is satirized by being placed in a new context. His plays, like 'Pataphysics,' are a perversion of logic—the impossible carried out in accordance with the laws by which the possible exists."[7] Wellwarth concludes that Simpson, although influenced by Ionesco, "is of all the current avant-garde dramatists—French or English— perhaps the closest in spirit to [Alfred] Jarry," and that Simpson's plays are "perfect examples of the drama of protest and paradox that sprang directly out of Jarry's *Ubu Roi*."[8] Simpson's heavy reliance on characters who act and talk like machines also places him in the comic tradition of Henri Bergson, in which unthinking and unfeeling replication or obsession, no matter how logical, creates comedy.

Martin Esslin calls attention to Simpson's brilliant parodies of British language, for example, legal language in *One Way Pendulum,* and sees the parodies as a "ferocious comment on English life" and on the "deep undercurrents of cruelty and sadism"[9] in the obsessive nature of the characters. In these respects Simpson joins Pinter, Orton, and Rudkin.

Simpson's remaining plays exhibit the characteristics discussed here in *A Resounding Tinkle* and *One Way Pendulum*. They include *Can You Hear Me?* and *Gladly Otherwise,* part of a revue entitled *One to Another* (1959); sketches in another revue, *You, Me and the Gatepost* (1960); *The Form* in the revue *Three* and some sketches in *One Over the Eight* (1961); *Oh!* (1961); *One Blast* and *Have Done* in *On the Avenue* (1961); *The Cresta Run* (1965); *Playback,* with Leopaldo Maler (1970); and *Was He Anyone* (1972). *Was He Anyone* is another ingenious variation on a Simpson theme, in its concern with the rescue of a man who has been treading water in the Mediterranean and with the subsequent bureaucratic arguments about whether to rescue him, arguments that stretch out his experience to twenty-seven months. Critical arguments broke out about the play: Is it the same Simpson, creator of the ludicrous, or is his concern with various charitable organizations involved in the debated rescue mission a change in the direction of direct social commentary? The play seems a prophecy of the many charitable attempts made by philanthropic organizations and musical groups in the 1980s on behalf of the starving in Africa and the poor in America.

Most important of all, perhaps, in any assessment of Simpson is his own description of his plays: "farce in a new dimension."

JOE ORTON

"A hostile sharpshooter using his wit to kill the past and defend himself from the present[,] Joe Orton was the only other person to make me laugh in the theatre the way my father did. In their unique ways, both men created the purest of theatrical experiences: joy."[10] So writes John Lahr, son of the famous American comic actor Bert Lahr, and biographer of Joe Orton. As Dionysus—the lord of misrule, the celebrant of sensual gratification, and finally the victim murdered by the ax of his lover, Kenneth Halliwell—Joe Orton, writer of uproarious farces, became a legend in his short life, a life that recalls that of another dramatist centuries earlier, Christopher Marlowe. Born on 1 January sometime between 1933 and 1939 to John and Elsie Kingsley Orton, a Leicester city gardener and a machinist, respectively, John Kingsley Orton became Joe Orton, a legend that has grown since his untimely death on 9 August 1967. In four years, between 1963 and

1967, he wrote three major dramas—*Entertaining Mr. Sloane, Loot,* and *What the Butler Saw,* produced in 1964, 1965, and 1969, respectively. Four more plays—*The Ruffian on the Stair* (1964), *The Erpingham Camp* (1966), and *The Good and Faithful Servant* and *Funeral Games* (1967)— round out a writing career that has bestowed on his vision and style an adjectival label, "Ortonesque," an honor conferred on few of the new-wave dramatists. Pinter, an acknowledged admirer of, and influence on, Orton, also earned a like honor.

Denounced by many, *Entertaining Mr. Sloane* evoked vituperative assaults, such as "absolutely filthy" by West End impresario Emile Littler, who went on to condemn the Royal Shakespeare Company for mounting, during one of their most brilliant seasons, the modern classics *Marat/Sade, Endgame, The Birthday Party,* and *Afore Night Come,* plays he described as a "programme of dirt."[11] It was the decade during which the new forces in the theater were at their peak, and Joe Orton was very much a part of the intoxicating freedoms and acclaim, negative and laudatory. Indeed, his own orgiastic life-style paralleled the near-total sense of release his plays exhibited. After all, the despised censorship laws, enforced by the lord chamberlain's office, were already headed for oblivion, although, ironically, they were not repealed until 1968, a year after the death of Orton.

Rare for emerging new dramatists was the commercial success of his first staged play in the West End, which provided Orton the financial means to live his Dionysian life, not that lack of money had necessarily prevented him from doing so earlier (both he and Halliwell had spent six months in prison for having defaced library books.) Flouting middle-class proprieties in his personal life, Orton wrote entertaining plays about incest, violence, homosexuality, bribery, and murder. Funerals (coffins seem a natural prop in an Orton play) and even a symbol of Sir Winston Churchill's phallus, held up by a detective dressed in Dionysian leopard skin, are part of Orton's comic, festive orgy and his new fertility rites.

The joy of life, a standard theme in Ibsen's plays, was given new meaning by Orton, whose aim as a playwright was "to write a play as good as *The Importance of Being Earnest.*"[12] Admiring Wilde's work but not his life, Orton went on to say, "I think you should put your genius into your work, not into your life."[13] He proceeded to do so, earning the deranged jealousy of his roommate, the vituperative criticism of influential critics and theatrical figures, and the encouragement of audiences and playwrights such as Rattigan and Pinter. In the double sense of his own title he is "entertaining Mr. Orton."

Admiring Tom Stoppard's idea in *Rosencrantz and Guildenstern Are Dead* ("How I wish I'd stumbled on it"), Orton tersely pinpoints his criticism of Stoppard's work, contending that it lacked action. "It should've been about the futility of students—always talking, talking, talking and never doing anything. Great events, murderers, adulteries, dreadful revenge happening all around them and they just talk."[14] On the other hand, "Orton fed his characters into farce's fun machine and made them bleed," writes Lahr.

The peculiar genius of Orton, then, is his ability to make uproariously funny the ultimate outrages and cruelty that society commits in the name of middle-class respectability and morality. His technique involves the dramatization, with the cool aplomb normally accorded the comedy of manners, of subjects usually associated with the revenge tragedies of the seventeenth century. An anarchist in his subject matter, Orton worked hard to realize a highly disciplined style. Lahr describes Orton's relish at the idea, suggested by a producer, that *What the Butler Saw* be staged at the "bastion of escapist bourgeois entertainment"—the Haymarket Theatre in the West End. " 'That'd be wonderful,' I [Orton] said. 'It'd be sort of a joke even putting *What the Butler Saw* on at the Haymarket—Theatre of Perfection.' We discussed the set. 'It should be beautiful. Nothing extraordinary. A lovely set. When the curtain goes up one should feel that we're right back in the the the old theatre of reassurance—roses, french windows, middle-class characters.' "[15]

Orton's first play, *The Ruffian on the Stair,* produced first on BBC Third Programme and two years later (1966) on stage, strongly suggests Pinter's influence. An intruder, Wilson, appears in a room occupied by a former prostitute, Joyce, and her boyfriend, Mike, a petty thief. Wilson turns out to be the brother of a man Mike has killed in a road accident. Taunting Joyce and then goading Mike into killing him, Wilson revenges his brother's death. Joyce, like Rose Hudd in Pinter's *Room,* has her security disrupted, as she will be left alone; like Meg Boles in *The Birthday Party,* she carries on a desultory breakfast conversation with Mike about the "nice" eggs and marmalade she has prepared. The Pinter pauses are there. After reading the rewritten script, Pinter wrote Orton that he thought he (Orton) was a "bloody marvelous writer."[16]

Entitled *The Boy Hairdresser* when it was first submitted to the BBC, *Ruffian on the Stair* derives from a poem by W. E. Henley:

> Madam Life's a piece in bloom
> Death goes dogging everywhere:
> She's the tenant of the room
> He's the ruffian on the stair.[17]

The poem not only conveys the basis for Orton's entire *ouevre* but ironically predicts his violent death.

Entertaining Mr. Sloane, Orton's first full-length stage play, deals with three members of a suburban family: Kath Kemp, a nymphomaniac; her homosexual brother Ed, a businessman, who visits occasionally; and her old father, who hasn't spoken to Ed for twenty years because of the son's "committing some kind of felony in the bedroom." A lodger, Mr. Sloane, appears, a fair-complexioned murderer on the loose; he wishes nothing more than a life of ease, and he soon finds it with Kath. Ed finds Sloane sexually delectable as well, and brother and sister casually dismiss Sloane's murder of their father as the outrageous ménage à trois continues its cozy life, with Mr. Sloane satisfying them as they satisfy him in return.

Orton's talent is that he manages to entertain an audience with tales of homosexuality, bribery, and murder. He does so by his realistic dramatization of the facades of genteel, civilized British life, manipulating the manners and language of his characters into societally approved fashion. Slowly the deceptive facades give way to their underlying realities. Yet the strong contrast between facade and reality is consistently maintained in the play. It is this balance between the two that provides the structural and aesthetic unity for Orton's plays. No less a master of the well-made play than Rattigan recognized immediately the classical underpinnings of Orton's work. "I wouldn't have liked *Sloane* if I hadn't seen its classic construction. . . . Orton understood that a play, if it's any good, has to have its basis in structure."[18]

Orton's social outrage is nowhere focused so sharply as in *Loot,* which during the 1986 season in New York received its first unanimously approving notices from American critics. In this play, Orton's farcical plot inventions grow to manic proportions as a young son and his friend manipulate his mother's body in a coffin in order to disguise wads of money from a bank theft. The mother's nurse, who has ingratiated herself with the father, superbly illustrates Orton's fun with hypocrisy. Mouthing Catholic platitudes throughout, she bows her head in prayer at the end, even as she is contemplating still another murder. The son, commenting that it would be a Freudian nightmare to see his mother in the nude, uses his mother's false teeth as castanets, and he plays with, and jokes about, her false eye, which has rolled from her head.

As though this situation isn't enough, still another character, who ultimately dominates the play, appears in the person of an investigator for the Metropolitan Water Board. He turns out to be Truscott of the Yard, a detective whose romp through Orton's lethally uproarious attack on sleuthing's logic outdoes his assault on the familial and religious hypocrisies of the son and the nurse. Even as Truscott recounts the nurse's record of having slain several husbands and eluded punishment, he and the audience are well aware of her next intended victim, the father. Intending to acquire the money himself, he decimates the young son with his bullying. "Under any other political system I'd have you on the floor in tears!"[19] He makes even the nurse (who states that she will never marry a man who isn't a Catholic, even though she has yet to marry a man she doesn't murder) seem sympathetic as he wields his authority over all the plot complications and the greedy characters, thus proving himself the master hypocrite, in true Ben Jonsonian style.

Frank Rich sees "Orton's lethal farce, [as] one of the funniest and meanest in the contemporary theater, in which the characters often act like prim, well-mannered, God-fearing representatives of the bourgeoisie, even as their every private deed and thought reek of greed, blasphemy, sadism and lust."[20] John Simon describes Zoe Wanamaker's rendition of the nurse as the "personification of female rottenness" even as she is "pursed and poised to perfection, overacting genteelly in a way that proves just right."[21] He asserts that *Loot* is Orton's funniest play, going about "its sacred mission of a total demolition job with unfailing good humor, reveling in its cool unraveling of the social fabric. Evil gets away with everything, without even the familiar cop-out of having to live with pangs of conscience or an enervating satiety amid its ill-gained wealth. . . . Language is bandied about, bent into every sort of paradox and play on words, twisted into sidesplitting non-sequiturs of impeccable pseudo-logic: 'It will put Paradise to shame.' 'Have you ever seen Paradise?' 'Only in photographs.' "[22]

Orton's *Erpingham Camp,* about a holiday camp for the old and disabled, similarly attacks societal conventions as one Mr. Laurie Russel of Market Harborough wins a disability bonus, even though he fell over twice while performing "the Twist and the Bossa Nova to a tune specified on the entrance form."[23] A melancholy, not there in earlier plays, pervades his second television play, *The Good and Faithful Servant,* about a retiree who discovers and marries an old love, his cleaning woman. *Funeral Games* and *What the Butler Saw* were staged posthumously, on television and stage, respectively. Ministers in the former and psychiatrists in the latter are the subjects of Orton's black humor. John Russell Taylor states that neither of these plays "did any service to his [Orton's] memory."[24] Ironically, Taylor and Lahr, for similar reasons, come to opposite conclusions about the merits of *What the Butler Saw.* Taylor writes that "Orton goes out of his way to demolish in nearly every line he writes. And if it is the conventions themselves Orton is making fun of, then he has got his and our lines inextricably crossed by trying to do so within a form which depends on convention for its essential structure and indeed its very existence."[25] Lahr, too, mentions the breakdown of all boundaries and personalities in a nightmare of disorder, but he adds that "the anarchy is transformed instantly into a fairy tale of harmony."[26] As in Shakespeare's later plays, the "all is forgiven"[27] ending works, and life returns to normality, even though no moral lesson has been learned in *What the Butler Saw,* or in any other of Orton's plays.

What the Butler Saw celebrates "neurotic patterns brilliantly illuminated by Orton on stage but dismissed by him offstage."[28] In a masterfully executed series of intrigues that include disguises, misunderstanding, and brilliant twists of logic, Orton unleashes his revenge on psychiatry's enormous appetite to explain everything. Not since T. S. Eliot's serious treatment of psychiatry in *The Cocktail Party* has the subject been the focus of a major play. The construction of the plot, with the obligatory important scene in which a bellhop and a secretary are revealed to be the twin son and daughter of two leading characters, follows the "foundling" themes of Shakespeare's *Comedy of Errors* and Shaw's *Major Barbara*. The Euripidean ending includes Sergeant Match wearing the secretary's bloodstained leopard-skin dress. The elements of Orton's earlier plays are here, in a sophisticated comedy of errors, manners, and revenge, its theme expressed in Orton's use of an epigram from Cyril Tourneur's seventeenth-century *Revenger's Tragedy:*

> Surely we're all mad people, and they
> Whom we think are, are not.

Impossible to summarize quickly, the labyrinthine windings of the action-packed plot are merely suggested here. It begins innocently enough with an interview conducted by Dr. Prentice with an attractive secretary, whom he attempts to seduce on the "professional" excuse of a physical examination. His attempt is interrupted by a series of intruders that include his wife, a nymphomaniac who has recently raped a young man; another psychiatrist by the name of Dr. Rance, who arrives as a government inspector; Nick, the young bellhop who is the current object of Mrs. Prentice's amorous advances; and Sergeant Match, who himself becomes a part of the complicated series of disguises, nudity included. Before the final disclosure that the bellhop and secretary-to-be are actually children of the Prentices, Geraldine, the secretary, under interrogation by Prentice, admits that her stepmother had an important part of Sir Winston Churchill's statue embedded in her. At the end of the play, Geraldine opens a box she has brought with her to the interview, to reveal the missing body part. In a revision of the play, the phallus was changed to a cigar, a symbol, Dr. Rance contends, "falling far short, as we all realize, of the object itself."[29] Promising to keep the revelation of "a number of remarkable peccadilloes" out of the papers, Match loudly shuts the lid of the box and tucks it under his arm as the play ends.

Attempts to illustrate the twists and turns of logic that the dialogue takes would wrench them out of context and run the risk of making them sound like gag lines. They are anything but that, as it is the inexorable logic by which a character derives his perverted argument that inevitably results in an absurd, sometimes monstrous conclusion. This technique begins at the outset of a drama and never lets down, to the end. For example, *What the Butler Saw* initiates its lunge into absurdity with Dr. Prentice's interrogation of Geraldine at the interview. Asking her to write down questions and then her answers underneath, he begins.

PRENTICE: . . . Who was your father? Put that at the head of the page.

    . . . .

GERALDINE: I've no idea who my father was.

    . . . .

PRENTICE: I'd better be frank, Miss Barclay. I can't employ you if you're in any way miraculous. It would be contrary to established practice. You did have a father?

GERALDINE: Oh, I'm sure I did. My mother was frugal in her habits, but she'd never economize unwisely.

PRENTICE: If you had a father why can't you produce him?

GERALDINE: He deserted my mother. Many years ago. She was the victim of an unpleasant attack.

PRENTICE: (*shrewdly*). She was a nun?

GERALDINE: No. She was a chambermaid at the Station Hotel. (*WBS*, 7–8)

The questions continue about her parents, leading to a discussion of Mrs. Barclay's death in an explosion from a faulty gas main that took off the roof of her home.

PRENTICE: Were there no other victims of the disaster?

GERALDINE: Yes. A recently erected statue of Sir Winston Churchill was so badly injured that the George medal has been talked of. Parts of the great man were actually embedded in my step-mother.

PRENTICE: Which parts?

    . . . .

PRENTICE: You've had a unique experience. It's not everyone that has their step-mother assassinated by the North Thames Gas Board. (*WBS*, 9)

In another dialogue, between Mrs. Prentice and the youth, Nick, whom she has just seduced, she complains of his hiring a photographer to take photographs of them, which he intends to use for blackmail. Her response to his admission about a concealed camera in the room is that her contract with him does not include cinematic rights. Earlier, in response to Mr. Prentice's comment that he can't "endure the torment of being in your company," Mrs. Prentice explains where she has been. "I arrived at the meeting to find the hall in an uproar. Helen Duncanon had declared herself to be in love with a man. And, as you know, the club is primarily for lesbians. I myself am exempt from the rule because you count as a woman. We expelled Helen and I spent the night at the Station Hotel" (*WBS*, 13).

Dialogues and long speeches, each gathering manic comic momentum, pile up on each other in a race to the play's conclusion. In *Loot* it is Detective Truscott who gathers into his logically twisted speeches the hypocrisy of the goings-on. In *What the Butler Saw*, the psychiatrist, Dr. Rance, picks up the anarchic complications and develops them to monstrous proportions in his absolute interpretation of events. Neither Rance nor Truscott is discovered, and neither, consequently, undergoes any punishment. Orton carries his farcical revenge on societal absurdities to their anarchic extremes. He turns the seventeenth-century *Revenger's Tragedy*, in fact, into a twentieth-century revenger's comedy.

Unlike the harmless absurdities dramatized by Stoppard and Simpson, those of Orton outrage conventional critics and audiences, as illustrated in the reaction to Sir Ralph Richardson's portrayal of Dr. Rance, when someone in the audience demanded that Richardson's knighthood be remanded. Indeed, it was only after a number of unsuccessful productions of both *Loot* and *What the Butler Saw* that they were given successful production, the latter at the Royal Court as late as 1975.

DAVID RUDKIN

Born on 29 June 1936, the son of David Jonathan Rudkin, an evangelical pastor, and Anne Alice Martin Rudkin, a teacher, David Rudkin was reared in an atmosphere of puritanical ethos that denied the pleasures of the world, even of the theater, except for Shakespeare. His concern with the dark side of things seems natural, with its focus on themes of evil, corruption, inexplicability, and lack of redemption.

A dramatist known primarily for one major stage play, *Afore Night Come,* Rudkin has captured the attention of critics and scholars for a vision of life that, as in the cases of Simpson and Orton, is uniquely his. Despite the obvious influence of Harold Pinter and despite the affinity with the theater of cruelty of the French playwright Jean Genet, he has a purity of dramatic voice that is shocking and stark. The play was his first and was produced by the Royal Shakespeare Company at the Arts Theatre in London in 1962. It belongs to the succès de scandale tradition that includes Orton's *Loot* (and, indeed, all of Orton's plays) and Pinter's plays such as *The Birthday Party.* Frederick Lumley refers to the focus on fear and on the "dark side of the moon" that has clearly established Rudkin as a "regional member of the Theatre of Cruelty."[30] Kenneth Tynan refers to Rudkin's theme of "primordial rustic violence," the "ancient satanic significance," and the "climactic scene of shrieking horror, silently observed by three tall pear-trees, a ritual slaughter straight out of *The Golden Bough*"[31] and the ancient scapegoat myth.

Afore Night Come begins innocently enough, as do Pinter's plays. Rudkin's characters are workers in a pear orchard, whose numbers grow with the arrival of some strangers. The realistic situation of pear harvesting gradually changes to one of growing hostility toward the strangers and ends with a ritual murder. As the change occurs, innocent details take on a dark luminosity. The setting is "an orchard in a rural pocket on the crust of the Black Country" near Birmingham, where the rustic dialect, even to an English audience, at times seems impenetrable, as though to ward off outsiders. Among the new arrivals in the work force are a leather-jacketed "Teddy"; a student; Hobnails, who has been released for the occasion from a nearby mental asylum; and an Irish tramp who evokes Davies of Pinter's *Caretaker.* The wrangling among the workers grows into a disturbance in which hostilities slowly focus on the tramp, who wears dark glasses, seems literate, and is altogether the foreigner of the group. All are slowly drawn into the hostilities, so that when the physical dismemberment of Shakespeare, the tramp, occurs, only the mentally deficient

Hobnails seems conscious of the horror of the violence as he attempts to draw the student away. The ritual horror of the tramp's murder includes impaling his head on a pitchfork, "as in the celebrated and unsolved 'witchcraft murder' which took place in the Midlands in 1945, and on which Mr. Rudkin's play may well be based."[32]

John Russell Taylor places the peculiar strength of the play in two areas: "the inexorable theatrical logic with which it carries us from its simple realistic opening to the weird, primitive ritual of its climax; and the efficacy of the play on a literal as well as metaphorical level."[33]

Rudkin has insisted on the documentary nature of the details, which include the hurried completion of the work because the men want to be put on a piecework basis. In the circle of pear trees, where the tramp sits at leisure and carries on a nonstop commentary, the foreman, Spens, plants his pitchfork and vanishes, whereupon four men close in on the tramp and behead him as the sky darkens. After the murder, normal existence resumes as the men go home to tea and the orchard empties.

Yet, in the gruesome events, the details take on mythic overtones: the Garden of Eden, Christ (Hobnails), the Euripidean orgy of violence in *The Bacchae,* and Golding's *Lord of the Flies.* It is the latent fear-driven instinct in man that is brought to the surface by the strange and the unknown. The universality carries to the end, where, as in Orton's farces, no learning takes place, nor is there a change in the participants, who continue the routines of their lives. The Conradian heart of darkness has once more asserted itself and will continue to do so, Rudkin seems to say.

What happens surrealistically to Stanley in *The Birthday Party* and to Gus in *The Dumbwaiter,* plays by Pinter, happens naturalistically to the tramp, and Rudkin's horror is made more palpable by the physicality of the action, the ordinariness of the pear-picking situation, and the primitive purity of the worker's dialect in contrast with that of the intruders. The societal outcasts—the lazy but harmless tramp and the innocent, gentle, weak-minded, and homosexual Hobnails—stand apart from the others in Rudkin's commentary on innocence trapped by evil. Both ancient (Euripides) and modern (Genet and Artaud) in its vision, *Afore Night Come* "caused considerable upset and found little enough favour during its brief stay at the Arts." Yet those critics not upset by its satanic darkness express views similar to those of Tynan, who sees in the play "signs of insolent originality at which the critic's soul quickens, recognizing the rare but always familiar stigmata that betoken genius."[34]

The reviewer Tom Milne described Rudkin's language as similar to Pinter's in exactness

but with a good deal more adventurousness. The rhythms of everyday speech are brilliantly caught, often used with devastatingly funny effect. But with the tramp's traditional Irish gift of gab, the language begins to take a step into biblical rhythms. Gradually it coalesces into a kind of wild-earthbound poetry, as in Ginger's denunciation of the tramp-witch: "I won't get my babby now. . . . His hands are the hands of a dead man . . . don't eat anything . . . don't drink nothing . . . grass do wither at his feet . . . why don't someone make him die then?"[35]

On the basis of just this play, Rudkin's uniqueness of style not only has earned him a first-play production by the prestigious Royal Shakespeare Company but has placed him squarely in both an ancient and a modern dramatic tradition.

After *Afore Night Come,* Rudkin spent ten years writing scenarios and librettos for operas, the most famous of which is his translation of Arnold Schönberg's *Moses and Aaron,* an opera in which orgiastic forces of license and darkness are unleashed. He also wrote plays for BBC Radio, for example, *Cries from Casement as His Bones Are Brought to Dublin* (1973), and other stage plays produced at small theaters. All contain the themes found in *Afore Night Come. Ashes* (1974), however, is generally regarded as the only one that carries on directly from *Afore Night Come.* Unlike Simpson and Orton, Rudkin does not write farce, yet like theirs, his voice is uniquely grotesque.

CHAPTER VII

NEW SOCIAL REALISTS

PETER NICHOLS, DAVID STOREY, SIMON GRAY

If the dramas by Beckett, Osborne, Pinter, Stoppard, Simpson, Orton, and Rudkin capture critical attention for reasons of innovation, uniqueness, or historical impact, those by Peter Nichols, David Storey, and Simon Gray are unsurpassed in their dramatization of the fabric of British middle-class life or the upwardly mobile lower class. Realistic, at times naturalistic, in their close scrutiny of domestic, professional, and national concerns, they have woven highly intricate patterns of relationships that seem not only a means to an end but an end in themselves. Whatever modicum of the angry young man, the detached ironist, the philosphical existentialist, or the farcical absurdist appears in their plays, there is a stylish and sophisticated fusion of the dramatic currents of the time with the tradition of the earlier problem plays of Shaw, Harley Granville-Barker, Pinero, and Maugham. Out of the fusion has emerged a series of distinguished plays rooted in recognizable personal and social realities.

Dramatists with some academic credentials, each has created his image of middle-class England with a freshness that has echoes of Chekhov as well as of the new-wave dramatists or the earlier social problem playwrights.

Nichols's image is that of the suburbanite whose bleak realities overtake his or her illusions/fantasies, and his image is combined with an increasingly quasi-Proustian "recognition that as we grow older we are likely to become our parents, to act out the same patterns of behavior over and over again."[1] Reality and illusion become more balanced with each of his plays, resulting in a tone of detached irony with fairly even mixtures of laughter and tears. How this balance is carried out—in the life of a young couple with a retarded child, in the lives of six patients in the British National Health program, or in the middle age of a modern affluent and cultured couple whose younger alter egos appear as real characters—constitutes the iconography of Nichols. Humor, satire, compassion, absurdity, and intelligence are some of the qualities that make his characters flesh-and-blood, credible human beings that playwrights such as Stoppard have difficulty realizing on stage. In the juxtaposition of fantasy and reality, the former exists only to dramatize the latter, a mutual dependency that is a hallmark of Nichols's style.

Storey's dramatic icon (exept for his early D. H. Lawrence–like plays about family life—*The Restoration of Arnold Middleton,* 1967, and *In Celebration,* 1969) has a Chekhovian plotlessness in its concern with the finely spun texture of personal lives rather than with the conventional suspense-creating actions of the stage. Complications and climaxes are not important. At the wedding of a contractor's daughter, what happens on stage is the erection and dismantling of the tent in which the festivities are held. The festive events that include the bride and groom are peripheral to the main action, which consists of the dialogue among the workers as they go about their duties, and of the random entrances of members of the wedding party. In another drama, the main sporting event is secondary to what goes on in the locker room during the halftime interval or before and after the game. In yet another drama, about the royalist-Puritan war of the seventeenth century, soldiers and citizens at large are depicted, randomly and sometimes confusingly going about their lives. In Storey's plays about family life, the image of dissolution dominates as educated sons and daughters of working-class parents find their ways into the middle class. Familial betrayals and disillusionments surface during reunions, celebrations, and various social gatherings. A distinguished novelist, Storey developed plays from his novels, and his plays make an interesting study of the way in which novelistic details become the substance of a drama.

Gray's dramatic vision has developed from Ortonesque imitation in *Wise Child* (1967) and *Dutch Uncle* (1969) to a Jimmy Porter–like character named Butley in *Butley* (1971) whose near-total detachment serves as a defensive mechanism against the outside world. Butley's vituperative and literate attacks on those around him, even those who would be his friends, are transformed into passivity in later characters such as Hench, an affluent publisher, in *Otherwise Engaged* (1975); the impassive Quartermaine, instructor of English for foreign students, in *Quartermaine's Terms* (1981); and an immobile family patriarch at a reunion in *Close of Play* (1979). All are variations of the withdrawn character whose emotional nullity forms a shell of imperviousness to people and events around him.

Nichols and Gray have been closely involved with the British academic world, and all three writers have written about education and its effects on people's lives. Each has written about teachers, collegial relationships, and the resultant personal, domestic, and professional conflicts. In particular, Gray came from Cambridge, the academic world so vividly realized in the television series *Glittering Prizes* by Frederic Raphael.

In addition, both Nichols and Gray, particularly the former, have come to the stage via the medium of television. For ten years Nichols wrote television plays, an experience that served both to develop his skills and to provide him with characters and situations for his stage dramas. The stage allowed more room for complexly developed characters, as in *A Day in the Death of Joe Egg,* and for a more sophisticated structural style, as in plays such as *National Health, Forget-Me-Not Lane,* and *Passion Play.* Because the subject of a retarded child and its effects on family lives was considered tasteless for a television audience, Nichols created the famous character of Joe Egg for the stage.

All three dramatists have been associated with the smaller experimental theatres. Storey had his first nine plays staged between 1967 and 1976 at the by-now legendary home of the new drama, the Royal Court. Nichols's plays were produced at the National, by the Royal Shakespeare Company at the Aldwych and later at the Barbican, as well as at some West End theaters. Gray's dramas were staged at a mixture of provincial, West End, and subsidized houses. Nichols, Storey, and Gray represent another growing tradition of theatrical production: that of a close association with a particular director, of Nichols with Michael Blakemore, Storey with Lindsay Anderson, and Gray with Pinter.

A final note in this introduction to the three dramatists concerns their plays of memory, in which past events invade the present in an attempt by characters to gain some perspective or control in their lives. In *Home* (1970) by Storey, about four old people in a mental institution, the silences and the random, dissociated thoughts of the characters suggest Pinter's influence. In fact, the play appeared a year before Pinter's own play, *Old Times,* about three early-middle-aged people reuniting and sharing memories. Storey's *Early Days* (1980), with Sir Ralph Richardson in his last stage appearance, is a highly controlled dramatization of the anarchic reflections of a successful public man. Nichols's *Forget-Me-Not Lane* (1971) appeared the same year as *Old Times,* and his *Passion Play* ten years later struck up the same tune, but with a bittersweet, sophisticated brilliance not present in the earlier work. And, distinguished by the acting of Sir Michael Redgrave in his last stage role, Gray's *Close of Play* (1979) deals with his recurrent familial theme: a family reunion at which repressed and destructive revelations swirl around the immobile and silent patriarch of the family.

The three dramatists extend their respective visions of personal and family life to the national level. Storey's *Cromwell* (1973) etches a fragmented society during the Civil Wars. Nichols's *Privates on Parade* (1977), drawn from his own Royal Air Force service in Malaysia, confronts the fading reality of British power. Gray's *Rear Column* (1978) is concerned with the members of Stanley's expedition to the Congo and their cruelty to the natives, a Conradian "heart of darkness" theme. The interestingly woven and highly textured cloth of British society dramatized by these writers includes specific domestic situations and events, such as the National Health settings of Nichols's *National Health* and two celebrated English murders in plays by Gray: *Dutch Uncle* (1969), about the bizarre Christie murders, and *Molly* (1977), about the Alma Rattenbury case of the middle 1930s (also dramatized in Terence Rattigan's *Cause Célèbre* in 1977).

PETER NICHOLS

Born the son of Richard George and Violet Annie Poole Nichols on 31 July 1927, Peter Richard Nichols grew up in Bristol, England, attending Bristol Grammar School and Bristol Old Vic Theatre School and later studying at Trent Park Teachers' Training College. If not of the Oxford–Cambridge tradition, Nichols's education was solid, and his

Bristol environment conducive to the development of theater interests. Pinter's early career had its roots here, including the important speech about his dramatic style to a Britol audience in 1962, as well as a production of an early play at the theater in Bristol. Stoppard also began his journalistic career in Bristol, his father having moved the family there, about the time that the new wave of drama began its swell.

For ten years Nichols wrote for both BBC and commercial television at a time when television writing provided a means of livelihood for many dramatists. From his early television work, Nichols drew subjects that he fully realized in major stage dramas such as *A Day in the Death of Joe Egg* (1967), *The National Health, or Nurse Norton's Affair* (1969), *Forget-Me-Not Lane* (1971), *Privates on Parade: A Play with Songs in Two Acts (1977),* and *Passion Play* (1981). Coming to the stage at the age of forty, Nichols had already established himself with his television drama, and it remained for public recognition by way of the stage to grant him the prestige that his work deserves. John Russell Taylor "popped him [Nichols] into the first edition of *Anger and After* [1962] . . . with some slightly sniffy but not . . . entirely unfair comment about 'sprightly invention sometimes a little dampened by the exigencies of working out' in television."[2] Taylor, however, opens his survey of British drama for the 1970s, *The Second Wave* (1971), with an entire chapter devoted to Nichols's television and stage work, focusing on the thematic concerns in Nichols's plays: 1) the "genetic family" trap, 2) the divisiveness between parents caused by children, and 3) adult-children conflicts, especially those of fathers and sons. To Taylor's list of themes could be added that of the extension of the conflicts into society at large, as these are evident in national institutions and, indeed, on the international level. The post–World War II economic difficulties of Great Britain and the decline of British political influence on the world scene are important threads in the texture of contemporary middle-class life as depicted in Nichols's plays. Writing about the success of Nichols's *National Health,* Taylor sees in that very success "a sign that we are now growing up sufficiently to take Peter Nichols as he comes, and even to take the world he pictures, our world, as that comes."[3]

Nichols's first two plays deal with subjects that would seem too harsh, some would say tasteless, for stage presentation, yet they have enjoyed strong critical support and a modest popularity. Their subjects, a spastic child and terminally ill patients, have autobiographical origins. Without the farcical style of Simpson or the grotesquerie of Orton, Nichols manages his harsh subjects with sympathetic laughter and tears, so that pure cynicism is avoided, as is its opposite, maudlin sentimentality. In speaking about *Joe Egg* in a *New York Times* interview, Nichols describes his style as a comedy in which "sane, witty, civilized people . . . have plenty of other troubles beside the child. . . . At first, of course, we were terribly stricken, but we got used to it. [The oldest of the Nichols's four children, Abigail, was born spastic in 1960 and died in 1971.] We could laugh, and so can the characters, and so should the audience."[4] In the interview Nichols talks about using the alienation techniques of Brecht, "but in the opposite way from Brecht, because they're supposed to involve you, draw you in, make the experience more intense. If the audience isn't moved by 'Joe Egg,' then I've failed."[5]

Nichols admits also to being influenced during his youth in Bristol when he saw a production of Thornton Wilder's *Skin of Our Teeth*. The tragedies of the human race over the ages, depicted in Wilder's comic-strip style, were discovered by Nichols to be his own voice, and it is that voice that is heard in all his dramas.

A Day in the Death of Joe Egg belongs to a steadily growing genre of plays dealing with the handicapped or terminally ill: Terence Rattigan's *In Praise of Love* (terminal cancer), Bernard Pomerance's *Elephant Man* (deformity), Brian Clark's *Whose Life Is It Anyway* (paralysis), and the American plays about the blind and about Aids victims, *Children of a Lesser God* and *The Normal Heart,* respectively.

Turned down by producers in London because of its subject matter, *A Day in the Death of Joe Egg* was first produced at the Glasgow Citizens' Theatre in 1967. As notices slowly but surely acclaimed the merits of the play, Nichols emerged into public notice out of the ten-year obscurity of writing for television, so that his next play, *The National Health,* was staged in 1969 by the prestigious National Theatre Company, then residing at the Old Vic.

A Day in the Death of Joe Egg, a drama about a schoolteacher, Bri, his wife, Sheila, and their spastic daughter, Joe Egg, is, as it turns out, essentially about the effect of the child on the marriage of Bri and Sheila and, as well, about attitudes of the outside world toward the situation. At the core of the two-act drama, however, the small day-to-day details that fill the lives of Bri and Sheila, in addition to those dealing directly with Joe, constitute a rich texture of life indicative of what Irving Wardle describes as Nichols's "power to put modern Britain on the stage and send the spectators away feeling more like members of the human race."[6] Wardle also says that of the many good playwrights in Britain, none has Nichols's power to do this.

The play opens with the discovery by the audience that as a teacher in a secondary school, much like that at which Nichols himself taught at one time, Bri finds little satisfaction. At home after school, he addresses the audience directly, clowning about the classroom problems of the day. His clowning takes the form of a dramatic, self-mocking monologue delivered in mimetic music-hall style, in which he reenacts his attempt to keep some control over his students. The audience has its first glimpse of Sheila as she arrives with a tea tray and then rushes back to push an animal out of the door with her foot. Over a minor incident involving a spider Bri has confiscated in the classroom, a small quibble occurs between him and Sheila. Additional details from Bri's day at school, for example, the "flashing" by a pupil, Scanlon, whom Bri calls Pithecanthropus Erectus, intensifies his attempt to make light of his basic disillusionment with teaching.

Sheila, on the other hand, is described by Bri as a woman who embraces everything. At the moment, she is involved in a rehearsal for a local amateur theatrical and must fend off Bri's amorous advances. She, too, has a turn at speaking directly to the audience while getting ready for her rehearsal. Bri, according to her, needs to do something he can be proud of. She expresses distaste for Bri's childish temper over Freddie, who appears with her in the local production. The bickering between Bri and Sheila veers in many directions, including possible reasons for the birth of their brain-damaged daughter, one of Sheila's theories being that her former promiscuous life and her subconscious shrinking from motherhood caused it, another being that the doctor botched the birth. In the course of feeding and diaper changing, they draw in Joe, who can only say, "Aaah!" In their serious joking, the parents speak on her behalf, making her a third participant in the dialogue. Reenacting humorously the results of brain tests performed on Joe, Bri imitates the German doctor, and Sheila picks up the playacting.

> BRI: Ach, nein. Zis vos a liddle biopsy to take a sample of her brain tissue.
>
> SHEILA: That's a relief. . . . I thought at first you'd bored a hole in her skull to let the devil out.[7]

Joking, playing games, and playacting are the means by which the parents cope with their problem.

At the end of act 1, in another long direct address to the audience, Sheila concedes that she joins in the jokes to please Bri. "If it helps him live with her, I can't see the harm, can you? He hasn't any faith she's ever going to improve. Where I have, you see. . . . I believe, even if she *showed* improvement, Bri wouldn't notice. He's dense about faith—faith isn't believing in fairy-tales, it's being in a receptive state of mind".[8]

The game playing is intensified and expanded in act 2 when Sheila brings home their friends, Freddie and Pam, who begin clawing at each other in the style of Albee's *Who's Afraid of Virginia Woolf?* Pam is jealous of Sheila, as Bri is of Freddie, because of the intimate roles played by Sheila and Freddie in the local play. The visiting couple are obviously more affluent than their hosts and are condescending in their appreciation of Bri's paintings of American cowboys and of Sheila's doing so much with so little in the way of home decor. Bri's impatience with the posh vulgarity of the visitors is obvious, and with growing irony he refers to "the Thalidomide Kid. Fastest gun in the West" (*JE,* 51–52). To Freddie's question about teaching, Bri replies, "It's not exactly Good-bye Mr. Chips" (*JE,* 53). When Bri's mother, Grace, arrives unannounced with a new "cardi" for Joe, the five-way conversation grows more abrasive as underlying hostilities surface. In the accusations and counteraccusations that follow, Sheila insists that Grace had spoiled Bri.

Finally, after a crisis in which Joe was taken to the hospital and returned home, the accumulated frustration takes its toll on Bri. He leaves Sheila and Joe on the pretext of an errand, knowing that Sheila will continue to fill her time, not only with Joe but with her life-embracing activities and her general optimism based on an acceptance of things. He leaves without the conventional parting quarrel or fare-well, without, in fact, Sheila's awareness that his is a final departure. The realistic naturalness of the events, including our experience and knowledge of Joe's basic "functions—how she eats, drinks, has fits, breathes, excretes, everything,"[9] has its own momentum, so that Bri's departure continues the rhythms, despite the inconclusiveness of what will become of Sheila or of him.

Nichols once told an interviewer, "I dislike very much the ap-proach that suggests it's a tense neurotic experience dealt with by a frantic family, or that the characters are desperately smiling through their tears."[10] Neither are his funny lines intended for "that part of the audience that barks with laughter quite senselessly. . . . But if under-standing is the end of it all, you manage to make the audience share your world-view for a moment, or give them a glimpse of things they wouldn't have seen if they hadn't gone to the theater, then you've achieved something through laughter."[11]

Even in this most tightly knit of Nichols's stage plays, there is present the episodic style of Brecht, which he admires, not one of events, however, but of the multitudinous details that fill the daily lives of average, middle-class families such as Bri, Sheila, and Joe. As characters in the drama, Bri and Sheila are participants, but as narra-tors who step out of character to provide commentary on the pain and the pleasure (in this play mostly a sexual pleasure), they are stylized into Brechtian representations of a problem, though without loss of their human dimensions. The understanding gained by the audience is thus achieved through layer upon layer of ironies that evolve from trivial details, such as Sheila's cat. At one point, Grace makes one of many references to the nuisance and recommends the "animal" be put to death. Bri's mishearing of her remark coincides with the idea of euthanasia, which has at several points been mentioned in connection with the spastic daughter. This melding of episodic details gathered from memories, anecdotes, popular attitudes toward the handicapped, and game playing makes a powerful statement on contemporary Brit-ish middle-class life, on the medical profession, and ultimately on the individual experiences of the main characters, caught in what Nichols calls the "genetic family" trap.

Nichols's second stage play, *The National Health, or Nurse Norton's Affair* (1969), is about two families of a different sort: the group of hospitalized male patients in varying states of disability; and the detached world of the nurses, doctors, and staff, who are incorporated into a television soap opera in which the fantasies of each are played out. Again Nichols writes from personal experience, and again he writes about the medical profession; only here medicine takes center stage. The link between the two worlds is an orderly named Barnet, who energetically interacts with the patients, at first encouraging them and then slowly displaying his hostility, as seen in his persuasion of a recovering alcoholic to resume old habits.

The multicharacter play is conducive to the episodic technique, which serves Nichols so well. The loose plot consists of the actions of the ulcerous Ash, an ex-schoolmaster (like Bri of the earlier play); Flagg, a patient with prostate problems who becomes a character of humors, those humors consisting of excretory functions; Mackie, terminally ill with cancer; Loach, an amnesiac; Foster, whose whole life consists of listening to radio programs; and Rees, an elderly doctor obsessed by the need to get clothes so that he can ride in a waiting taxi. The characters, indeed, are their humors, much as in the Renaissance comedy of humors by Ben Jonson, where each character is marked by one ruling temperament, or humor—sanguine, phlegmatic, choleric, or melancholic.

In a second series of actions, the soap opera entitled *Nurse Norton's Affair* provides the antidote of fantasy to the bleak hospital milieu. Parodying the banal dialogue of soap opera, Nichols produces laughter with the melodrama of a black nurse in love with a Scottish doctor and of Nurse Norton's spontaneous donation of a kidney to Neil, Dr. Boyd's son. Soap opera fantasies are deftly worked in with the depressing, yet frequently comic, actions of the patients. Barnet's narration of the actions of the hospital staff during the interludes of the soap opera is similar to the commentaries of Bri and Sheila directed at the audience in *Joe Egg*. His role was originally played by Jim Dale, a master of music-hall routines, and in an American revival of *Joe Egg* in 1985, the part of Bri was also played by Dale. Both productions were critically applauded.

In his third stage play, *Forget-Me-Not Lane* (1971), Nichols returns to the family situation and to autobiographical experience. Covering three generations, the play uses a central character, Frank, who is narrator as well. The cast includes Charles and Amy; their son, Frank, and his wife, Ursula; and Frank's son (young Frank) and his friend Tom. In addition, Frank and Ursula appear as separate youthful characters (young Frank and young Urse), at times causing some confusion to the unwary reader or audience.

Stepping in and out of his dual roles, Frank is Nichols's most Brechtian character. Although deployed in the earlier plays, the techniques have a brilliance and effortlessness not present in *Joe Egg* and *The National Health*. Harold Hobson of the *Sunday Times* sees Nichols as "at the very top of his form"[12]; Frank Marcus of the *Sunday Telegraph* writes that "Mr. Nichols' profound compassion gets an immediate response from his audience and his uncannily accurate eye for the minutiae of family life and for the remembered absurdities of wartime England cause continuous waves of laughter. It is the laughter of recognition, and it is deep and true."[13] John Russell Taylor regards it as "the play Peter Nichols has been in training to write for the last ten years. Not only does it bring together elements from at least five television plays, but it neatly resumes most of his leading themes."[14] Critics agree the play is Nichols's most successful, popularly as well as critically.

Two actors depict Frank as ego and alter ego. His wife, Ursula, appears also as young Urse. Although the action focuses on the conflicts between father (Charles) and son, other characters, who include the mother (Amy), a friend (Ivor), his wife (Ursula), and his son (Frank), are very much a part of past conflicts that continue in a new form into the present. Nichols includes an enormous range of details by means of a series of doors that swing open to allow a character from the past to enter and leave fluidly. England's version of Thornton Wilder's *Our Town,* Nichols's play is more savagely funny and more sharply focused than Wilder's because of its limitation to four or five main characters. As the play swings backward and forward in time, the movement becomes a stylistic rhythm never broken, even though the narrator steps in and out of the action, a dramatic feat of its kind perhaps unparalleled elsewhere. The laughter, as well as the motion, is continuous, building ironies to their highest points when

Frank, in semi-Proustian fashion, finds himself to have become the same father that he so rebelled against in his own youth. Charles, the puritanical father, is repressive, so the curious Frank and his friend conduct secretly their explorations of forbidden matters such as sex. They discuss, for example, hearsay about sexual coupling in which the woman freezes from fear, sometimes necessitating medical removal of the male organ.

Laughter deflates the guilt and pain of the experiences, and Frank's metamorphosis into his own father deflates what might otherwise be a cynically satiric portrait of Charles. Frank's own son, Frank, chides his father when the latter balks at his request for money and explains that Ursula, now divorced, "gets nearly all I earn." The son reponds: "You married her. You left her."[15] Young Frank has his own friend, Tom, owner of a motorbike, just as Frank (Charles's son, a generation earlier) conducted his exploits with his friend Ivor.

Nichols's many-layered dramatic "cake" is set mostly in the 1940s, the time during which life in World War II England was most austere and the big band era and pinup girls counterpoised the realities of bombing raids and bomb shelters. The nostalgia of the past is cut by the unromantic present, as Frank now is disturbed by the noise of motorbikes. Youthful excitement fades into reality and then back into the illusions of memory. The illusions of the 1940s era are recalled in Nichols's use of the music of Duke Ellington, the Andrews Sisters, Bing Crosby, and others. In the costume and makeup of a Chinese magician, Mister Magic, a middle-aged man, performs his tricks as Amy sings "There'll always be an England." These music-hall routines are part of Nichols's Brechtian interruptive techniques.

Two more plays about bourgeois life—*Chez Nous*(1974) and *The Freeway* (1974)—continue Nichols's exploration of Britain's contemporary patterns of middle-class behavior. The former is about an experiment in modern living by two English couples living in France. The latter, with a spectacular stage set, occurs on a modern highway as a family in a motor home waits out a huge traffic jam. Like Barnet in *The National Health,* the affluent owners of the motorhome help people of lesser means at the start, but soon the good deeds change as time and impatience take their toll. In both plays, underlying hostilities surface even in the warmest of relationships and the best-intended efforts.

In *Privates on Parade: A Play with Songs in Two Acts* (1977), Nichols lets out all his music-hall stops as he dramatizes an entertainment troupe on a tour of duty in Southeast Asia. The play belongs to a time-honored tradition, practiced by dramatists such as Pinero (*Trelawney of the Wells*), Rattigan (*Harlequinade*), and Osborne (*The Entertainer*), to mention only a few. The *Observer* critic writes in his review that Nichols "remains supreme, too, as a fashioner of one-liners, dead in character and dead funny."[16]

Born in the Gardens (1979) returns once more to a family theme, this time that of a widow and her three sons. Two sons, Hedley and Queenie, one of whom is a twin, are successful in politics and journalism, respectively, and the third, Mo, remains at home with his mother, Maud, in a secluded life that resists all efforts by his brothers to entice him to enter the present. Maud and Mo prefer the past in Bristol (Nichols's home town) to the vacuous and vulgar present.

In *Passion Play* (1981), Nichols returns to the marital couples of *Joe Egg* and *Chez Nous*. An average middle-class, middle-aged couple, enclosed in the claustrophobic coziness of their lives, undergo painful change. Nichols splits his two main characters into four in a dramatization of egos and alter egos that recalls a similar technique used in *Forget-Me-Not Lane*. James needs a lover, not a friend, and so he has an affair with a young woman, who soon tires of him. Their affair sets in motion an intricate pattern of lies, letters, rows, disclosures by friends, reconciliations, and a suicide attempt—a painfully complicated situation, made all the more tragic by the deep affection each feels for the other. The balance between laughter and tragic disillusionment is perfectly poised, as egos and alter egos are juxtaposed in a near-deadly, yet ironically moving, unsentimentality.

Passion Play evokes Pinter's *Betrayal,* staged a few years earlier. The two dramas pose an interesting contrast of similar subject matter dramatized in totally opposite styles: one a lushly detailed, intricate pattern of colors and the other a sparse, minimalist configuration of black (words) and white (silences).

Nichols's plays have won many awards and enjoyed near-unanimity of critical applause, although their commercial success has been moderate. When Albert Finney played the part of Bri in New York, *Joe Egg* ran to sold-out houses. When Finney was replaced, the production soon folded. *Joe Egg,* a first play, won the John Whiting Award (shared), the *Evening Standard* Drama Award, and the Society of West End Theatre Managers Award for the best comedy in 1978. Nichols's kaleidosopic techniques have been consistently successful from his very first stage play, as have been his complex explorations of personal, social, and national problems, as seen in his dramatizations of suburban, middle-class England in the post–World War II era.

DAVID STOREY

A Yorkshire miner's son, an artist, teacher, rugby footballer, member of a tent crew, postman, and farm worker, David Storey transmutes real experiences into award-winning novels and dramas. From his novels he draws material for his plays. His own life reads like the seemingly random, dissociated and dispersed situations, characters, and plots of his plays. Born in 1933, Storey rejected his parents' wishes that their talented son settle for a comfortable schoolmaster's life and instead attended London's Slade School of Art during the week, traveling north to play rugby on weekends. Like his own varied activities, the plotless actions of Storey's dramas consist of peripheral activities surrounding a major event, rather than the event itself. The pre- and postdinner gatherings of a family at the celebration of a wedding anniversary, the interactions of athletes in a locker room before and after a rugby match and during the halftime, the erection and subsequent dismantling of a wedding tent: these fringe goings-on become central in Storey's plotting style.

Chekhov, more than a half century earlier, wrote plays about the arrivals and departures of family and friends for events such as a birthday party or the sale of a family estate. The surrounding actions and situations, rather than the main event, scatter the traditional suspense, climax, and progressive actions audiences have come to expect. So it is with Storey's plays.

If Peter Nichols dramatizes family life in English suburbia, Storey writes about emotional dislocations among family members as new generations from working-class parents find their way into middle-class professions and life. The texture of those dislocations and the minutiae of day-to-day relationships in fringe events are easily recognizable hallmarks of Storey's vision of contemporary life. Admitting to the naturalism of his style, he defines naturalism as "a poetic convention of drama quite distinct from literalism, where you try to represent life photographically."[17]

Storey belongs to the sizable number of English dramatists who come from, and write about, life in the Midlands and the north of England. The regional flavor, he contends, is part of any good play. "It's got to be rooted."[18]

Storey's methods of writing seem as random as his life and his plots. His irregular writing habits, for example, can be seen in the events surrounding the production of his first play, *The Restoration of Arnold Middleton* (1967), at the Royal Court (where Storey even served for a short time as artistic director and where most of his plays were directed by the same person, Lindsay Anderson, a fortuitous choice for creating on stage Storey's distinctive flavor). Storey wrote the drama in about 1958, but it was not staged until—encouraged to submit a play—he exhumed this one from a shelf where it had lain with other unpublished material. When *The Restoration of Arnold Middleton* proved successful, he went home and quickly dashed off a series of plays, all produced in rapid succession at the Royal Court: *Home* (1970), *The Changing Room* (1971), *Cromwell* and *The Farm* (1973), *Life Class* (1974), *Mother's Day* (1976); then *Sisters* at Manchester (1978) and *Early Days* at the National Company's Cottesloe Theatre (1980).

Working without a plan, Storey insists that his writing writes itself, and he frequently works on several novels and plays at a time. Like *The Restoration of Arnold Middleton*, *Early Days* had been written five years before its production. Storey's unfinished manuscripts include three or four plays, all untitled except one, which is tentatively titled "Women." "Maybe it will end, like so many, in the ash-can. Or maybe, just maybe, it will succeed in writing itself."[19] In his own words: "This reservoir of plays that built up inside me . . . simply had to find a way to pour out."[20]

Prizes also poured in for Storey who had been an award-winning student in art school. His first novel, *This Sporting Life* (1960), was awarded the Macmillan Fiction Prize. A second novel, *Flight Into Cam-*

den (also 1960), won the John Llewelyn Rhys Memorial Prize in 1961 and the Somerset Maugham Award in 1963. Most of his plays won prizes, with *The Contractor* (1969) standing at the head of the list: an *Evening Standard* award, the London Theatre Critics Award in 1970, and the New York Drama Critics Circle Award in 1974. Hardly a play or novel did not receive some recognition.

The year of the production of *The Restoration of Arnold Middleton,* 1967, was a vintage year on the English stage. Nichols's first successful stage drama, *A Day in the Death of Joe Egg,* Gray's first play, *Wise Child,* and Stoppard's *Rosencrantz and Guildenstern Are Dead* were produced. For his play, Storey won the *Evening Standard* award as the most promising playwright of 1967.

His vision of contemporary life focuses on the people who are caught, possibly trapped, in the painful change from lower- to middle-class life. Arnold Middleton is such a character. His comfortable but boringly routine schoolmaster's existence takes its toll, so he collects medieval suits of armor as an escape. He escapes, also, in actions that verge on madness and in drunkenness. When his working-class parents cancel a visit to Arnold's household, where he lives with his wife and his widowed mother-in-law, he throws a party, at which he threatens the guests with a gun. The attempt is futile, as the gun has no firing pin. Like the abortive shooting by Uncle Vanya in Chekhov's play by that title, even this action fails. Arnold's acrimonious exchanges with a fellow teacher are reminiscent of Osborne's Jimmy Porter and of Butley, a character in a later play by Gray. Arnold belongs to a generation of disillusioned antiheroes.

Especially in his early plays, Storey invests his family situations with strong evocations of D. H. Lawrence. Arnold's parents are working-class; his wife's family is middle-class. By their absence at the party, Arnold's parents contrast with his wife and his mother-in-law, who observe the niceties and proprieties of the middle class. Through this contrast, Storey hints at the reason for the emptiness that drives Arnold to near-insanity. He is "restored" when the mother-in-law, who at times suggests a sympathy for Arnold and a Lawrentian competition with his wife, leaves her daughter and her son-in-law to pick up the pieces of their marriage.

In Celebration, Storey's next play, focuses on the intense estrangement and guilt that surface when three educated sons who have made their respective ways in life return to their provincial home for their parents' fortieth anniversary. The claustrophobically small rooms of a small house in a small village, in which neighbors drop in to offer cheery and comfortable greetings, slowly grow into a metaphor for the past and present lives of all five members of the family. The anniversary dinner at a restaurant in town happens offstage. In its place as the central action are the arrival of the sons, as they reacquaint themselves with each other and with their parents, and the postdinner drinks at home. These occasions provide opportunities for family revelations of past and present. This tripled version of Arnold Middleton's frustrations fills in and amplifies the details missing in the earlier play. The resemblance to Lawrence's *Sons and Lovers* is unmistakable.

The father, Harry Shaw, is in failing health after forty-nine years in the mines. Helen, the genteel mother, claims the background of a smallholder, whereas Harry describes her family's source of income as pig breeding. Andrew at forty, suggesting Jimmy Porter in his railing against the world, has given up law practice to become a painter. Colin, the middle son, the peacemaker in the family, is in a business in which he must deal with strikers. Stephen, the youngest, teaches school and has been working on a book. (It is difficult not to see Stephen as David Storey, also the third son in his family. In addition, one of Storey's older brothers, Anthony, has written novels and has taught at Cambridge.) Lawrentian guilt surfaces when it is revealed that Andrew was farmed out to a neighbor while Helen was carrying Stephen. There is also some residual guilt about the firstborn son, who died suddenly at the age of seven. Family skeletons are only half the plot, as the present situations of the sons are in the process of changing. Colin cries and cannot sleep, consumed by his marriage (which includes four children) and the drudgery of schoolteaching. Andrew, having realized his parent's desire for his education and a better life than theirs, rebels and still resents having been sent to neighbors when his parents had their own personal problems and therefore could not handle him. To his disapproving parents, Colin announces his intention of marrying a dentist. At the end, maintaining their stolid exteriors even in the face of the increasingly painful confrontations, the parents, although disappointed that their sons have not become the successes they intended, observe the conventional goodbyes as the sons leave the next morning.

The sense of dispersal and dissociation pervades individuals and the family unit. The ironic counterpoint to the disunity is Storey's use of two old neighbors of the family, one a drunk and the other a gossip, who drop in while the family is away at dinner. The two comment on the celebratory dinner as well-deserved by the couple who had worked so hard to provide for their sons. The finely spun details of the family past are the substance of the play, with the focus deliberately fragmented in five directions, not as in *The Restoration of Arnold Middleton,* in which one central character dominates. The fragmentation in subsequent plays is even more noticeable, so that in retrospect these first two plays seem early attempts to find the directions that *Home, The Contractor,* and *The Changing Room,* possibly his three major plays, take.

Storey's third play, *The Contractor* (1969), is his first to illustrate with a vivid clarity the style that has become his hallmark. In three acts, the construction of a wedding tent occupying acts 1 and 2 and its dismantling act 3, the play seems at times to exist primarily for the visible and palpable fascination that physical work frequently holds for people. In Pinter's *Birthday Party,* McCann shreds a sheet of newspaper, column by column, as the audience concentrates on his action, waiting for a slip of the finger or for some significance to attach to the tearing. But the action seems to exist in and of itself. Storey takes just such an event, only on a larger scale, and creates a whole drama from it. Harold Hobson of the *Sunday Times* describes it as a play with no "superficially dramatic incident, yet it awakens in us a sense of infinite mystery."[21] Frank Marcus of the *Sunday Telegraph* describes it as "altogether an enthralling experience . . . [that] exercises hypnotic fascination,"[22] and B. A. Young of the *Financial Times* speaks of "a play that is as gripping as it is original, and as shapely as it is simple. . . . [It] kept me fascinated."[23]

Yet the mechanical construction of the tent is evenly balanced by the human interactions among five workers, three Yorkshiremen and two Irishmen, and three generations of the Ewbanks family: old Mr. and Mrs. Ewbank; their son, the contractor, and his wife; the contractor's daughter, whose wedding to Maurice happens offstage between acts 2 and 3; and finally their son Paul, who seems more sympathetic to the laborers than to his family. In their comradely joking and story telling with rich Yorkshire and Irish dialects, the workmen prove as fascinating as the erecting and dismantling of the tent. Revelations occur about the not-so-friendly contractor-laborer attitudes toward each other, about the generational differences in the family, and about the empty prosperity of the contractor, as both his son and daughter for different reasons seem indifferent to it. Ronald Bryden of the *Observer* calls the play "a subtle and poetic parable about the nature and joy of skilled work, the meaning of community and the effect of its loss."[24] And Hobson sees it "as exquisite as Keats's 'Ode on a Grecian Urn' and, like that poem, it is about a work of art, how it is fashioned, what regrets and happiness it enshrines, and the poignancy of its contrast with human experience."[25]

If the unraveling of the personal, familial, and social fabric of characters' lives is in process in Storey's first three plays, *Home* (1970) dramatizes the unraveled state in its completion. Four characters, in what is a vaguely identified setting, at first speak in disjointed, dissociated, random fashion about anything, frequently about very trivial details of their lives. Suggestive of Pinter's style, in which information about plot and characters is withheld, and in which silences and pauses occupy the dramatic spaces, *Home* produces mysterious nuances. If there is little plot in Storey's other plays, there is even less in this one. The sense of dispersal is so dominant as almost to eliminate action and character altogether and in their place to render a musical performance. Taylor writes that "the actors seemed to be moving, speaking, falling silent, as though to some musical pattern which they could hear and we could not—and the effect was breathtaking. So perfect was the spell cast, indeed, that on the second night during one of the deeper silences, a mouse strolled on stage, looked calmly around, and having satisfied its curiosity wandered off again."[26]

We first see and hear the two male inmates in a long conversation about trivial matters, as though careful to disguise their innermost selves, using what Pinter describes as the language locked beneath the ordinary spoken speech. They leave, and two women replace them in their chairs. Soon the two couples meet, and by the end of act 1 it is clear that the location is a mental institution. Distinguished by the acting of Ralph Richardson and John Gielgud in London and New York, the play received strong critical plaudits, its style "as austere as Pinter or even Beckett, but nearer to common experience, almost naturalistic."[27]

In *The Changing Room* (1971), Storey returns to the tangible world and also to the structural style of *The Contractor.* The fringe situations here are the interactions of players, owners, trainers, and sundry persons such as the janitor, as they dress for the game, arrive during halftime, and then return after the game to dress in street attire. Individualized portraits of the players and managers are realized in the unusually rich physical details of the language, dress, hopes, and concerns of each. One competent, silent player wishes to save money for his education; an older player hopes to stay healthy until he wins big betting on the horses; still another is proud of the toolbox he has bought.

As a depiction of one slice of British society, the play does not contain the psychological or sociological commentary implicit in the characterizations of Storey's other plays. It is almost as though Storey, the rugby player, relives the situations of his own playing days in a realistic style that is closer to the literal, photographic level than in his other dramas.

Segments of British history and contemporary life continue to be the subject of plays such as *Cromwell, The Farm, Life Class, Mother's Day, Sisters,* and *Early Days.* The titles speak clearly for the plays, sometimes ironically, as in the case of Cromwell, the Puritan leader in England's seventeenth-century civil war, who does not even appear in the play by that title (1973). Storey concentrates on various characters on both sides of the conflict, who at times seem ignorant or confused by the issues. The loss and confusion people feel during a war situation is sometimes expressed in antiphonal chanting, a stylistic means by which the author articulates and shapes the random nature of the suffering. The play did not enjoy the critical or popular approval of earlier plays, possibly because this vague, generalized comment about the waste of war lacks the imaginative and metaphorical nuances that distinguish his earlier writing.

The Farm (1973) returns to the situation of *In Celebration,* this time three daughters replacing the three sons as the main characters. The two older daughters are schoolteachers, one of whom exihibits strength and stability while the other, the middle daughter, has a succession of men in her life. The third daughter, revolutionary in her ideas, has a local factory worker as her boyfriend. The father is a hard-drinking farmer, and the mother, again as in D. H. Lawrence's stories, is sympathetic to the son, who announces that he is going to marry an older, divorced woman with two children. The mother and the sisters, each for her own reasons, side with the son against the father. Storey once more works in an intricate web of shifting familial relationships that at times evoke Lawrence's *Sons and Lovers* and at times seem like an updated version of Chekhov's *Three Sisters*. But the play remains Storey's own, not an imitative or influenced drama, for he retains the strong emotional and physical detail of Yorkshire England as only his unerring ear and eye have been able to reproduce so richly on the English stage.

Life Class (1974), like *The Changing Room,* concerns a specific segment of Storey's own experience as an art student. Like *The Contractor* and *The Changing Room, Life Class* contains much banter, this time among a class of art students. Storey returns, however, to his early style in *The Restoration of Arnold Middleton* with his use of an event that unifies a series of individualized characterizations. During a class, a chaotic situation results when a male student goes up to the nude model and stages a mock coupling. The commentary on the separateness of art and life, as well as the reversion to conventional style, diminishes the play's effectiveness.

Mother's Day (1976) is another reworking of a family gathering, this time of two sons and two daughters, a housepainter father, and the usual Lawrentian mother. The tone of the play is comic rather than dramatic. In *Sisters* (1978), Storey changes his setting from the small village to a housing estate in the North, where Adrienne visits her sister, Carol. The emphasis here is on the present rather than the past, in particular on Adrienne's involvement with a prostitution scheme run by Carol and her husband, a former professional footballer.

After this series of mediocre plays, Storey recoups some of his losses in *Early Days* (1980). Like *Home,* the play is musical enchantment, as an aging gentlemen, of substance and public accomplishment, finds himself isolated and regarded by his daughter and servants as unable to take care of himself. The theme of insanity and the Beckettian sense of diminishment, as he struggles to maintain his independence and to remain intact, are delicately etched in Storey's finest form. Played by Ralph Richardson in his last stage appearance, an actor whose idiosyncratic ways are legend, the main character, Kitchen, is viewed as wilful, obstreperous, and childish by the sane around him. Storey's vision of dispersion and decline is total, as Kitchen slowly dissociates himself from life. In the last scene, ignoring his daughter's question, he speaks his wandering thoughts, heard by Bristol, the butler. "What seaport do we leave from? Is this cottage at the edge of the wood, or is it amongst the trees? When the peasants sing in the evening are they from the village, or are they gypsies? Are gypsies allowed there? Are people free?"[28] When, in answer to Kitchen's questions, Bristol replies that the children do not even know whom he [Bristol] works for, Kitchen's thoughts revert to images of his dissociation. "I can't see you, if you stand behind. I was telling Mat . . . So tall, I thought the bridge would fall. So high, the people on it looked like flies. . . . All those strange faces gazing down . . . Ellen . . . [turns] Ellen!" (*ED*, 53).

With the focus on one character in *Early Days,* Storey returns to the one-character style of his first play, *The Restoration of Arnold Middleton,* but in its stylistic maturity, the play is distinguished by pure lyricism, just as in the more physically palpable plays, like *The Contractor,* the earthy lyricism of the tent construction fascinates.

SIMON GRAY

More than Nichols and Storey, Simon Gray is associated with the academic tradition. Born in 1936, he traveled between England and Canada during and after World War II and took an honors degree in English from Dalhousie University in Canada and a second degree in English at Cambridge University. Following these achievements, he took up lecturing in English at the University of British Columbia, supervising in English at Trinity College, Cambridge, and, later, lecturing at Queen Mary College, London. It is not surprising, then, that his first successful play, *Butley* (1971), is set in a faculty office at London University. If there is one name from Gray's works one remembers, it is Butley, primarily because he is a forceful and fascinating version of Jimmy Porter, made famous by Osborne fifteen years earlier. Butley's immediate fame was partly due to the fine direction by Pinter and the acting of Alan Bates, who had played the role of Cliff in the original production of *Look Back in Anger*. Like the playwright-director duos of Nichols–Blakemore and Storey–Anderson, that of Gray and Pinter effectively continued into 1982, when Pinter directed *The Common Pursuit*.

Before *Butley,* other plays by Gray had been produced: *Wise Child* (1967, the year of Nichols's *Joe Egg* and of Storey's *Arnold Middleton*), *Spoiled* (television version, 1968), *Dutch Uncle* (1969), and an adaptation of Dostoyevski's *Idiot* (1970). His first two original stage plays, *Wise Child* and *Dutch Uncle,* with their bizarre, melodramatic plots, received poor notices, mostly because of what critics saw as labored imitations of Joe Orton's grotesque comedies. In *Wise Child,* a criminal wanted for mail robbery evades the police by dressing as a woman. A murdered homosexual landlord, a black maid, and the strange relationship between two criminals suggest the manic events of an Orton play. The plot of *Dutch Uncle* is drawn from the notorious Reginald Christie murders, a series of crimes committed by an ex-constable, who sealed his victims, including his wife, in the kitchen walls. In the play, the main character is a married chiropodist, Godboy, who is attracted to a police inspector. The actions of the stereotypically inefficient inspector and the equally inefficient chiropodist who would murder his wife prove a lame attempt at Ortonesque comedy. Both plays, however, contain elements of the dark subterranean forces in man that appear in later plays. In *Spoiled,* with its triangular plot involving a schoolteacher, his pregnant wife, and a male student, Gray probes the undercurrents of middle-class psyches. The teacher in special French lessons presses the boy, and the relationship eventually concludes in a seduction.

It is but a step from *Spoiled* and its limitations as a television drama to a much more profound study of Ben Butley, the teacher in *Butley,* who is disillusioned, angry, bitter, vituperative, and very articulate. As with Nichols's Bri and Storey's Arnold Middleton, Butley's life is in the process of distintegration, and we discover that process through his own lashing out at those around him. Like Jimmy Porter, he cannot specifically identify the cause or target of his anger, and so he unleashes his invective on his wife, students, and colleagues. He articulates brilliantly his contempt for those who cannot match the knifelike logic with which he devastates their arguments. His intellectual attacks on them develop into psychological and moral battles.

Butley shares his office at London University and his flat with Joey, a quiet, homosexual member of the faculty, who is applying for promotion. Two faculty members, Edna Shaft, who has been working for twenty years on a study of Byron, and James, who does not appear on stage, are important to Joey's promotion. In the course of one day in the life of Ben Butley (Storey not only observes the classical unities in the drama but also has his characters talk about them), the audience is given full insight into Butley's complex personal and professional relationships. The means by which Storey realizes clarity and a unity in the tangled web of verbal and psychological games that Butley plays is the theme of domination, Butley's only way of coping with life. He presses each of his victims for information about themselves and for motives for their actions, abusing their trust until, out of sheer exhaustion, they are driven from his life. So Joey moves out of Butley's office and into Edna's. He moves, as well, out of Butley's apartment into Reg Nuttall's. Butley's wife, Anne, and their small daughter have left him, and Anne is planning to marry someone whom she finds dull but, even so, preferable to Butley. Butley not only ruins his own marriage but attempts to ruin the liaison between Anne and Tom, as well as their professional status at the school at which Tom teaches and Anne hopes to work. He proselytizes tutorial students away from Edna, and he spends the entire day attempting to separate Joey and Reg. Although Butley dominates, he loses, for he is left alone at the end, dismissing Gardner, the student whom he does not find interesting anymore. In small ways, even though Anne, Joey, Reg, and Edna lose their intellectual battles with Butley, they win, as each leaves and settles for less stimulating but more stable and rewarding situations and friends. Anne, with the daughter, Marina, settles down with Tom and with a job. Joey wants to get on with his book on Herrick, and he will do so in a quiet life with Reg. Edna does finally finish her work on Byron, despite Butley's continual slurs. Butley, however, has not progressed with his study of T. S. Eliot. His family and friends all understand that Butley's only way of coping with his disintegrating life is the verbal assault. Once he begins, there is no stopping him until he reaches rock bottom, only to begin the process over again with the next visitor or telephone caller.

English education, the cornerstone of British civilization, comes under scrutiny by Gray in an elegiac note struck by Edna. "Nobody takes anything seriously any more. But the Universities were serious once, yes they were. But they despise them, yes, they do, just as they despise me. Just as you two [Butley and the student, Gardner] despise me!"[29]

Butley's long series of brilliant verbal attacks on his office mate and his visitors shows the slow corrosion of the main character and the effect of this corrosion on the lives of others. In the end, Butley victimizes only himself.

The domination-submission theme in *Butley,* common in Gray's writing, derives from *Spoiled.* Butley, like the schoolmaster in the earlier play, attempts personal and professional human relationships, as seen in his increasingly desperate but ultimately futile efforts to wangle an invitation to dinner with Reg and Joey. Psychologically, his lacerating sadism, like Jimmy Porter's, is eventually seen as masochism. Morally, the use to which he puts his store of literary knowledge, his powers of reasoning, and his keen insights into the weaknesses of others is an attempted Faustian corruption of good.

In *Otherwise Engaged* (1975), the main character, Simon Hench, a publisher, is possibly an expansion of a character in *Butley*—Reg, who is in publishing. At the center of events that swirl about him, Hench remains detached from those events. In a reversal of the roles of victim and victimizer in *Butley,* he is the recipient of the searing wit turned on him by a sociology student—a squatter-tenant of Hench's—and by others who freely arrive and depart his domicile. The weapon Hench uses against the onslaughts of the outside world is passivity, in sharp contrast to Butley's tormenting tirades and offensive intrusions into the lives of others. At home to all who would enter his tastefully appointed apartment in crises of their lives, Hench protects himself from their pain and anguish by merely being there without reacting, impervious to their problems. Throughout the play, Hench listens to Wagner records and registers annoyance only when visitors intrude on his listening, his particular form of being "otherwise engaged." Only when he throws a glass of whiskey at Jeff, a literary critic and friend, does Hench display any emotion. But even after this brief outburst, he resumes listening to Wagnerian music. Hench's passivity extends even to the arrangement with his wife, a marital situation in which neither love nor divorce is necessary. In Gray's gallery of characters, he seems to be a midpoint between the extroverted Butley and the paralyzed Jasper of *Close of Play*.

T. S. Eliot's theory of the dissociation of sensibility seems to have found residence in the chilling character of Hench, who is as disturbing in his passivity as is Butley in his active humiliation of others. Nicholas de Jongh's review of the play calls attention to the emotional and moral dissociation found in Gray's characters much like that found in the seventeenth-century comedies of William Wycherley.[30]

Like *Butley*, *Otherwise Engaged* observes the classical unities of time, place, and action. Also, like *Butley*, the play was directed by Pinter, who succeeded in realizing the isolation of Hench, as he had with the earlier Butley.

Otherwise Engaged was followed by productions of *Dog Days* (1976) and *Molly* (1977) in provincial theaters at Oxford and Watford. *Dog Days* is an early, less satisfactory version of *Otherwise Engaged*, and Gray reluctantly allowed it to be staged. *Molly* represents a return to the type of subject matter Gray dramatized in *Dutch Uncle*, the murder mystery in this case being the Alma Rattenbury case of the mid-1930s, successfully dramatized by Rattigan in *Cause Célèbre* the same year as Gray's play. *Stage Struck* (1979), a thriller compared frequently to Anthony Shaffer's *Sleuth* or Ira Levin's *Deathtrap*, belongs to the dark melodrama of *Wise Child*, *Dutch Uncle*, and *Molly*.

In the tradition of dramas about Britain's guilty past, *Rear Column* (1978) combines a historical event with Gray's favorite theme, the cruelty of detachment. Setting his drama in the context of Stanley's expedition to the Congo, Gray focuses his sights on a major event in England's colonial past. Domination and dissociative cruelty are illustrated in the actions of Jameson, a kind man on the surface, who buys a native girl and sells her to cannibals in the interest of photographing the event.

The term "chilling" recurs in reviews of Gray's plays, and succeeding dramas—*Close of Play* (1979) and *Quartermaine's Terms* (1981)—

follow on the heels of *Butley* and *Otherwise Engaged* in the exploration of the dark forces in the human psyche. Both plays deal with the silent, rather than the loquacious, form of that darkness. In *Close of Play* (1980), a rare treatment of children and parents in place of Gray's usual husband-and-wife subject, a family patriarch, Jasper, sits dumbly listening to family revelations poured out by his children, their spouses, and their children. Only once does he attempt speech, as he struggles to get up from his chair, only to go unnoticed even by his wife. His comment is "The door is open . . . ," part of a chant from Eliot spoken earlier in the play. Gray's favorite poet is obviously Eliot, whose hollow men seem the basis for Gray's own characters.

Quartermaine's Terms (1981), again about a schoolmaster, this time in an English school for foreigners like that in which Gray himself taught in France, features a character similar to Butley, Hench, and Jasper. Quartermaine, who has no family, refers to the faculty as his family. The action of the play consists of conversations in the faculty room as various members enter and exit, revealing their personal problems. Quartermaine alone has nothing to say, because he has no family and none of the personal problems associated with a family. Impeccably mannered, he has been reduced to a shell of a human being, relying, for human ties, on babysitting and being a dinner guest. Although the faculty work, as one character admits, is a job for failures, their lives contain compassion, and they are human and, therefore, good. Quartermaine is the epitome of Eliot's hollow man.

The Common Pursuit (1984) is a transference of Gray's Cambridge days on to the stage. About a group of Cambridge students, the play develops their lives as each experiences a marriage, divorce, a publishing success or failure, etc. These are the idealists of the days of F. R. Leavis, from whose book the play derives its title. His donnish wit at its most playful, Gray entertains and, according to Frank Rich, most closely resembles Frederic Raphael's *Glittering Prizes,* the televised series about the brightest and the best from England's major universities.[31] There are the historian, the critic, the philosopher-poet and even the untalented person who lives vicariously through others. If there is a hero in the play, he is the one person who destroys only his own life. The theme of dissociation, however, is dispersed among the many characters, and the drama suffers from the absence of concentration on one character.

In an interestingly autobiographical sense, Gray's concern with the idea of dissociation is present in his published running account of the production stages of *The Common Pursuit*. He describes the director, Pinter, as a "figure of benevolent reassurance" and "ferocious geniality" and decidedly casts Pinter in the supporting role of his own "unflappable and patient ego."[32]

Gray, like Nichols and Storey, is remarkable for the fine detail with which he has painted the social canvas of postwar England and the shifting realities of middle-class English life, encompassing the personal, societal, and national ideals and disillusionments. The three writers are not so much innovators or rebels of the stage as they are a refinement of the new trends in drama. They are not, however, imitative, as each brings a fresh voice and vision to contemporary man that go beyond their timeliness to universal matters of the human spirit.

CHAPTER VIII

LEFTISTS

Some writers from the group that Kenneth Tynan had labeled as the "hairy men," those dramatists espousing use of the stage as a forum for matters of social conscience, went so far as to protest the very basis of English society: its values and the institutions representing those values. Unlike those who merely criticized abuses or advocated reform, the New Left writers frequently dramatized nothing less than the necessity of abolishing those values and institutions, some offering nothing to take their place, others recommending a form of enlightened socialism. Anarchy sometimes seemed preferable to the cruelty or injustices of the establishment.

As Harold Hobson points out, the difference between the milder dramatists of commitment, like Osborne and Wesker, and those of radical persuasion is that in the latter, hatred for the oppressor is much stronger than sympathy for the oppressed.[1] Instead of the personalized situations of Jimmy and Alison Porter, the allegorical/historical approach frequently characterizes the work of writers such as Howard Barker, Peter Barnes, Edward Bond, Howard Brenton, David Edgar, Trevor Griffiths, and David Hare. The impetus to this politicized writing came mainly from the flourishing fringe theaters in London and environs. The most influential of these stages was the Royal Court, but the Traverse in Edinburgh and the RSC's Warehouse in London encouraged the new drama as the larger theaters could not. Hobson describes "the most famous outpost of the Alternative Theatre . . . [,] not in London, but in Edinburgh . . . [,] [as] a sinister little room half way up a winding stone staircase ideally suited to medieval plotting and murder, the Traverse."[2]

Politicization grew bolder with the advent of the new heads of the government-subsidized Royal Shakespeare Company and the National Theatre, Peter Hall and Trevor Nunn, who mixed traditional and experimental plays in the offerings at their theaters.

The radical drama, seen in perspective, is not as radical as it may have seemed at first. In fact, it can be viewed as an extension of Shaw's plays, in which shockingly new ideas were debated with brilliance—with an eye to satirizing middle-class respectability—and also as the British extension of Brecht's plays, in which capitalistic values and institutions were turned upside down with entertaining verve. With the new freedom of stage language that accompanied the 1956 production of *Look Back in Anger,* and with the repeal of censorship laws and those against homosexuality in the 1960s, the continuance of the ideas of those two iconoclasts—Shaw and Brecht—seems only natural.

What is so unusual about the proliferation of leftist drama is the relatively little formal opposition to it from the institutions that came under attack: the government, the church, and, in general, middle-class morality. Shocking though the use of obscenities, nudity, homosexuality, antichauvinism, anticolonialism, and even brutality—such as the stoning of a baby in Bond's *Saved*—seemed at first, radical writers, like their milder contemporaries, managed to enjoy subsidies from the government. Some dramatists enjoyed increasingly broad acceptance as their plays moved from tiny fringe stages to larger, subsidized experimental theaters, and then to the West End commercial houses. Even the comfortable middle-class theater audience of "Aunt Ednas," who were used to the politely spoken and acted dramas of Coward and Rattigan, was slowly familiarized with the stylistically intriguing plays of Pinter and Stoppard. The process of "mainstreaming" was underway, so that by the 1980s the shocks of even the leftist dramas had been absorbed. At least part of the reason for the absorption was the participation of the old generation of knighted actors, such as Ralph Richardson, John Gielgud, and Laurence Olivier, in plays by Osborne, Pinter, Stoppard, and Storey.

If, as Harold Hobson asserts, Beckett, Osborne, Pinter, and Brecht are the "forces that transformed the theatre built up by Galsworthy, Maugham, and Shaw, by Eliot and Priestley and Fry,"[3] then Bond, Brenton, and Hare represent unabashedly political drama and stand out from those contemporaries who merely attack systemic abuses or who focus on the victims of those abuses (Arnold Wesker, Peter Terson,

Henry Livings, David Mercer). They stand out also from those of their contemporaries who write penetrating social and psychological realism (Nichols, Storey, Gray) and, as well, from those who explore the dark or fantastic regions of the individual and societal psyches (Rudkin, Orton, Simpson, Heathcote Williams). Not as well known, certainly to American audiences and possibly even to the general English audience, they comprise a formidable group of dramatists.

Most of them launched and developed their careers in alternate theater. Bond, Barker, and Brenton have had plays produced at the Royal Court and ultimately at one or the other of the two major national companies, the Old Vic or the Aldwych, or at one of their smaller houses, such as the Warehouse. Although seldom commercially viable, they remain an important force in the theater revolution. Ties among the radical dramatists are strong, and their closeness has resulted in a number of collaborative writing efforts, to be discussed in their appropriate contexts in this chapter.

EDWARD BOND

Like many of his contemporaries, Bond, born on 18 July 1934, is of lower-class origins (Holloway in North London) and saw fields and countryside for the first time as a wartime evacuee. Although his plays have been frequently described as Pinteresque because of the absence of motivational details about his characters' actions, he has, unlike Pinter, espoused the actively committed theater. In his protest of injustices, he has become one of the most controversial of the politicized writers. An attack on a baby in a London park by hoodlums—in *Saved*—has been described as the single most horrible and controversial scene in post–World War II drama. His powerful images of violence in the modern age, along with his technique of withheld information, has drawn critical attention to both his substance and his style. In his early plays, naturalistic images are so vivid that their significance as parables for the twentieth century sometimes is lost. However controversial, he remains a major figure of the Left among both the first and second waves of new dramatists.

Bond's first five plays, including a translation of Chekhov's *Cherry Orchard,* were produced at the Royal Court. Among these, his most controversial play, *Saved* (1965), is a vivid dramatization of his chief dramatic concern: the fate of innocence in an age in which violence is the new form of pornography. In an interview, he commented that just as sex was the pornography of the Victorian era, violence is the pornography of the post–World War II age. Violence pervades a competitive society: "There is no alternative, because this is the whole dialectic of violence—I threaten you, you threaten me, and finally you have to carry out your threats, otherwise there is no credence behind them."[4]

Four of Bond's plays are discussed here, in illustration of his treatment of his subject by means of three different approaches: the naturalistic, the historical/allegorical, and the mythic.

In an early play, *The Pope's Wedding* (1962), a naturalistic play about violence in a rural family in which the only method of communication was silence, that silence eventually erupts into violence: Scopey, a young farm worker, becomes obsessed with an old hermit, whom he must eventually kill and replace. In *Saved,* a similar family situation is transplanted to a London working-class family in which a sensitive young man, Len, lives with Pam and her parents, a couple who haven't spoken to each other in years. Their marital silence is broken when Pam's mother and Len become comically involved in what seems like a mutual seduction, a scene violently interrupted by the father. The most horror-filled incident of the play occurs in a park, where hoodlums, among them the alleged father, stone Pam's baby to death, having rubbed excrement on the baby's face as well. The violence of silence in the family is renewed as the family resumes its living routines, with Len breaking the otherwise wordless last scene in its only spoken line—"Fetch me 'ammer"—as he is seen at work. The salvation of the play's title resides in the goodness of Len as he lives in a world alien to that goodness. One may assume that the release of the pent-up violence in both the comic and the tragic situations is a form of salvation, despite the family's resumption of their nonspeaking relationships. But a Kafka-like pall haunts the play even at the end.

If *The Pope's Wedding* and *Saved* with their indelibly horrible scenes depict Bond's concerns naturalistically, *Narrow Road to the Deep North* explores the creation of powerful political forces that have their origins in a passive violence. His exploration takes the form of a Brechtian epic play set in Japan in either the seventeenth, eighteenth, or nineteenth century; the historical accuracy is unimportant. What is important is the truth that the poet Basho learns thirty years after he had done nothing upon seeing a baby abandoned by its parents. A native tyrant, Shogo, is deposed and replaced by an equally, if more subtly, oppressive British commodore and his evangelist sister, Georgina. Shogo then attempts unsuccessfully to recover his power and is executed; the evangelist goes mad; Kiro, a young priest-idealist figure, commits suicide after becoming involved with Shogo. Basho learns that the baby he had failed to help had grown into the tyrant Shogo.

British colonialism, secular and religious, is attacked by Bond and shown to be no less violent than that of Shogo; barbaric and civilized brutalities, both destructive, clash. Basho, the poet, is an ivory-tower idealist who has failed the baby who grew into the tyrant. Fascinatingly, Bond deploys a second baby in the person of the son of the murdered king.

The old man in *The Pope's Wedding,* the baby in *Saved,* and the two babies in *Narrow Road to the Deep North* are allegories of innocence betrayed and destroyed. As adults, Scopey, Len, and Basho represent vestiges of that innocence. John Russell Taylor points out Georgina's "cynical manipulation of the forms of Christianity as . . . a way of keeping the masses subservient . . . with overtones of Bond's Queen Victoria [in the play *Early Morning*]."[5]

Lear (1971) is Bond's reworking of the mythic origins of Shakespeare's drama. In Bond's version, the two sisters displace a despotic father and go on to repeat his tyranny. Cordelia, loyal to her father, finally succeeds the sisters but, like them, is part of the revolutionary violence and part of the continuing cycle of violence. Bond's plea is that the cycle be broken, and he ends the play with Lear's plea to Cordelia to keep pity, the only means by which she can remain sane. As he dies, Lear attempts to dig up his great wall, the symbol of the new social order that he had envisioned but ultimately betrayed.

The fate of innocence in a violent world, then, is the continuing center of Bond's plays. Although he proposes no solutions, and although his characters are not fleshed out, his images remain vivid and theatrically compelling. His curious amalgamation of the spare techniques of Pinter and the epic narrative of Brecht, "smooth" and "hairy" dramatists, respectively, results in the distinction to which his drama lays claim.

Bond's political iconoclasm extends to his literary views. In an irreverent response to an interviewer's question about his assessment of Brecht and Beckett, he expresses admiration for Brecht, tempered by a skepticism regarding Brecht's praise of the Communists and condemnation of the Nazis for the same thing. And he contends that Beckett should not be made a cultural hero, accusing him of writing plays "not true to his experience" (*NTV*, 35).

HOWARD BRENTON

Unlike Bond, Brenton, who was born on 13 December 1942, comes from a middle-class background, his father a policeman-turned-minister (Methodist) with a bent for the theater. Brenton describes his father as a "social," rather than a fanatic clergyman. Also unlike Bond, Brenton enjoyed the advantages of a Cambridge education. His socialist leanings have always been open and direct, and unquestionably a natural subject for his plays. In a 1974 interview, he discounted both the existing capitalism and the "alternative society" (Labour's socialist programs), claiming that "reality is remorseless," and that "if you're going to change the world, well there's only one set of tools, and they're bloody and stained but realistic. I mean communist tools. Not pleasant. If only the gentle, dreamy, alternative society had worked" (*NTV*, 92).

He represents a distinguishing characteristic of leftist dramatists in his close relationship with fellow writers, resulting in a number of collaborations: *Lay By* (1971) with Brian Clark, Griffiths, Hare, Stephen Poliakoff, Hugh Stoddard and Snoo Wilson; *England's Ireland* (1972) with Edgar, Tony Bicat, Brian Clark, Frances Fuchs, Hare, and Wilson; *Deeds* (1978) with Griffiths, Ken Campbell, and Hare; and *Brassneck* (1973) and *Pravda* (1985) with Hare. His plays—except for *Weapons of Happiness* (1976, Lyttelton Theatre) and *The Romans in Britain* (1980, Olivier Theatre)—were produced at the small Upstairs Theatre at the Royal Court, or at other fringe and provincial theaters. His *Weapons of Happiness* was the first play to enjoy a premiere at the new National Theatre.

The impact of his plays on the London stage is aptly described in

Theatre Quarterly as "petrol bombs through the proscenium arch" (*NTV,* 85). The "bombs" literally refer to a petrol bomb thrown against a theater wall in his play *Fruit.* Like Bond, Brenton deploys violence in his plays. Frequently at the center of the violence is a policeman or other government official, who is there ostensibly to uphold the law but who reverts to violence in a criminal act.

Revenge (1969) deals with a criminal, Hepple, bent on killing MacLeish of Scotland Yard. One operates by the code of the mobster, the other by Calvinist morality. Vaudevillian scenes and jokes liberally employing the colorful language of the criminal world are the metier of the drama. At the end both men die, caricatured in a scene in which they bite blood bags.

It was during the run of this play at the Royal Court that Brenton met Hare and their long-standing collaboration in both writing and directing was established. Brenton was commissioned by Hare's Portable Theatre to write his play *Christie in Love* (1969), about a real-life criminal, in which the inspector and constable prove as violent in their middle-class morality as Christie is.

Two plays, *Lay By,* a collaborative drama mentioned earlier, and *Scott of the Antarctic; What God Didn't See* (1971), illustrate the kind of cannibalistic imagery he is associated with. In the latter, American astronaut Neil Armstrong feeds on the bodies of Scott's party. In *Lay By,* explicit sexual imagery dramatizes the plight of three offenders, whose treatment by the law echoes with vivid theatricality the same kinds of systemic injustices suffered by victims in an earlier twentieth-century drama, Galsworthy's *Justice.*

Another early play, *Magnificence* (1973), is about young radicals who abortively attempt peaceful, then violent, actions. Two of them are accidentally blown up, but it is the brutality of the police that is treated harshly with Brenton's usual violent imagery.

In *Brassneck,* Brenton traces the fortunes of the Bagley family over thirty years, the individuals of that family having risen by means of murder, bribery, and drug trafficking. Even Labour politicians join the long procession of corrupted denizens of the play. The decay of England, allegorically depicted in various Osborne plays, is unremitting and unrelieved in this generational treatment of an English family. In two other works, *The Churchill Play* (1974) and *The Romans in*

Britain (1980), Brenton uses history to attack the English policing of Ireland as the ultimate in police brutality, for it is the English people as a whole, and not just specific individuals, who are the policemen.

Brenton's *Thirteenth Night* (1981), a fantasy-parody of *Macbeth,* is ambivalent in both justifying and criticizing violence. A socialist minister murders the prime minister, who is unduly influenced by the United States, and events culminate in a gulag. Although leftist in his political orientation, Brenton does not hesitate to point out brutality wherever it occurs, in rightist or leftist regimes. Like Bond in *Lear,* Brenton reinvents a Shakespearean play, but his insistence on the necessity of violence in some situations contrasts sharply with Bond's abhorrence of it.

Weapons of Happiness (1976), its title taken from a comment by one of the radicals in an earlier play, *Magnificence,* is about a Czech émigré who, even when disillusioned by Stalinism, refuses to relinquish his communist beliefs. Brenton has described this play as anti-Stalinist but procommunist. Brenton won an *Evening Standard* award for *Weapons of Happiness,* even though his extreme views evoked controversy, as the infant killing in Bond's *Saved* did. *Pravda* is yet another vitriolic attack, this time on the journalism world, as epitomized by a character based on the wealthy Australian newspaperman Rupert Murdock. Again, no one of the huge cast of characters seems immune from the corruption.

A strong believer in the force of the theater as a forum, Brenton says that he dreams of "a play acting like a brushfire, smouldering into public consciousness. Or like hammering on the pipes being heard all through a tenement." He doesn't wish to convert, he states, but "to stir things up. . . . When it comes to agitprop, I like the agit, the prop I'm very bad at. I'm not wise enough. Yet" (*NTV,* 97).

Regarded by some critics as a major figure among the younger, intensely politicized dramatists who emerged forcefully in the 1970s, Brenton invited controversy and skepticism in his early plays. But the vast Brechtian historical canvases on stage have convinced critics of his firm grasp of style. Despite his strong attacks on English history and current English society, he has enjoyed the premieres of two plays, *Weapons of Happiness* and *The Romans in Britain,* at the governmentally subsidized National Theatre. Condemning official violence at home (police against strikers) and abroad (the military in Ireland), Brenton also shows the Irish rebels killing English officers, and he is aware of Stalinist atrocities. In dramatizing some of the violence on the part of revolutionary forces, he has gained acceptance by those critics skeptical about his one-sidedness.

DAVID HARE

With *Lay By, England's Ireland, Brassneck,* and *Pravda* among his writing collaborations with Brenton, in addition to similar associations with Nick Bicat, Tony Bicat, Edgar, Griffiths, Poliakoff, and Wilson, Hare, nevertheless, has attracted attention with his singly written plays: *Slag* (1970), *Knuckle* (1974), *Teeth and Smiles* (1975), for which Nick and Tony Bicat wrote songs, *Plenty* (1978), and *A Map of the World* (1983). Cambridge-educated like Brenton, Hare, who was born 5 June 1947, has his political dissatisfactions with both conservative and liberal wings. From his earliest plays, he has been concerned with the lies by which his characters live and act. His subtle and complex handling of how people play around with truths frequently confuses audiences, sometimes leaving them without even the smallest presumption of truth. It is this vacuum that permeates the characters in *A Map of the World,* a play in which participants in a world hunger conference in a third-world country debate their positions. Similarly, in *Slag* three schoolmistresses at Brackenhurst School, with varying neuroses of their own, manage in their experimentation with education to reduce an already small enrollment to zero. In his concern with the moral void of contemporary culture, nothing has changed in Hare's later plays, except that he has sophisticated his style and intriguingly varied his situations. His style is marked by articulate dialogue and a cinematically rapid flow of scenes, rather than by plot narrative or character development. This *Pictures at an Exhibition* style is illustrated in *Knuckle,* a play about the connivance and greed in both the upper- and the working-class characters.

If Hare doesn't see much possibility for political change in his own culture, he seems to in China, the setting for his drama *Fanshen: A Documentary of Revolution in a Chinese Village* (1967). Truth and change, even optimism—rarities for Hare—contrast with the pessimism of his other plays.

Teeth and Smiles is Hare's admittedly autobiographical play about a rock group whose self-destructive habits result in consequences similar to those of the three schoolmistresses of *Slag*. *Plenty* similarly deals with a moral vacuum, experienced by a former female French resistance fighter. His subject allows Hare to move quickly through a succession of scenes in her life, leaving the audience again with the impression that nothing has changed or that nothing has been gained, as in the international canvas of *A Map of the World*.

Director of the Portable Theatre when it was founded in 1968 and literary manager at the Royal Court, Hare, according to his *Theatre Quarterly* interviewers, straddles the line between the alternative and the institutional theaters, hoping "to break into Shaftesbury Avenue" (*NTV,* 110). He has been active in directing not only his own plays but those of others, such as Christopher Hampton's *Total Eclipse* (1981). Hampton's plays, like Hare's, frequently dramatize ethical and moral bankruptcy in the behavior of their characters.

Like many other members of what has been described as "the wild bunch" of leftist dramatists, Hare expands his individual situations to the national level, making them symbols of the bankruptcy of England and of Western civilization. As such, they would seem to be the cynical second-wave extension of Osborne's angry Jimmy Porter and, before Porter, of characters in Shaw's *Heartbreak House.*

DAVID EDGAR

Associated with General Will, an overtly political theater group, David Edgar has realized international popularity for his dramatization of Charles Dickens's novel *Nicholas Nickleby,* a mammoth RSC production in 1980 that garnered strong critical reviews on both sides of the Atlantic. Born in Birmingham on 26 February 1948 to a father who was a television producer and a mother who was an actress, Edgar early on developed political and theatrical interests. Graduating from Manchester University and working as a political reporter for a few years, he enjoyed encouragement from the Bradford University Theatre and demonstrated his political bent in the strongly topical nature of his plays. *Tedderella* (1971) and *Dick Deterred* (1974), for example, deal with Edward Heath and the Common Market and with Richard Nixon's Watergate scandal, respectively.

In addition to his *Nicholas Nickleby* adaptation, Edgar is known to general audiences for two dramas especially. *Destiny* (1976) attacks the Nazi-like tactics of the right-wing activists, like Sir Oswald Mosely, who led public opinion against Asian immigration. Its central point is "that there is no God-given reason why a national socialist movement should not arise in Britain" (*NTV*, 171). The play was Edgar's means for alerting Britishers to the danger of racial bigots.

Prolific in his writing, Edgar adapts characters from real life, for example, Mary Barnes, in a play of this title (1978) and Albie Sachs. *The Jail Diary of Albie Sachs* (1978), a study of a man "bored into submission in a way that wasn't boring" (p. 170), gave Edgar experience in solving the structural problems of taking a book and honing it down, as a sculptor would a piece of stone.

Edgar frequently deals directly with economic issues of an England that was increasingly becoming a culture of the haves and the have-nots. Some of these plays take on a documentary style. *The Case of the Workers' Plane* (1973) and *Events Following the Closure of a Motorcycle Factory* (1976) are but two plays whose weakness is their unmanageable structure, as well as their topical nature. Edgar has admitted to writing "gut" plays, sometimes completing a play in a week. His didactic message suggests the optimistic tone of Brecht as the plays of the more pessimistic political dramatists do not.

HOWARD BARKER

Although not associated with the collaborative writers or with any closely knit groups such as the Portable Theatre of Hare and Brenton, Howard Barker has in common with them his strong anticapitalist and antiestablishment sympathies. He enjoys a direct link with Bond in that his second produced play, *No One Was Saved* (1970), was written in direct response to Bond's *Saved*. Barker's reason for that response is that he doesn't find convincing Bond's optimism expressed in the final scene, in which Len is mending furniture. In fact, he "took up the gang of youths from *Saved* and used them in *No One Was Saved*"

(*NTV*, 186), a play in which a John Lennon figure exploits a lonely woman, Eleanor, for his song writing purposes. Eleanor's name derives from the Lennon-McCartney song "Eleanor Rigby."

In response to questions regarding his pessimism, Barker, born on 28 June 1946, refers to his interest in history, in which he received an M.A. from Sussex University in 1968, the annus mirabilis of national and world events. Barker says he shares with Brenton a fury, because "in our society now [1980] the progressive forces exist, the analysis of the problems exists, but for historical reasons it is difficult to assemble the opposition" (*NTV*, 196).

Their dramas, however, present sharp contrasts. Brenton expresses his fury in outrageous situations in which sexuality, politics, and financial greed combine to create extravagant caricatures, made entertaining with verbal exuberance and sharp wit. Barker's satire, however, was not as well received as Brenton's. It is to "that range of middlebrow critic" (*NTV*, 195)—Michael Billington or Irving Wardle—that he attributes an active hostility to his plays, particularly because they agree with those who say he fails "to understand the laws of structure" (*NTV*, 186). Although the subject of Barker's comedies of class conflict is in the mainstream of the new drama, it is his lampooning style that contributed to his not being regarded as a serious dramatist.

In his play *Edward,* Barker sees "Toryism as a manifestation of life-hatred" (*NTV*, 188). He asserts that there are only two options for the classic communist position of a Tom Driberg: "to remain here, in the Labour Party, and become a gossip columnist, or to become an outright traitor" (*NTV*, 192). This choice is the subject of his play *Heaven.* Not only Tories but Labourites, as well, are his targets. And, as might be expected, in *The Loud Boys' Life,* right-wing bigots like Enoch Powell join Barker's long gallery of caricatures.

Claw and Stripwell are characters whose names, in typical Barker fashion, reflect their qualities. Pimping under the alias Claw in Barker's play of that title (1975), Noel deliberately uses his profession as a means of acting out his politics. In *Stripwell* (also 1975), a judge by that name, after a series of ludicrous scenes—such as his socialist son's capitalist plans to smuggle heroin in the vaginas of elephants and his wife's sexual intercourse with a Tory on the floor of the House of

Commons—comes to the conclusion that his options are reduced to living with the hypocrisy of one or the ineffectuality of the other.

Barker's interest in history becomes the subject or setting for his later plays. *The Power of the Dogg* (1985) is set in the 1945 Yalta meetings, at which Stalin and Churchill divided Europe after World War II. *Pity in History* (1985) is about the English civil war. And in 1985 three history plays were produced at the RSC's small Pit Theater: *Downchild, Crimes in Hot Centuries,* and *The Castle.*

Barker has remained essentially a fringe dramatist, and he is keenly sensitive to the fact. He wishes for his plays "a texture which is uniquely mine against the headlong rush of naturalism. . . . I think every convention is a form of decay. I'd like to rediscover the rhetoric and power images of an earlier theatre, say the Jacobean."[6] His drama is, if anything, one of images.

TREVOR GRIFFITHS

Born on 4 April 1935 and older than the political dramatists that compose a large segment of the second wave that swept Britain during the 1970s, Griffiths was thus almost thirty-five when his first play, *The Wages of Thin* (1969), was produced in Manchester. His sympathies, however, are with the younger group, some of whom he has collaborated with. His dramas reflect the necessity for systemic uprooting, a theme basic to the radicals, rather than the advocacy of systemic reform, expressed or implied in the plays of the writers of his generation, the first wave of postwar dramatists. Leaving no doubt about the leftist genesis of his writing career, he told an interviewer that "it started with a number of images, really. It started with 1968, in France [with the student demonstrations]. And the American universities, the Blacks in Detroit, Watts. It started with the experience of the Friday night meetings at Tony Garnett's, where sixty or seventy people would cram into a room, and the whole sense, the aching need to . . . to do more, to get it right, to be correct, to read the situation as a first step towards changing it utterly" (*NTV,* 131).

His collaborations include the aforementioned *Lay By* and *Deeds* with Brenton, Hare, and others. But it is his single plays that have attracted wide critical attention, especially *Occupations* (1970), *The*

Party (1973), and *The Comedians* (1975). What distinguishes all three plays is the representations by the characters of a variety of viewpoints and, indeed, of many subtle shadings of a viewpoint, resulting in articulate, witty, substantive debates that evoked from one interviewer questions regarding the Shavian nature of his plays. Griffiths's response to these questions includes his reservations that Shaw "takes more pleasure in the forms of argument than out of the substance," and that Shaw lacks "any particular passion *about* the issues he raises or for the issues, or for the solution of the issues" (*NTV*, 131).

In *Occupations,* set in Turin, Italy, during the 1920 Fiat labor unrest, two spokesmen for the Left—a local intellectual Marxist and his pragmatic and ruthless Soviet opponent—clash, in demonstration of the author's interest in presenting a variety of views and approaches within the left wing. *The Party* is similarly set during a political upheaval, this time the French anti-Gaullist student demonstrations of May 1968. In the London home of a television producer, representatives of left-wing constituencies from all over Britain discuss varying views of, and approaches to, possible political changes. The complexities in the personal lives of the characters and in their intellectual positions create a compelling and vivid scene of "people who were deeply rooted in their arguments," although "the rooting was different in each case" (*NTV*, 131).

In *The Comedians* Griffiths assembles yet another group, this time six comedians participating in a local talent show. Each comedian is explored for the personal and social roots of his comedy. The focus gradually sharpens on an older comedian, Eddie Waters, who sees the younger version of himself in Gethin Price. As in *Occupations* and *The Party, The Comedians* provides the audience with a spectrum of radical political views. Griffiths describes the two major traditions represented as the social-democratic and the revolutionary. One is the "rational and humane . . . arguing . . . for . . . change through education" (*NTV*, 131). The other, younger tradition opts for anger and violence. Waters appeals to compassion in spite of his disillusionment, contrasting with Price, a symbol of the cynicism of the new generation. As an exploration of both the art of comedy and of varying political attitudes, *The Comedians* remains Griffiths's major play and a potent drama in the New Left tradition.

Even Harold Hobson, a London *Times* critic regarded as old-fashioned by the New Left, describes *The Party* as containing a "political discussion of a *gravitas* and a quickness of mind which had not been seen since the heyday of Bernard Shaw."[7]

In 1986 the RSC's Pit Theatre staged *Dreams,* still another of Griffiths's dramas about revolutionaries, this time a group of young radical Americans in the process of holding up an A&P store in the midwest. The same dilemmas are present as in Griffiths's other plays, as some members of the holdup group confront the possibility of violent action.

ANDREW (SNOO) WILSON AND STEPHEN POLIAKOFF

The youngest among the politically committed dramatists, Snoo Wilson, born on 2 August 1948, and Stephen Poliakoff, born in 1952, are essentially "un-mainstreamed" dramatists. At university (Wilson at East Anglia and Poliakoff at Cambridge) during the height of the political unrest in 1968, they soon found their place with Brenton, Hare, Griffiths, etc., and joined in the collaborative writing of *Lay By.* Both remain substantially fringe dramatists. Neither has had the impact on the new drama that Brenton, Hare, and Griffiths have had.

Poliakoff has drawn notice with his *Strawberry Fields* (1977) and *Breaking the Silence* (1984), the former at the small Cottesloe Theatre in the National Theatre complex and the latter at the small Pit Theatre. *Strawberry Fields* illustrates Poliakoff's favorite subjects, young people caught in the economic and political turbulence of their time. Their actions spring more from the generally confusing, sometimes wantonly cruel, spirit of the times than from clearly defined convictions or ideas. A middle-class liberal young woman, Charlotte, becomes a victim of her encounters with right-wing revolutionaries, as was a policeman earlier in the play.

Breaking the Silence reflects Poliakoff's personal Russian heritage, his father an émigré to England in 1924. Again, what remains dominant throughout the play is an atmosphere of swirling events in which people are caught up uncontrollably. Pesiakoff (except for two letters in the name, the similarity to Poliakoff's is obvious), the protagonist, is an inventor (Poliakoff's father is a physicist turned businessman) who experiments with talking movies in a railway car, even as events force him to keep moving, leaving family behind. The situation of the individual dislocated by historical events evokes the experience of Pasternak's Dr. Zhivago.

Whether writing about the members of the younger or the older generation, Poliakoff depicts them in symbolic and frequently blurred terms, the dominant image being one of debilitation, futility, and dispossession at times of routine or impersonal cruelty. *Clever Soldiers* (1974) treats young public-school graduates who enjoy class privileges during World War I. Tawdriness dominates *American Days* (1979), about a recording company and three young singers who try to land a record contract. The pop culture of this frantic life experienced by both executives and singers seems as dreary as the poverty of the society that encloses it. The spiritual poverty is concentrated in the young people and in the popular trends of the time.

Snoo Wilson, known almost as much for his association with the Portable Theatre group of Brenton and Hare as for his own particular plays, admits that his political development was "a lamentably slow one" (*NTV,* 173), that he is influenced by Beckett, and that he is interested in the contiguity of the interior and exterior worlds. He claims surrealism as his métier because of its suitability to his interest in the occult and the unconscious.

Vampire (1973) contains "bizarre images of Freud and Jung on stilts, the appearance of a rampant talking ox and Enoch Powell [a right-wing ideologue] delivering his 'Rivers of Blood' speech as he rises from a coffin."[8] Titles such as *Blowjob, Vampire, Pignight,* and *The Beast*—the last-mentioned his best known play—suggest the wildly imaginative quality of his writing.

He speaks of being obsessive about certain things, so that one may "return and look at them from different angles . . . as if the past were a series of stills-like holograms, which you can examine from any angle" (*NTV,* 175). In *Vampire,* events race over a period of a hundred years, in Wilson's hope that as people watch changes happening, their "ideas about the world are changing and other changes are going on as well because they're living in a universe which isn't totally in their grasp at any particular time" (*NTV,* 178). The rapidity of pace and the huge volume of events subjected plays like *Vampire* to charges of lack of structure. His *England England,* a musical about twins, one mad and one sane, who achieve power and ultimately "are taken away," he describes as a play from which people "stayed away in droves" (*NTV,* 179). Of the political dramatists, he is probably the least political in any specific sense. But he remains firm in his insistence that audiences be discomfited. Stylistically, he is a candidate for being the wildest among the "wild bunch."

PETER BARNES AND C. P. TAYLOR

Like writers Alan Plater and John Hopkins, Peter Barnes, born on 10 January 1933, and C. P. Taylor, born in 1929, are known as much for their television/screen plays and adaptations as for their stage dramas. Barnes's *Ruling Class* (1968) and Taylor's *Good* (1981), however, deserve mention as original stage dramas. The former is a satire in which members of the House of Lords are depicted as corpses, and in which the estate of a Tory earl, who believes himself to be God, eventually becomes the property of a butler, a card-carrying Communist. *Good,* a morality play for the twentieth century, explores Nazi values through characters who are metamorphosed into Nazis in a compellingly civilized and rational manner, so that distinctions between good and evil disappear in the process.

Barnes has adapted a number of dramas, such as Frank Wedekind's *Lulu* and *The Singer;* Ben Jonson's *Alchemist, The Devil Is an Ass,* and *Bartholomew Fair;* and two plays by John Marston under the title *Antonio*—seventeenth-century plays about societies in decay.

JOHN ARDEN AND MARGARETTA D'ARCY

Collaborative drama is nowhere so solidly present as in the writing of Yorkshire-born John Arden and his Irish actress-wife, Margaretta D'Arcy. They have written together about two dozen plays. Although they belong chronologically to the angry generation of the late 1950s and early 1960s, they have written about the social evils of their time not in anger but in the antirealist and poetic tradition, combining history, song, verse—frequently doggerel—and poetic imagery, to create a British version of Brechtian drama, in which the protagonists are survivors in a society and a life continually threatened by extinction.

Born on 26 October 1930 and a graduate of Cambridge, Arden received a degree in architecture from the Edinburgh College of Art. His career as architect, however, was short-lived after the production of his play *The Waters of Babylon* (1957), when he decided to become a full-time dramatist. Play followed play in a distinguished career that includes as collaborators not only his wife but also theater groups like the Muswell Hill Street Theatre, the Socialist Labour League, Writers against Repression, and the Galway Theatre Workshop. Their critical acclaim can be judged from the impressive array of theaters on which they were staged: the Royal Court, the Chichester Festival Theatre, the Glasgow Citizens' Theatre, and the Mermaid and Aldwych theaters. Yet, early in the 1970s, the Ardens chose to retire from the impressive stages to the smaller Galway Theatre Workshop, perhaps to be closer to the poetic tradition in drama. Even though removed by generation, geography, and literary tradition from the political "wild bunch" of Brenton, Hare, and others, the Ardens are, like their younger counterparts, very much committed to political drama.

Sergeant Musgrave's Dance: An Unhistorical Parable (1959), *The Workhouse Donkey: A Vulgar Melodrama* (1963), and *Armstrong's Last Goodnight: An Exercise in Diplomacy* (1964) are among Arden's best-known dramas. In *Sergeant Musgrave's Dance,* Arden focuses on the everyday occurrences of a small town when a soldier returns home during a mining strike. Ostensibly a recruiting team, the soldier and his buddies turn things upside down when they are revealed as deserters bringing home the bones of a local youth, a type of revenge on the town.

Unknown to the townspeople, Sergeant Musgrave's desertion of the army is a protest against war in general. As the soldiers and the townspeople mix and a squabble between two soldiers results in the death of one, the routine life of a small town slowly turns to horror as Musgrave's plans slowly emerge: to kill five men in order to avenge the death by a sniper of the local youth, Billy Hicks. The logic by which wars are fought multiplies itself, as even more citizens must be killed to avenge other deaths. In a chilling scene, Musgrave, increasingly taking on a posture of authority and power, publicly exhibits

Billy's skeleton and speaks to the gathered townspeople about his desire to stop the logic by which killing only perpetuates itself. He mentions the "Queen's Book, which eighteen years I've lived, it's turned inside out for me. There used to be my duty: now there's a disease"[9]

At the end Musgrave is visited in jail by a townswoman with a glass of port for him. In response to her comment that he has brought to the town a different kind of war, he claims that he has "brought it in to end it" (*SMD,* 102). What is most chilling, perhaps, is that life returns to normal in the small town, and Walsh, a collier, bitterly remarks: "The community's been saved. Peace and prosperity rules. We're all friends and neighbours for the rest of today. We're all sorted out. We're back where we were. So what do we do?" (*SMD,* 99).

The play is based on an incident that occurred in Cyprus, an event in which women and children were killed by British soldiers searching for the killer of one of their own men. In having the atrocities of war slowly infect the rhythms of life in a small town, Arden resembles the Swiss dramatist Deurenmatt, who wrote one of the most powerful of modern dramas, *The Visit,* about the way in which normal individual and community life is changed by events into the enactment of ritual evil. In different circumstances, this same ritual is enacted in Rudkin's *Afore Night Come.*

Philip Barnes echoes the sentiments of many in describing Arden's "powerful and innovative" drama as "the best English play in the Brechtian mode to have been produced."[10] Arden's use of song, poetry, and color (black and red) is at its finest in this, the play for which he is best known.

In *Armstrong's Last Goodnight* (1964), Arden turns to sixteenth-century Scotland to dramatize an obscure but ambitious outlaw, James Armstrong of Gilnoclie, who betrays those below and above him and in the end, after he has escaped authority, assumes authority over others. With the romance of history replacing the small town realism of *Sergeant Musgrave's Dance, Armstrong's Last Goodnight* focuses on the mythic aspect of what was so shockingly dramatized in the earlier play.

Arden and D'Arcy's collaborative dramas are most strikingly represented by *The Ballygombeen Bequest* (1972), *The Island of the Mighty: A*

Play on a Traditional British Theme (1972) and *The Non-stop Connolly Show* (1974). All three consist of a long series of political or historical events. *The Island of the Mighty* "gathers most of Arden's themes and techniques into one mighty plot."[11] In the play, the authors reshape King Arthur's downfall (treated in an earlier play) with strongly Marxian overtones. And in *The Non-stop Connolly Show,* the efforts of an international socialist leader, James Connolly, are dramatized as he organizes labor unions in Ireland, America, and England. In its huge cast—which includes the American labor leader Eugene Debs, as well as Lenin and Yeats—and its sweep of historical events, the play resembles the epic film *Reds,* produced in the same general time period.

In his departure from the London scene, Arden is seen by John Russell Taylor as having deprived London of "one of its most individual voices,"[12] succeeding where T. S. Eliot had failed, as a poet in the theater. Laurence Kitchen "suggests that *Sergeant Musgrave's Dance* is 'an achievement to justify anyone's entire career.' "[13] In the history of the political drama of post–World War II England, he is the first in a long line of voices. In the opinion of some, his is the richest, most compelling voice, as illustrated in plays such as *Sergeant Musgrave's Dance.*

PAM GEMS

Women dramatists are relatively few in the new drama of postwar England. Joan Littlewood made her impact in the collaborative movement and in proletariat drama. Shelagh Delaney attracted attention for one stage play, *A Taste of Honey*. Pam Gems, however, remains the single woman to write consistently, over a period of time, plays about womanhood in its totality in the tradition of her novelist contemporary, Margaret Drabble.

Born on 1 August 1925 the daughter of working-class parents, brought up by a mother and grandmothers whose husbands had died early, Gems served in the armed forces during the war, afterwards read psychology at the University of Manchester, married an architect-turned-manufacturer of models, and reared three children, the youngest of whom was born with Down's syndrome. Production of her first play occurred when she was in her late forties. Feminist in her concern with the intimate and complex problems of women, Gems has written nearly two dozen plays, most of them produced within a ten-year period at fringe theaters such as the Cockpit, Almost Free, Round-house, and Soho Poly. Three of them—*Betty's Wonderful Christmas, My Warren,* and *The Amiable Courtship of Miz Venus and Wild Bill*—appeared in one year, 1973. Her work includes adaptations—Chekhov's *Uncle Vanya* (1979) and Ibsen's *A Doll's House* (1980)—and an historical drama, *Queen Christina* (1977), rejected by the Royal Court because of its sprawling nature but then produced by the Royal Shakespeare Company at its small theater, the Other Place.

The two plays of Gems's that attracted the attention of major critics are *Dusa, Fish, Stas and Vi* (1976) and *Piaf* (1978). After premieres at the Edinburgh Festival and at the Other Place, respectively, they were produced at, or transferred to, commercial stages, *Piaf* reaching New York in 1981.

Originally titled *Dead Fish* and written for the Women's Company, *Dusa, Fish, Stas and Vi* is about four urban women in their twenties living together. Each has her distinctive problems. Dusa's husband has kidnapped her children, even though she had been granted custody of them. Fish, a middle-class activist, provides much-needed help for the others but in her own personal life has increasing problems. Stas works as a psychotherapist in a hospital during the day and as a prostitute at night, with hopes of becoming a marine biologist. Drug-addicted and anorexic Vi, from the working class, works her way through her illness with antidepressants, and Dusa is reunited with her children, but these positive events are counteracted by the suicide of Fish.

The episodic style consists of a series of scenes that alternate the different problems of the women, the major one being the return of Dusa's children. Critics call attention to the humanity with which the play pulsates—in its moments of desperation as well as those of joy—its many ironies, the uncertainties with which women live, and in general their attempts to gain some control over their lives. Gems's admitted purpose is to "show women as they are now, against mechanised, urban backgrounds, isolated in eyries, breeding sometimes, more often divorced from their mothers . . . trying to live the revolution with their fellers, and so often getting knocked back in what is still so inexorably a man's world."[14]

Written earlier but produced later than *Dusa*, *Piaf*, about the famous French songstress, contains the thematic threads of *Dusa*, although here they are focused on one character. The technique remains the same, however, as in scene after scene Gems dramatizes the sordid and funny pastiche that was Piaf's life. Some reviewers criticize the play for not emphasizing Piaf's art and the way in which her art transcended the coarseness of her life. Despite the objections of audiences and some critics to what they saw simply as vulgarities, the play won the coveted Tony Award in New York in 1981.

ANN JELLICOE

Frequently associated by critics with Bond and Wesker and the early days of ferment at the Royal Court, Ann Jellicoe, like Joan Littlewood, demonstrates one of the emerging trends of the time—the increasing importance of the director. Born on 15 July 1927, she began her career directing in repertory theaters and working as staff producer at London's Central School of Speech and Drama. Eventually she founded her own open-stage theater club at the Cockpit Theatre in London. In fact, she wrote her first play, *The Sport of My Mad Mother* (1958), in order to sharpen her skills as a director and—together with the mover behind the experimentation at the Royal Court, George Devine—even directed her own play.

Having written stage adaptations of Ibsen's *Rosmersholm* and *Lady of the Sea*, Friedrich Kind's libretto, *Die Freischutz*, and Chekhov's *Seagull*, she is best known for her original work *The Knack* (1961, Cambridge, and 1962, London). Two other plays, *The Sport of My Mad Mother* and *Shelley; or the Idealist* (1965), complete her trio of major works.

The directorial influence on her writing can be seen in her attempt to make the play, even in its written form, seem improvisational, with the pieces eventually falling into place and creating the sense of a whole. Using loosely related words, gestures, rhythms, noises, and visual actions (her own terms), she hopes to communicate with her audience by emotional rather than logical and intellectual means. Loose though her technique may seem, she insists that the effect is not so, as she intends to "use every possible effect that the theatre can offer to stir up the audience—to get at them through their emotions."[14] The physical impact of words, disjointed words, and non sequitur dialogue are all a part of her attempt to create a poetic stage language, an attempt likened by some to that of Christopher Fry and T. S. Eliot. Her rationale is that people are driven by their emotions, fears, and insecurities rather than, as is the common perception, their rationality and intelligence.

The Sport of My Mad Mother, a play that won third prize in the *Observer* competition, demonstrates Jellicoe's technique. The characters, a group of instinct-dominated East End teenagers and their leader—a woman named Greta who at the end gives birth on stage to a child she names Kali, after the Indian goddess of creation and destruction, a mad mother to whom all creation is a sport—are reduced to dialogue in which noises, sounds, and cries create a Pinter-like sense of menace and evolve into a demonic ritual chant.

The Knack (a reference to sexual prowess) continues the idea of sport in the earlier play, but in terms of three articulate, middle-class, intelligent youths, whose civility breaks down at the point that, like the East End gang of the earlier play, they are dominated by their insecurities and fears. Colin, landlord in the house where all three live, and Tolen become involved with an apparently naive girl, Nancy, in a sexual competition which Tom watches with ironical detachment. As the competitive sex game is played and new plans for woman sharing are in the making, Nancy changes things with her claim that she was raped, while unconscious, by Colin. Tolen departs, leaving the trio of Nancy, Colin, and Tom, with the last-mentioned ever the observer. In a remarkable scene, Colin and Tom draw Nancy into their fantasy of the bed as a "piano, of 'pings' and 'plongs,' variously distributing and extending over some three pages of the script."[16]

Appearing in 1958, the same year as Delaney's *Taste of Honey,* also about the problems of youth, *The Knack* became the best known of Jellicoe's plays, largely due, according to Frederick Lumley, to its "splendid film adaptation, where the camera takes over verbal situations and plays a visual ping-pong."[17]

The third play for which Jellicoe is known is *Shelley,* about the women in the poet's life who find themselves in a male-dominated society. In a departure from the nonlogical style of her earlier plays, she arranges scenes in a direct near-documentary account of episodes in Shelley's life. In yet other departures, she uses words in logical sequence as the means of communication, and adults, rather than teenagers, as characters, all these changes evoking disappointment from critics who regard as her distinctive qualities her keen insights into the behavioral reality of youths, their viscerally or imaginatively illogical forms of communication, and their inner drives as these take control of their actions.

Jellicoe, along with Littlewood, Delaney, Gems, and Churchill, is an important voice in the socially conscious creativity that flourished in the new drama, particularly at the Royal Court.

CARYL CHURCHILL

With the distinction of being the first female resident dramatist at the Royal Court Caryl Churchill, born in London on 3 September 1938, enjoyed the benefits of middle-class English society, her father a car-toonist and her mother a model and actress. Churchill read English at Oxford University and had her first three plays produced there: *Down-stairs* (1958), *Having a Wonderful Time* (1960) and *Easy Death* (1962). Like Gems, Churchill married, reared a family (three sons), and even-tually, with her barrister-husband, who left his practice to join a legal aid group, changed her conventional middle-class life. Unlike Gems, however, Churchill combined her feminism with her leftist political views. Her first play at the Royal Court, *Owners* (1972), for example, is about a woman who in her real-estate success finds herself progres-sively moving away from her sordid environment, which includes her butcher husband.

Cloud Nine (1979) won Churchill serious attention from the critics. Earlier, she had begun to widen her political consciousness with his-torical perspective, as in *Light Shining in Buckinghamshire* (1976), set in the Cromwellian period, and in *Vinegar Tom* (also 1976), about witch-craft in the seventeenth century. In *Cloud Nine*, set in the nineteenth century in colonial Africa, Churchill creates farcical distortions of char-acters in her treatment of colonialist repression. Working with images of what John Barber calls "a nest of Tartuffes," in a drama "emphati-cally not for prudes," Churchill entertained critics like Barber who responded to her explosion of myths and to her honesty in shining "a curious torch into dark erotic corners . . . with . . . an all-saving sense of humour."[18]

Francis King, however, finds her stereotypes of Victorian characters with their hypocritical behavioral patterns of "adultery, pederasty and sapphism" finally "weary, stale and flat."[19] Although King's judgment of Churchill's work is supported by the relatively short runs of her plays and her tenuous position in critical and scholarly works, she represents a pioneering cultural force in the new drama. She maintains a lively and imaginative presence in her sociopolitical protest, in which sexual repression is an integral part of colonialist imperialism.

In addition to *Cloud Nine,* Churchill has won increasing recognition with *Top Girls* (1982), which she describes as "about a lot of dead women having coffee with someone from the present and an idea about women doing all kinds of jobs"; *Fen* (1983)—set in the farming land of East Anglia—about the poverty resulting from shifting land relationships; *Softcops* (1984), dealing with the difference between "hardcops," who use force in their policing activities, and "softcops," who, although detached, maintain a friendliness with the people with whom they must deal; and *Serious Money* (1987), a searing, hard-hitting drama about the greed of the young, upwardly mobile English versions of American "yuppies." Written in rhymed couplets, *Serious Money* was composed during the reelection campaign of Margaret Thatcher. The play ends in a devastatingly ironic choral chant of "five more glorious years," the slogan of the campaign. The irony embraces the financial events of the year of the Ivan Boesky insider-trading scandal in the United States and of the Guinness stock manipulations in England that preceded the worldwide stock market upheavals that occurred on Black Monday, 19 October, 1987.

Churchill has enjoyed a close liaison with the American stage, *Cloud Nine* being directed by Tommy Tune at the off-Broadway Theater de Lys in New York, and *Top Girls, Fen,* and *Serious Money* being produced at Joseph Papp's New York Public Shakespeare Theater. Her plays are finally reaching the commercial theater audience, with *Serious Money,* sold out for the limited run at the Public, moved to a Broadway theater.

CHAPTER IX

WORKING-CLASS WRITERS

Without the vituperative anger and social alienation of a Jimmy Porter or the radical politics of the second generation of new playwrights, a sizable group of writers—Arnold Wesker the most impressive of them—have written what may be called social protest of the working-class kind. To judge Wesker and others as only social critics, however, is to deny them the stature that is theirs by virtue of the complexity of human issues with which they deal, and to deny as well their distinctive styles. The grouping, thus, is an arbitrary one, based primarily on their use of characters from working-class backgrounds. Like the social realists (discussed in another chapter), who dramatize the variegated texture of a newly emerging middle class, Wesker draws portraits of his particular class—the Stepney life of East London—with vividly detailed characterizations of individuals within that class. If Nichols composes the rhythms of life in a hospital, Gray those of life in the teaching profession, and Storey those of provincial life among an emerging new middle class, Wesker orchestrates the rhythms of life of a social stratum heretofore ignored as subject for serious consideration on the stage, except perhaps as pitiable victims (Galsworthy) or as suitable subjects for comedy (Shakespeare, Shaw).

In plays such as Gorky's *Lower Depths* or Eugene O'Neill's *Iceman Cometh,* a Zolaesque naturalism gives the impoverished a certain stage validity. But naturalism is a limited dramatic style and prescribes boundaries for its characters, focusing on their powerlessness to have any control over their lives. It is the limitations of these earlier treatments of the poor and the working class that Wesker and the new dramatists expand or destroy.

The playwrights considered in this chapter are so different from each other, and each different sometimes even within his or her own body of plays, that the grouping of them together raises valid questions. Certainly Wesker and Livings are hardly comparable in the style or specific thrust of their plays. These differences are discussed in this chapter within their common concern for the working class as proper subject for the stage.

The dramatists here are mostly from London's fertile East End (Wesker) or from provinces such as Lancashire (Delaney), Yorkshire (Mercer), and Newcastle-on-Tyne (Terson). With few exceptions, they had their stage beginnings in small repertory or fringe theaters. Labels like "kitchen sink" and "proletariat" have been attached to them, sometimes with contempt.

Populist theater—represented by Joan Littlewood at the Theatre Royal in Stratford and London, and by two American transplants associated with traveling street and school theater, Charles Marowitz and Ed Berman—brought drama to the very young and the poor in a fashion unprecedented, perhaps, since the days of the medieval religious plays staged on traveling wagons. Accessibility of the working classes to English drama was taken seriously by writers, directors, and producers in their attempts to give dignity and articulation to the underprivileged and to give individuals in that class the universality previously accorded only to the privileged.

ARNOLD WESKER

Arnold Wesker's family background and Pinter's have much in common. Both are from London's north and east Jewish ghetto—Hackney and Stepney, respectively—their fathers both tailors. Wesker's mother and Pinter's parents are Hungarian, and both dramatists—Pinter is two years older than Wesker—underwent the familiar experience of evacuation to the country during World War II. Both realized critical approval early, their first plays having been produced in the late 1950s, shortly after the advent of Jimmy Porter. Wesker was born on 24 May 1932. His early employment consisted of a variety of jobs as carpenter, plumber, bookshop assistant, farm worker, and cook. Cooking and food figure prominently in his plays and are responsible for the designation of his plays as "kitchen-sink drama," used to describe a realistic depiction of life among the working class.

His third produced play, *The Kitchen* (1959), evokes a technique

Nikolay Gogol used in one of his short stories, "Nevsky Prospect," in which the reader is taken through the various times of the day—dawn through night—each time giving the city of Leningrad a character wholly different from that of its predecessor. In similar fashion, the rhythms of life in the kitchen are created from the opening moments, when the porter lights the ovens, the center of activity, through the lunch hour rush, and then through the rush of the dinner hours. Characters like a new Irish employee (Kevin), a Cypriot (Dimitri), a pastry cook (Paul), a German fried-fish cook, waitresses, and the beleaguered owner (Marango) interact. As they do so, they establish highly individualized views of themselves and the world, the kitchen itself a microcosm of the large outside world. Like the tenement of Gorky's *Lower Depths* and the orchard in Chekhov's *Cherry Orchard,* the kitchen is the bond among his disparate characters. And as the appearance of Luka in the Gorky play and the sale of the cherry orchard in Chekhov's drama catalyze the interweaving strands of lives, Wesker's German cook, disappointed in love, wreaks havoc in his kitchen, shutting down the ovens and bringing the play to its conclusion.

Three other plays, Wesker's famous trilogy, along with *The Kitchen,* remain the dramas for which Wesker is best known: *Chicken Soup with Barley* (1958), *Roots* (1959), and *I'm Talking about Jerusalem* (1960). With the exception of *The Kitchen,* these early plays were first produced at the Belgrade Theatre in Coventry before their staging at the Royal Court in London. All four plays are about working-class families drawn from his own experience and, as well, about Wesker's convictions on the necessity for change. All four have drawn both praise and criticism, the latter on the basis that there is not always enough aesthetic distance between the dramatist and his subject. With his unremittingly working-class subject matter—workers and their work—in these first plays, Wesker established himself as a compassionate advocate of the dignity and humanity of his own personal social subclass as worthy of the attention of the middle class. In one of his many newspaper and journal articles, Wesker states his plays are not merely for those who already acknowledge the legitimate stage "but for those to whom the phrase 'form of expression' may mean nothing whatsoever. It is the bus driver, the housewife, the miner and the Teddy boy to whom I should like to address myself."[1]

As close as *The Kitchen* may be to Wesker's own experience as a cook, the trilogy is rooted even more deeply in his family relationships. Details such as the constant quarreling of his parents create a thickly textured sense of family that includes the community of relatives and neighbors as well. The first play of the trilogy, *Chicken Soup with Barley,* is set against the background of the fascist Mosley marches in the Jewish east end of London in the mid-1930s. Against these foes, the communists demonstrate with strong support from the Jewish community, especially from the family of Harry and Sarah Kahn. The play spans nearly twenty-five years in its three acts. In act 1, even among the domestic quarrels and petty thievery, the larger issues of the fascist threats absorb them, and their social idealism lends a semblance of optimism and hope to their lives. Act 2 shifts to 1946 and finds the daughter, Ada, waiting for her husband, Dave, to be discharged from the service, and the son, Ronnie, still as fervent as ever in his antifascist feelings. Then the action shifts to 1956, when Ronnie returns from abroad, disillusioned by the Russian invasion of Hungary. The father has had paralyzing strokes, and things have not gone well for the family. Though their early optimism is dimmed, the mother shouts the last words of the play to the departing Ronnie: "If you don't care, you'll die."[2] The title of the play derives from Sarah's remarks about Mrs. Bernstein, the only person who is there to help when needed, with her chicken soup and barley.

In the second play of the trilogy, *Roots,* the setting shifts from the Kahns in London to a family in Norfolk, the Bryants, whose daughter, Beatie, is awaiting the arrival of Ronnie, her fiancé. In the last act, however, rather than Ronnie himself, a letter from Ronnie, in which he withdraws his proposal, arrives. He describes his ideas about a new kind of life as useless and romantic, claiming they wouldn't work and finding, also, his coward's way out of their plans during the two weeks they have been apart. "We couldn't build a world even if we were given the reins of government—not yet, [at] any rate" (*WT,* 142). The sudden change in wedding plans causes bewilderment among her friends and relatives, but Beatie does learn from Ronnie and in that learning discovers herself. In the final scene of the play, she delivers a ringing assertion of independence from the inertia of provincial life with its stultifying resistance to change. Ronnie's rejection is the catalyst for her change, and she exclaims at the end: "God in Heaven, Ronnie! It does work, it's happening to me, I can feel it's happened, I'm beginning, on my own two feet—I'm beginning" (*WT*, 147).

Tynan describes *Roots* as "an intensely moving play [built] out of the raw materials of old-fashioned kitchen comedy, if not of outright farce," and he goes on to compare it with Chekhov, as "the most affecting last act in contemporary drama."[3]

I'm Talking about Jerusalem, the third play in the trilogy, also set in Norfolk, where Wesker had spent some time, returns to the Kahn family. Dave has been demobilized, and he and Ada move into their new home with the help of Ronnie. An old friend of Dave's visits, and they talk of their disillusionment about things. Dave's attempts to set himself up in business fail. Harry, the father, has been taken to an asylum, and the play ends on the note of a Conservative election victory in 1959. Even in their disillusionment, however, Sarah, the mother, retains a fragment of hope that though things haven't turned out as they had wished, something, however small, has been realized. The contrast in mood between the pessimism of the third play and the optimism of the first is considerable. Yet the trilogy as a whole is an affirmation of personal ideals in the face of only very small gains.

Chips with Everything (1962) deals with military life in the Royal Air Force. Having served his term of duty in the RAF, Wesker again draws from his experience. The antihero here is Pip Thompson, middle-class in origin, who rejects the privileges he might have enjoyed among his working-class companions. Even the officers' attempts to sway him from his unconventional insistence on abandoning the principles of his upbringing are futile. Wesker wrote letters during his years in service, asking recipients to keep them. These letters provided him with much material for this play, composed in the epic tradition of Brecht. First written as a novel, the drama retains the order of the scenes in the novel. Again left-wing critics such as Tynan approved, and more conservative critics such as Frank McGuinness of the *London Magazine* objected to Wesker's view of modern British class structure.

With increasing frequency, Wesker focused on personal relationships. Having integrated these relationships in his early plays with the sociopolitical events of the time, he then turned to poetic drama after an unsuccessful work, *Their Very Own and Golden City* (1965), an unwieldy structure of two acts and twenty-nine scenes that flash "forward" rather than "back." The drama integrates Wesker's leftist vision of utopia through one Andrew Cobham, a dreamer, a fictional Bevin, who retains his hopes even though they are considerably dimmed at the end.

In *The Four Seasons* (1966), set in a deserted house, Adam and Beatie, each disappointed in their marital or extramarital partners, weave their theories about love in discussions and in images, such as Beatie's decorating Adam with bluebells while he sleeps and Adam's cooking an apple strudel. Wesker's attempt at a poetic drama about love seemed too vaguely realized for critics and audiences accustomed to the concreteness of a kitchen, family debates, and an RAF base. Although more concrete and focused, *Friends* (1970) suffers from a similar vagueness of ideas and emotions. A group of six friends, on the occasion of the death of a mutual friend, discuss matters of life and death. All seven characters are engaged in the interior decorating business, the unifying detail in their relationships.

The Old Ones (1972), *The Wedding Feast* (1974, drawn from Dostoevsky's *Unpleasant Permission*), *The Journalists* (1975), *Love Letters on Blue Paper* (1976), *The Merchant* (1976, from Shakespeare), *Caritas* (1981), and *Four Portraits* (1982)—all illustrate a mixture of the two styles of Wesker's drama. *The Journalists,* for example, returns to the rhythmical movements of *The Kitchen,* and *Letters on Blue Paper* to the style of *Friends.*

Wesker, like his characters, remains idealistic. He has been actively involved in Centre 42, formed to implement Resolution 42 of a trades union congress. The resolution recognizes the importance of the arts for working classes. Wesker remains open to the criticism that his ideas need clearer definition and that his plays are haunted by a lack of Eliot's objective correlatives. Tynan, on the other hand, writes that "among living playwrights Mr. Wesker has few peers when it comes to evoking an atmosphere of family cohesiveness."[4] Like those of Pinter's, Wesker's "characters live immured in a room, vaguely intimidated by the world outside, fearful of direct communication with each other, and therefore talking about everything except what most deeply concerns them."[5] Tynan goes on to say that Wesker's vision may be blurred and that his talking about Jerusalem may not be what

John Whiting "means by art: but it is what most of us mean by theatre."[6]

BERNARD KOPS

The author of fewer than ten stage dramas, Bernard Kops, like Shelagh Delaney, is known primarily for one play: *The Hamlet of Stepney Green* (1958), a contemporary Jewish version of Shakespeare's play. Kops was born in September 1926. His origins in Stepney Green, his East European Jewish ancestry, his onetime job as a cook, and the choice of his play *Enter Solly Gold* (1962) as the first production of Centre 42, in which Wesker was so active: all these place Kops in the working-class tradition of Wesker, in particular, and in the larger tradition of the new dramatists from London's Jewish east end.

In *The Hamlet of Stepney Green,* David Levy, in his aspiration to become a crooner, is a prototype of Kops's other antiheroes, "the dreamer-poet-rebel type."[7] His ties to his mother are strong, so that when she wishes to remarry after his father's death, a naive outline of Shakespeare's plot takes form, as the father appears to his sensitive son and directs him, in a seance, to go along with the marriage as a form of revenge. On his deathbed, Sam, the father, had mumbled something about having been poisoned by life, his wife being his life. At the end of the play, he gives David a love potion under the pretense that it is poison, and under its influence David realizes that he loves "Ophelia," his stepfather's daughter, Hara. Too self-conscious in its attempt, and lacking sophistication of thought, plot, and language, *The Hamlet of Stepney Green* can do little but suffer from its obvious comparison with its famous Shakespearean source.

Kops's remaining plays, none having attracted the attention of this first play, include *Goodbye World* (1959), *Change for the Angel* (1960), *The Dream of Peter Mann* (1960), *Stray Cats and Empty Bottles* (1961), *Ezra* (1981), and the aforementioned *Enter Solly Gold.*

JOAN LITTLEWOOD

Improvisational drama, given modern legitimacy by Pirandello in the first half of the twentieth century—its roots in a long tradition of Italian commedia del'arte—holds a special place in the history of the new British drama. Its outstanding British advocate and practitioner, Joan Littlewood, born in 1914 and the oldest among the new voices on the stage, is also one of the most revolutionary and the most populist. Spanning the decades from the 1930s through the 1960s, with a brief return in 1973 to one of the many theater groups she established, the Theatre Royal at Stratford in East London, she enjoys a unique position as the only nonwriter of the dramatists considered in this volume.

Functioning primarily as a director, she has, more than anyone else, brought the stage closer to the cinema in the power of the director not only to shape a play but to bring new ideas to it and even to write or rewrite a script. In her theater, however, the director, as well, must allow the actors/actresses to contribute to the ideas or the language or the situations, which never do achieve a final form.

> I do not believe in the supremacy of the director, designer, actor or even of the writer. It is through collaboration that this knockabout art of the theatre survives and kicks. It was true at The Globe, The Curtain, The Crown, and in the "illustration theatre" of Moliere and it can work here today.
>
> No one mind or imagination can foresee what a play will become until all physical and intellectual stimuli, which are crystallised in the poetry of the author, have been understood by a company, and then tried in terms of mime, discussion and the precise music of grammar: words and movement allied and integrated. The smallest contact between characters in a remote corner of the stage must become objectively true and relevant. The actor must be freed from the necessity of making effective generalisations.
>
> I could go on but you too know how the theatre must function if it is to reflect the genius of a people, in a complex day and age. Only a company of artists can do this. It is no use the critics proclaiming overnight the genius of the individual writer; these writers must graft in company with other artists if we are to get what we want and what our people need, a great theatre.[8]

Littlewood's theories of collaborative drama are as old as drama itself and as new as the plays of Tom Stoppard, an established dramatist of the second wave, who allowed, for example, Mike Nichols, a highly esteemed American director, to adapt *The Real Thing* in its New York production, in the process creating a quite different play from the one London audiences had seen. What Stoppard and collaborative dramatists such as Hare and Brenton practice in a limited way, Littlewood depends on for the very essence and, indeed, for the totality of her productions.

Consequently, listed among her credits are *The Quare Fellow,* after Brendan Behan's play (1956); *A Taste of Honey,* after Shelagh Delaney's play (1958); and *The Hostage,* after Behan's play (1958). Among her other productions are adaptations of Lewis Carroll, Dickens, Stevenson, and Balzac, and semiadaptations of contemporary scripts by Henry Chapman, Frank Norman, Wolf Mankowitz, Stephen Lewis, John Wells, and Richard Ingram. With Charles Chilton as a cowriter, she has staged *Oh, What a Lovely War!,* the play for which she is best known.

Frequently Littlewood would ask a writer to rehearse the role of a character to give all those involved in the production some idea of his intent. Sometimes that intent underwent transformation, as in the case of Frank Norman's *Fings Ain't What They Used to Be,* where the author complained that his conception changed with every day that passed until he "was hardly able to identify with the antics on the stage at all."[9]

In the 1930s, Littlewood formed the Theatre of Action with Ewan McColl (real name Jimmy Miller), who had been working in the theater in the Manchester area. The son of a steel worker, he left school at fourteen and became active in drama as a vehicle for social change: agitational propaganda, or agitprop. After World War II, McColl and Littlewood formed a new group, the Theatre Workshop. In 1953, the company moved to the stage for which she became famous: the Theatre Royal at Stratford in East London. It was here that she staged two dramas by Brendan Behan and one by Shelagh Delaney, dramas that became widely recognized among the early experiments by new writers. These three dramas are discussed later in this chapter.

As a populist figure of her time, Littlewood espoused antiestablishment causes, particularly those of her Manchester origins: the unemployed, the coal miners and industrial workers, antinuclear activities, the military, prison life, etc.

Oh, What a Lovely War! (1963) developed from ideas by Littlewood's colleagues Gerry Raffles, Gwyn Thomas, and Ted Allan—the latter two writing the scripts. Ronald Hayman describes the production of this antiwar play as a combination of farce and horror, without which "Joe Orton would probably never have written as he did."[10]

About World War I, the play utilizes historical facts and statistics, "whisking the narrative dizzyingly between songs, fiction, facts and figures. . . . On a screen [the width of the stage], picked out in moving lights were the grim statistics—so many thousand lives lost, so many hundred yards gained—which counterpointed the clowning and caricature in the foreground."[11] Hayman concludes that the theatricality was of a type "that no playwright could have evolved while sitting at his typewriter."[12] Littlewood's style was indeed epic, in both popular and Brechtian senses of the term.

A view of the drama of the second half of the twentieth century would be incomplete without including mention of the importance of Littlewood in reviving a dramatic tradition practiced by Shakespeare and Molière. Her importance resides also in her efforts to bring drama to the underprivileged and in her dignifying them as subjects, in Tynan's words, fit for presentation on the stage. She strongly disliked the West End and the comfortable middle class, the negative symbols of her antiestablishment place in dramatic history.

Littlewood left England in the middle 1960s to pursue her endeavors elsewhere, returning only for very brief visits. Ironically, in 1984, she ghostwrote *Milady Vine: The Autobiography of Philippe de Rothschild,* about an individual who is the very essence of the excessive living of the rich and the famous. David Pryce Jones, reviewing the book, calls attention to the "scoop for Baron Philippe to have collared Joan Littlewood as his ghost-writer. . . . She now calls him 'the Guv' and it is his hope [having invited her to stay at his winemaking establishment] that she will stay on at Mouton forever."[13] The proletariat and the overprivileged have made what seems to many an ironic accommodation of each other.

BRENDAN BEHAN AND SHELAGH DELANEY

The author of only five produced plays, Brendan Behan remained throughout his life a rebel whose main cause, embracing his lesser ones, was the inhumanity of man to man. Two of his plays—*The Quare Fellow* (1954) and *The Hostage,* originally titled *An Giall* (1958), gained international attention and remain dramas of importance in the social-protest genre of dramatic literature. Behan could not be anything but a rebel, having been reared in a family that consisted of a father who was a housepainter, union leader and jailed IRA activist when Brendan was born on 19 February 1923; a mother who sang revolutionary songs; an uncle who wrote the Irish national anthem, and a grandmother who at seventy-three years of age was arrested for terrorist activities. Behan carried on the family tradition. In 1961, he was not allowed to march in the St. Patrick's Day parade in New York City because of his "bad boy" image.

Like Hemingway, Behan created antiheroes in his plays and novels and lived the lives of those antiheroes. His excesses in drinking and womanizing became a caricature of his own fictional creations. On American campuses, he became a cult figure at speaking engagements, where he sometimes was unable to perform because of intoxication.

The "quare fellow" of Behan's play title is, like the father in Ibsen's *Ghosts* and in Williams's *Glass Menagerie,* an important character who never appears in the play. Instead, it is the occasion of his hanging the next morning that the author uses to delineate other characters. These include a prison guard who performs his job out of duty, even though he opposes the injustices of the judicial system. Other Irish prisoners, like the ineffectual Irish males of O'Casey's dramas and those of Synge's *Playboy of the Western World,* settle for a drink, a cigarette, or a joke. Only one other prisoner, Gaelic-speaking Kerry, stands out in contrast, his innocence not yet corrupted into indifference. Other employees of the justice system are interested mostly in advancing themselves. Behan's gallows humor and his obsessive need to fight systemic injustices find a perfect vehicle in the Brechtian style, in which stories, jokes, songs, and episodes form a rich tapestry of bawdiness, sympathy, and, finally, horror. There is no plot, in the tightly knit sense of the realistic play, so that the improvisational nature of Littlewood's Theatre Workshop was as perfectly suited to Behan's play as his subject was to his chosen style.

Anti-English though Behan remained throughout his life, he was even more vehement in his general condemnation of inhumanity, whatever form it took and whomever it involved. The second play of the two on which his reputation rests, *The Hostage,* also has for its central character a prisoner, this time an English soldier, who similarly experiences brutality, but at the hands of Behan's own IRA. Yet, despite his sympathy for the Englishman, Behan never loses sight of the cause of Irish rebels against England.

Unlike O'Casey and Beckett, who exiled themselves to England and France, respectively, Behan, like Yeats, maintained his ties with the politics and the theater (for him, the Pike Theatre Club) of Ireland. More outrageous in his personal life than any of the other writers whose work outraged the Irish public—O'Casey and Joyce in particular—Behan provided only more reason for that outrage every year, even from the New York Irish, while he enjoyed the adulation of American academia. He died on 20 March 1964.

Linked with Behan by their common Irish ancestry and association with Littlewood's theatre, Shelagh Delaney, who was born in industrial Lancashire on 25 November 1939 to a bus inspector of Irish heritage, became famous for one play, *A Taste of Honey* (1958). With one other stage play, *The Lion in Love* (1960), Delaney has since devoted her writing to the screen, radio, and television. In the years since *A Taste of Honey,* for which she also wrote the screenplay, Delaney seems to have become famous almost as much for the reason for her writing the drama as for the drama itself. Upon seeing Margaret Leighton, one of England's finest actresses in the twentieth century, in Rattigan's *Variation on a Theme,* she complained of the waste of so much talent in so poor a play. She claimed that if Rattigan could write such a play, she certainly could do better, whereupon at the age of eighteen she wrote *A Taste of Honey* in two weeks. In two more weeks, the play began its rehearsal at Littlewood's Theatre Royal at Stratford in East London. (In a sequel to Delaney's Rattigan-based motivation for her play, David Mercer told *Theatre Quarterly* interviewers after seeing *A Taste of Honey* that "if that's a good play, I'm bloody sure I can do better. So I wrote a play in 1959–60, which became the first of *The Generations* trilogy, *Where the Difference Begins.*"[14])

Melodramatic in its premise, *A Taste of Honey* is about Jo, the daughter of a "loose woman," Helen, and about their efforts to survive. Left on her own from time to time, Jo meets a black sailor, who impregnates her and then leaves. A gentle homosexual art student, Geoff, moves in with Jo during one of her mother's frequent absences and takes on housekeeping responsibilities. Helen returns and asks

Geoff to leave. What strikes John Russell Taylor about the play is the excessive detail with which Jo is shown "in the real world outside—at school: working, surprisingly efficiently in the shoe shop. . . . , how she gets involved with her coloured sailor and, later, her first meetings with Geoffrey. . . . In the process, the special quality the play has of just letting things happen, one after another (like in a dream), disappears, and modifications clearly intended to strengthen the material succeed . . . only in making it seem thinner and more contrived."[15] Taylor attributes the success of the play to the "true genius of Joan Littlewood . . . to bring out the best in the author's work while staying completely true to its spirit."[16] Yet it is Delaney's ear for the rhythms of Lancashire dialogue that is impeccable, as is "her skill in noting down precisely what she hears."[17] In her other stage play, *The Lion in Love,* however, "her critical sense and her ability to select seem at times to have deserted her."[18] Even the genius of Littlewood failed in this case. The word "freakish" is sometimes used in connection with Delaney's status as a one-play writer. Her rebellion, unlike Behan's, was directed at a minor target, Rattigan's play, and, unlike Behan's, her talent is minor.

PETER TERSON

With a reputation as one of the most prolific dramatists of his time, Peter Terson has, according to one source, written more than sixty-five plays, in addition to his radio and television dramas. Born Peter Patterson in Newcastle-on-Tyne on 14 February 1932, he joins earlier writers like Arnold Bennett, the novelist of the pottery towns, and A. E. Housman in their portrayal of provincial life. In fact, three of his plays are adaptations of Bennett's novels: *Jock on the Go, The Heroism of Thomas Chadwick,* and *Clayhanger.*

With his often-expressed dislike for the solitary life of the writer, Terson, like Joan Littlewood, is perfectly suited to the practice of collaborative drama, regarding any completed play of his as only the beginning of the final production. He has enjoyed a long association with two directors: Peter Cheeseman at the Victoria Theatre in Stoke-on-Trent and Michael Croft at the National Youth Theatre in London. These two homes for his dramas, in fact, define the two kinds of plays that Terson has consistently written: those about inhabitants and traditions in the Vale of Evesham area and those about youth, the former rural and the latter usually urban in their settings.

Among the best known of the plays for youth are *Zigger-Zagger* (1967), *The Apprentices* (1968), *Fuzz* (1969) and *Spring-heeled Jack* (1970). In *Zigger-Zagger,* a spectacular reproduction of soccer bleachers on stage forms the backdrop for the conflict within Harry Philton, the main character, who is torn between the advice of his elders and that of his young friends, who aimlessly follow their soccer team from game to game. Harry chooses to become an apprentice rather than follow the advice of his peers. Though the name of the main character changes in *The Apprentices,* it might just as well be Harry, for the play, set in a factory, takes up another set of conflicts within the youth as he makes choices arising from the transition from adolescence into adulthood. In this play, the bleak factory setting with which Terson is so familiar seems almost to absorb the characters into itself, in much the same way as the soccer stadium in the earlier play.

As most critics have asserted, Terson's best plays are those dealing with life in the north of England. His cycle of dramas set in the Vale of Evesham, A. E. Housman country, are Terson's most powerful. These include *A Night to Make the Angels Weep* (1964), *I'm in Charge of the Ruins* (1966), *All Honour Mr. Todd* (1966), *The Mighty Reservoy* (1967), and *Mooney and His Caravans* (1968). The plays deal with such subjects as "the growing delusions of a Midlands village community about returning to a feudal way of life, . . . the possible psychological and social effects of a new reservoir upon the lives of two men who have markedly different personalities, . . . [and] the disruption of rural life by the digging of a sewer."[19]

The images in the dramas are powerful, such as the "glowering new power stations" dominating what on another side of the stage are "the crumbling remains of a medieval castle, watched over by a pathetic, almost equally ruinous old guide."[20] It is obvious from such images as this one, from *I'm in Charge of These Ruins,* where the author's sympathies lie. In the shadows of his giant images, the experiences of the characters are poignant and sometimes seem minuscule, such as those of Church and Dron in *The Mighty Reservoy*. The two men, of vastly different educational backgrounds, one an office worker and the other a keeper of a new reservoir, establish an acquaintance, the force of the reservoir making its presence felt throughout the play. What appears to be a disaster caused by a crack that Dron discovers turns out in the end to be a figment of his imagination.

In the idiom of his time and people, Terson explores the man-versus-nature theme that D. H. Lawrence earlier in the century wrote about in his novels. Frequently described as primitive, Terson's dramas lack the complexity and power of Rudkin in *Afore Night Come,* with its ritualistic treatment of the ultimate savagery of man. Terson's is a gentler, even romantic, world. Sympathetic with natural man, his bent for the primitive does carry its own "crude force and vigour, and if Terson suffers from the obvious comparison between him and David Rudkin, he does still have a quality which is all his own."[21]

One can see in Terson's dramas the limitations of writing collaboratively and of writing about the same themes. A sense of predictability eventually sets in. The adolescent choices between peer and adult pressures in his plays on youth and, in the Evesham plays, the effects of mechanization on the individual and on the life of a community unable or unwilling to change are themes that take on the nature of a modern morality play, frequently simplistic and sometimes crude in both conception and execution.

The soccer spectaculars, the crowds, the factories, reservoirs, and sewers take on ritual significance, as they dwarf the individuals caught up in the conflicts created. There is a giantism about Terson himself, who in sheer number of dramas stands out, unique in his consistency in forging exclusively collaborative drama over his entire career.

DAVID MERCER

As a distinguished television writer and, in a lesser way, a stage dramatist, David Mercer, perhaps more than any other of the new dramatists, evades attempts at even the most general classification or evaluation: thematic, stylistic, geographical, or political. One scholar notes that one large concern does emerge in his work as a whole, the "birthpangs of a private man."[22] The wrenching experience of sons who return to their rural or provincial homes is a common subject in the new drama, David Storey's *In Celebration* being one of the best known in this genre. Writing almost an entire body of plays on the subject and confronting the ultimate inescapability of one's past in order to create a personal self from one's familial, political, and cultural identities have rarely been accomplished as effectively as in Mercer's work.

Mercer's life represents a composite of those of many of the new dramatists. He was born on 27 June 1928 and brought up in Yorkshire. Having failed grammar school examinations, he left school at fourteen, worked at odd jobs, served in the merchant navy, enrolled at Durham University, and finally graduated with an honors degree in art from Kings College, Newcastle, in 1953. A voracious reader of psychology, philosophy, and history, he soon formed strong liberal views, which underwent changes to socialism and even communism, but without party affiliation. Important in the formulation of his attitudes is his working-class background, his father having been an engine driver. Like many of his contemporaries, he even taught for a few years. His treatment at Tavistock Clinic for psychiatric help during a time of marital difficulties became the basis for an early play, *A Suitable Case for Treatment*. His acquaintance with the famous psychiatrist R. D. Laing followed the televising of this drama. A subject in a number of his plays, insanity, or what society regards as insanity, is seen in his plays as merely the attempt of the artist to develop or express himself.

His television dramas outnumbering his stage plays, Mercer was one of the earliest of the new dramatists to establish writing for television and film as equal to writing for the stage. Unlike many contemporaries, whose plays were produced primarily in provincial or fringe theaters, Mercer gained stage exposure at the Royal Shakespeare's Aldwych Theatre in London, at the Picadilly and Criterion theaters in the West End, and at the more prestigious small houses, such as the Hampstead, Bush, Kings' Head (pub), and Warehouse theaters.

After Haggerty and *Flint* (both 1970) are among his most highly regarded dramas. In *After Haggerty,* the techniques of television are readily evident in the fluid succession of scenes from the past and the present, by means of which the author is able to "link" the three areas in the life of Bernard Link, a drama critic: his lectures on the state of the drama; his working-class roots, particularly his Labourite but racially bigoted father; and his present involvement with an American, Claire, who, since the vanishing of her husband (the father of her son, Raskolnikov Haggerty), insists on remaining in the apartment that Bernard occupies. From time to time, Haggerty sends messages from mysterious places. Bernard's lectures on modern British dramas—in Budapest, Moscow, or wherever—begin with references to Osborne's *Look Back in Anger,* a play that Mercer, in his *Theatre Quarterly* interview, said both affected and infected him.

In the last scene of the play, Bernard, his father, and Claire—along with Chris and Roger, workers who have just finished redecorating the flat—talk, drinks in their hands. As a result of Claire's shocking (for the father, anyway) remark about wanting to "fuck" Haggerty, father and son argue, and the father leaves after accusing his son of lack of respect. In a final, Ortonesque scene, a coffin arrives with a plaque containing a macabre poem and a final message from Haggerty, informing Claire of his death in a skirmish between government and guerilla forces in Africa. After reading aloud the message, Claire leaves, and the play ends. *After Haggerty* illustrates Mercer's basic style of quickly moving cinematic scenes.

Flint is the story of a rogue clergyman by that name, whose wife after their wedding night promptly took to a wheelchair, leaving him free to enjoy her sister, who lives with them, and, after her, other women who may catch his roving eye. Again the scenes in the play move rapidly, the last being in Rome and in Greece, where, in a motorcycle accident, Flint is killed trying to get his current young pregnant mistress, Dixie, to a hospital. Like Raskolnikov of *After Haggerty,* her baby has an unusual name, Prometheus, Prom for short. Mercer's characters, like Joe Orton's, carry out farcically outrageous actions with great aplomb. For example, when Flint's wife Esme is buried, Flint, responding to a comment by Inspector Hounslow, comments with utter seriousness: "By the standards of many, she was a virtuous woman. . . . Virtuous people are . . . so . . . unassailable."[23] This juxtaposition of conventional behavior with flagrantly outrageous reality constitutes a good part of the art of Mercer.

Not angry like Jimmy Porter, primarily political like Hare and Brenton, socially realistic like Nichols and Storey, proletarian like Wesker, or moralistic like Bond, Mercer has transmuted elements of all these into a highly stylized portrayal of all the forces in his personal and cultural life. He regards *After Haggerty,* along with his television Kelvin trilogy, as a summing-up play, "gathering together strands going back into the past, both personally and artistically, and they may represent the end of one particular direction for me."[24] He goes on to say that he "is searching in a more painful way than ever to create an invented world, in which the preoccupations of my middle age will begin to express themselves."[25]

The sense of the grotesque in Mercer's work is seen in an early television play, *A Suitable Case for Treatment,* a title taken from a psychiatrist's diagnosis of Mercer at the Tavistock Clinic. About Mercer's own experience at the time, the play dramatizes a collision between the inner and outer worlds of an artist. As with other Mercer characters, strands of the working-class past and of the liberated present, in itself not altogether satisfactory, intertwine and link in a continuous process.

Like Wesker, Mercer wrote dramas about several generations. An early play ended up as part of a trilogy entitled *The Generations* (televised 1961, 1962, 1963): *Where the Difference Begins, A Climate of Fear,* and *The Birth of a Private Man. On the Eve of Publication* (1969), *The Cellar and the Almond Tree* (1970), and *Emma's Time* (1970), also television dramas, constitute still another generational trilogy. Although he incorporates personal experience in his plays, the details of his working-class background and of his breakaway life never even border on the sentimental or the melodramatic. Instead, his style transmutes the particular into a universal experience shared by many of the post–Jimmy Porter generation of the first and second waves. He died on 8 August 1980.

HENRY LIVINGS

Henry Livings, born Lancashire on 20 September 1929, attended university (Liverpool) without taking a degree, served time in the Royal Air Force, and held varied jobs, among these acting with the Century Mobile Theatre in Leicestershire and then with Joan Littlewood's Theatre Workshop in London, where he played the role of Prisoner C in Behan's *Hostage.*

Applauded for his regional tang, Livings, like Mercer, writes about realistic situations of the working man, but in nonrealistic style, causing him to be one of the most misunderstood playwrights of his time, according to Michael Weimer. The confusion lies in the inevitable comparison with Spike Milligan, scriptwriter for the English television program "The Goon Show." In his view of the modern stage, Allardyce Nicoll places Livings between Rudkin, who dredges "up from man's depths an irrational bestiality" and Simpson, with his "fantastic world," loose English versions of the European theater of cruelty and the theater of the absurd. Nicoll refers to the satiric bitterness of Livings's *Stop It, Whoever You Are* and the bustling extravagance of *Eh?*[26]

Livings's self-described style involves choosing "simple stories and corny situations" and breaking his story down "into 'units' of about ten minutes each—about as long, I reckoned, as you can hold a new situation clearly and totally in mind."[27] At times his savage satire reminds one of the anger of a Jimmy Porter. When the anger takes the form of farce, Livings's plays suggest the absurd drama of Ionesco or Beckett. His subjects remain, however, the boiler-room worker or the factory janitor, characters who must work within the boundaries of the conventional but whose natural impulses fight those boundaries. They insist, as does one character (Warbeck) after he is dead, that "I might have gone down to the grave not knowing what a hairy baboon I was. I didn't. I did it. I'm entirely dead now, and you can heap words on me. You can heap six foot of dirt on me, for that matter. But I shall have been entirely alive."[28]

These words are spoken by William Perkin Warbeck—a character named after a fifteenth-century pretender to the English throne who had been hanged after challenging Henry VII. In Livings's first play, *Stop It, Whoever You Are* (1961), Warbeck is a janitor falsely charged by the police. Vengefully sabotaging the public opening of a local library, he eventually lapses into mental difficulties in which he imagines himself to be a clock. Like Gogol's civil servant in the story "The Overcoat," Warbeck enjoys his revenge in the afterlife, here in a séance conducted by the mother of the adolescent who had seduced him. Livings transforms with manic force the "slices of life" approach, usually used by naturalistic writers, into a combination of wit, fantasy, and surrealism that make for a lively and entertaining style with its touch of the Ortonesque.

The sketch style of Livings's work is indicated by some of his later titles: *Pongo Plays 1–6: Six Short Plays* and *Six More Pongo Plays,* unproduced but published. Some of these are children's plays.

Nil Carborundum (1962), like Wesker's *Chips With Everything,* is based on Livings's experiences in the Royal Air Force. Also like Wesker, Livings is an expert cook, and he sets his RAF play in a kitchen. Tynan, commenting on the language of the play, imagines Livings "crowing with glee as he taps out the words, each sentence treading on the heels of its predecessor, each page ripped from the typewriter and flung to the floor at random."[29] *Kelley's Eye* (1963) is a tension-filled drama about a young fugitive murderer who develops a close relationship with a girl, much to the disapproval of her parents.

In *Eh?* (1964), Livings, at his farcical best, deals once more with the resistance of the natural man to those unnatural forces in life of which he is unable to be a part. In the boiler room of a modern factory, Val's efforts are divided between maintenance of the boiler pipes and tending the seedboxes of mushrooms. Plotless, the play focuses on Val's maneuvers between the two and his increasing helplessness to maintain the mechanical functioning of the boiler. Noises such as the hissing of steam counterpoint his increasingly frantic attempts. The concluding noise is a loud boom as the boiler explodes, emitting steam, smoke, and soot.

As with the bohemian characters in Mercer's plays, Livings's eccentrics resist mechanization that disrupts their natural rhythms. His characters, however, are ordinary people with no creative outlet except for the manically obsessive turns their fancies take. A boiler or a toilet is more than a symbol; it assumes the dimensions of an antagonist and is even used as a weapon of revenge. Mechanization in Livings's plays evokes the absurdist world of Ionesco, in which characters have deteriorated into unthinking and unfeeling entities. In Livings, however, the small man resists and wreaks revenge of a sort, however unintentionally.

Livings's obsession with words, frequently mentioned in reviews, also suggests Ionesco's situations and characters, whose deterioration is expressed in the diminishment of language from long, deductively reasoned explanations to one-sentence platitudes and, finally, to words, sounds, and silence. This fascination with words and sounds pervades Livings's dramas as an active force in the lively imaginations of the characters, illustrated in the increasing tension between Val and the boiler in *Eh?*. Livings provides detailed instructions regarding sounds, such as "the regurgitative double gurk"[30] of the phone. Kelley, in *Kelley's Eye,* is aware that "there's too many people been at the words before I got round to needing them."[31] The sounds of words take on the quality of noises or, conversely, noises become words in the conflicts experienced by Kelley or Val.

In addition to the stage dramas, Livings has to his credits a long list of television plays. Describing his own work, he writes, "I go mostly for laughter, because for me laughter is the shock reaction to a new way of looking at something; even a pun questions our security in the solidity of words."[32]

CHAPTER X

TRADITIONALISTS

Resisting the experimentation of their times and incurring the criticism, sometimes contempt, of the New Critics, a number of dramatists have continued the conventions of the traditional farce or of the well-made play. For his farces, many of them produced in the West End and later at the National Theatre, Alan Ayckbourn has been labeled a commercial playwright, the English counterpart of the American Neil Simon. Robert Bolt, too, for his refusal to experiment with style, has been consistently judged traditional in a time when the prevailing fashion was innovation. Other writers—Michael Frayn, Christopher Hampton, John Mortimer, James Saunders, Anthony Shaffer, Peter Shaffer, and John Whiting among them—not only write in established forms but have avoided, some deliberately, characteristics of what have come to be designated as the theaters of anger, absurdity, and cruelty; kitchen-sink drama; antitheater; the comedy of menace; and other trends.

ALAN AYCKBOURN

Illustrating Allardyce Nicoll's assertion, quoted in the Introduction, that what is important in dramatic history is the element of continuity, the traditionalists for the most part found homes on West End stages, although Ayckbourn, who was solidly associated with the Scarborough Theatre in Yorkshire, has enjoyed a nearly equal number of productions in regional and West End houses, a balance achieved by few dramatists of the postwar era.

In 1971 John Russell Taylor stated that in his opinion "no one would ever be tempted to classify Ayckbourn as an important dramatist."[1] Guido Almansi, however, disagrees with those who once described Ayckbourn as only a pure farceur. If audiences merely laughed at Colin in *Absent Friends,* Almansi sees him as "a character who is so well-meaning in his sickly unctuous sentimentality that he carries laughter to the borderline of disgust. . . . And this is obviously far beyond the traditional boundaries of farce."[2] In plot unity, "only Shaw can be compared with Ayckbourn's clockwork combines. If instead we pay attention to the latter's search for a plot to defy all plots, an all-encompassing structure which challenges the limitations of narrative and dramatic equilibrium, then only our medieval ancestors knew such ecstasy and underwent such pangs: the visionary embrace of an Ars Combinatoria in which all varieties of human emotions and experiences were resolved in a circular unity."[3] In support of what may seem to some excessive praise by Almansi, Ayckbourn's reputation has been steadily rising, and his new plays continue to be produced at prestigious houses on an annual basis, whereas early new-wave dramatists such as Pinter and Stoppard have noticeably diminished in their writing. This phenomenon in itself may be an indication of the direction of British drama in the 1980s. In the United States, Ayckbourn's dramas have not fared well, whereas those by others such as Simon Gray have enjoyed long runs. According to Rich, the reasons may include the expense of large casts or the fact that the plays are "too provincial a slice of Mrs. Thatcher's England or worse, too horrifically close to home."[4]

Born in Hampstead, London, on 12 April 1939 to Irene Maud Worley and Horace Ayckbourn (a journalist and a deputy leader of the London Symphony Orchestra, respectively, divorced when their son was five years old) Alan spent his early years moving from one Sussex town to another, as his stepfather's bank-managing jobs dictated. Unlike many of the new dramatists, Ayckbourn is from the prosperous south of England—the Home Counties. When at seventeen years of age he found employment at the Library Theatre in Scarborough, a resort in the north of England, he worked at various jobs in the theater, including acting. Eventually realizing that he was a better writer than actor, he gave up acting, and since 1959 he has turned out plays on an annual basis. In 1975 five of his plays ran concurrently in London.

His track record in the theater would seem to indicate that Ayckbourn has had the best of all worlds. Originally enjoying the plaudits of audiences but dismissed by the critics as a writer of well-made plays and a stage trickster, he has gradually won the respect of critics. To the British, however, he is more than an English Neil Simon, as he has been labeled by American critics. Increasingly the darker elements have been more prominent in his farces: his obsessive concerns with the sterility of modern suburbia, particularly in marital and familial relationships, and with the materialistic greed that frequently reminds one of the objects of the satiric spirit in Ben Jonson's comedies.

Ayckbourn has acknowledged the influences of William Congreve, Oscar Wilde, Georges Feydeau, Anton Chekhov, Noel Coward, Terrence Rattigan, J. B. Priestley, and Harold Pinter.[5] In his forging of traditionalist and experimental theatrical techniques and themes, he has given the farce his unique stamp, transforming the popular British drawing-room comedy into a "living-dining area" comedy of the suburban Home Counties. In *Absurd Person Singular* (1973) three different kitchens, and in *How the Other Half Loves* (1969) two different upscale living rooms, become the arena for the intrigues and domestic wars that express Ayckbourn's serious concerns. In spite of his chosen genre, he appears increasingly to be in consort with the spirit of the new dramas—absurd, angry, and so on—in his depiction of the bleak suburban landscape, perhaps not so different from the desertlike voids of Beckett's dramas. His subjects are the domestic wrangles, sterile marital situations, infidelities, and materialistic greed that pervade every profession and every facet of contemporary British middle-class life, even as these are channeled in hilariously farcical style. Ayckbourn's wife, who lives in Leeds with their two sons, has stated "that she would be among the richest women in the world if she claimed royalties for all the fodder she has provided for his bitter, biting domestic comedies."[6]

As audiences have become educated by the critics about Ayckbourn's underlying seriousness, what they were theretofore entertained by has become disconcerting and tinged with discomfort. Taylor describes *Relatively Speaking* as "deriving entirely from variations on embarrassment."[7] Thus a new term, the theater of embarrassment, has joined others, like comedy of menace (Pinter), angry theater (Osborne), and kitchen-sink drama (revived in Wesker) in the critical lexicon of the new British drama.

Ayckbourn, having written several failed or mediocre plays, found in *Relatively Speaking* (1967) the turning point in his career. In the manner of England's most famous farce, Wilde's *The Importance of Being Earnest,* and originally titled *Meet My Father,* the drama is about adventures similar to the Bunburying exploits of Wilde's Algernon and Jack. But the play also contains the situation of multiple adulterous couples, a subject that has become the mainstay of each succeeding drama. With each play the seriousness of the subject has deepened, darkening the farcical element critics and audiences had come to expect.

This gradual change in mood has been accompanied by Ayckbourn's breaking away from the strictures of the well-made play, even as he has continued to use some of the traditional techniques—well-timed exits and entrances, complicated romantic intrigues, central misunderstandings, quid pro quos, and secrets known to the audience and not to the characters, for example. In the preface to *Relatively Speaking,* Ayckbourn explains his intent: "I did set out consciously to write a 'well-made' play. I think this is most important for a playwright to do at least once in his life, since as in any science he cannot begin to shatter theatrical convention or break golden rules until he is reasonably sure in himself what they are and how they were arrived at."[8] He shatters conventions through the rejection of suspense-creating teeter-totter action—including the big or obligatory scene—that moves linearly toward a predictable ending. Instead, he breaks the linearity of action by disarranging the artificial sequence of scenes, acts, and even whole plays, creating at times the mood of Chekhov's static drama.

His restructuring of the farce formula is most vividly illustrated in a trilogy of plays, *The Norman Conquests* (1973 at Scarborough's Library Theatre and 1974 at the Globe Theatre in London, a pattern of production throughout his long career), and also in *Sisterly Feelings* (1979 in Scarborough and 1980 in London).

With a title that trivializes Britain's heroic past, *The Norman Conquests* focuses on a character named Norman, around whom are arranged the marital and extramarital adventures of Ayckbourn's usual "three-couple" intrigues, with variations of an intruder or outside fourth couple thrown in to further the plot. The individual play titles— *Table Manners, Living Together* and *Round and Round the Garden*— indicate the specific areas of a rundown Victorian country house in which three related couples gather in order to relieve one of their members, Annie, of the care of an invalid mother. The central misunderstanding of the play is Annie's secret plan for a "dirty weekend" in East Grinstead with Norman, the husband of her sister Ruth. Irresistibly attractive to women, Norman enjoys his conquests for the sake of conquest, reducing whatever expectations the women may have to sordid encounters in each of the three areas indicated in the titles: a corner of the dining room, a rug in the living room, and a bush in the garden. Adding to the hilarious antics as each character attempts to keep his secret from the other is a neighbor, a local veterinarian, whom the family assumes to be Annie's partner for her holiday. Dull-witted and likable, he serves as a straight man to the intriguing maneuvers of the women, providing much of the hilarity.

What is ingenious in Ayckbourn's structural arrangement is that each of the three plays dramatizes the same events, so that what happens offstage in one of the plays becomes the onstage event for another. Thus, to understand a joke in a second play, for example, one should have seen the first. The three plays are to be seen in three successive performances, with any one of the three a possible starter and with each being complete in itself. It is possible to rearrange all the scenes from all three plays in a traditional interlocking sequence, but the author has deliberately rejected this order.

Sisterly Feelings illustrates yet another inventive structure. Again there are three related couples: two sisters and a brother with their respective spouse, lover, and fiancée. Abigail is married to a businessman; Dorcas, a newscaster, is currently involved with a poet; and Melvin is engaged to Brenda. Instead of the sick mother of *The Norman Conquests,* the occasion for the family gathering is their mother's funeral. A picnic has been arranged by the father at the site at which he and his wife first met. Instead of the neighbor, Tom, in the earlier play, the outsider here is Brenda's brother, Simon, for whose attention the sisters vie. When rain ends the picnic and available automobiles cannot transport all the picnickers, the sisters toss a coin to determine who will remain behind to walk home with Simon. The sister who wins then dominates the next picnic and next scene, entitled either "Dorcas's Picnic" or "Abigail's Picnic." The scenes in the play are so constructed and titled that in a given performance they can be transposed. The chosen order of a performance then determines which of the sisters walks home with Simon. Although whims, such as an actor's choice or a toss of a coin, determine which order is followed in a particular performance, the fourth scene, "The Wedding," remains constant. The wedding is that of Melvin, who, like Andrey of Chekhov's *Three Sisters,* marries the bossy (and pregnant) Brenda. What actually happens in the sisters' battle for Simon, however, is determined by chance, and in both cases the consequences of that chance are similar: the jealousy of the other sister and the displeasure of the husband/lover.

In an earlier play, *Absurd Person Singular* (1973), three unhappily married couples entertain on three successive Christmas Eves, with the onstage action occurring in their respective kitchens. Each kitchen contrasts with the other two, the first being in a small suburban home, the second in a fourth-floor flat, and the third in a Victorian house. In each case, the kitchen serves as a refuge from an undesirable circumstance: the boring jokes of another guest, a threatening dog, and uninvited guests, respectively, in acts 1, 2 and 3.

In later comedies, *A Chorus of Disapproval* (1986) and *A Small Family Business* (1987), Ayckbourn "is no longer the farcical tactician," but "a savage, if compassionate, observer of the same middle class his work once humored. His structural experiments with time and setting have been subordinated to his unblinking portrayal of an increasingly faceless suburbia."[9] Drawn from his own theater experiences in the provinces, *A Chorus of Disapproval* is about a provincial group of players in need of an actor for a role made vacant by illness. An unlikely character not only evolves into the major role of Mac in the company's production of Brecht's *Threepenny Opera,* but like Norman and Simon in the earlier farces, he beds the bored women who throw themselves at him, unable or unwilling to offer resistance to the sordid sexual sallies.

In *A Small Family Business,* in a set reminiscent of Arthur Miller's *Death of a Salesman,* four rooms occupy a two-level stage. Four related households make up what Frank Rich calls a "poisoned community."[10] The action in all four rooms is sometimes concurrent, other times in sequence, in a drama in which marital abuse and Mafia-like business actions dominate. The play begins with a party that culminates in what Rich describes as "the most hilarious farcical gag I've seen since *Noises Off,*" and the play ends with a less festive party in which "a teen-age daughter of the celebrating family hides in the bathroom, shivering from the effects of heroin addiction."[11] In the play, "loneliness and boredom give rise to abject greed and materialism, wife swapping and a new generation of alienated teenagers destined to join the swollen unemployment rolls of the Thatcher economy."[12]

Thus, in an ironic twist, Ayckbourn's critical stature has evolved from an early reputation as "appallingly cute"[13] in *Mr. Whatnot* (1963) to that of a committed dramatist who "charts a moral cancer through a family and the surrounding community"[14] in *A Small Family Business*. There are the concerns of the social realists in his depiction of the barrenness of suburban life. In both *A Chorus of Disapproval* and *A Small Family Business,* the laughter is chilling, the latter "more ferociously political than the exercise in boilerplate leftism"[15] of an overtly political play, Dusty Hughes's *Jenkin's Ear,* which ran concurrently at the Royal Court. Ayckbourn echoes the themes of Nichols, Gray, Storey, and Osborne.

Self-admittedly influenced early in his Scarborough years by the way Pinter bends words, he frequently invokes echoes of Pinter in his dialogues. So, although his early farces may be, as some have asserted, mindless, there has been a steady development in which laughter as an end in itself has been deflected. Linearity of scene movement has given way to circularity, increasingly suggesting the static "states-of-being" drama, in which characters allow a Chekhovian loneliness or frustration to break through surface farce. In the multiple suburban couples who inhabit his contemporary landscapes, Ayckbourn penetrates the disguises of everyday familial and societal relationships, expressing in farcical terms the anger of Osborne's Jimmy Porter, the menace in Pinter's comedies, or the sterility in Ionesco's middle-class couples such as the Martins and the Smiths of *The Bald Soprano*.

In his review of *The Norman Conquests,* Michael Billington defies "anyone to sit through it all and not feel that he has been given a funny, serious, moving, and comprehensive account of the awfulness of middle-class family rituals un-fuelled by love or understanding."[16] Commenting on *Absurd Person Singular* (1972), Ian Watson sees "the familiar totems of middle class life . . . twisted; competitive sports in *Time and Time Again* [1971] and in *Joking Apart* [1978], counterpointing far more basic competitions on a personal level . . . and do-it-yourself pursuits . . . in both *Bedroom Farce* [1975] and *Just Between*

Ourselves [1976], as a sublimation of a responsive and responsible marital relationship."[17]

Among Ayckbourn's many other plays are the musical *Jeeves* [1975], for which he wrote the book and lyrics, with music by Andrew Lloyd Webber, in an adaptation of stories by P. G. Wodehouse; *Men on Women on Men* (1978); two short pieces for lunchtime theater, *First Course* and *Second Helping;* and *Suburban Strains* (1980). Turning his domestic comedies into musical versions, Ayckbourn has evoked frequent comparisons with Noel Coward.

The author of more than thirty plays, he has been active at the National Theatre, where, in 1987, the innovation of several production-acting companies was introduced, each group headed by a director. Numbered among the directors, in addition to Ayckbourn, were Peter Hall, Michael Rudman, Richard Eyre, Mike Alfred, and Di Trevis. Ayckbourn directed his play, *A Small Family Business,* in this capacity.

MICHAEL FRAYN

Satirist-journalist, novelist, Russian language interpreter, television producer, screen and television writer, Wittgensteinian, and dramatist, Michael Frayn is, according to Benedict Nightingale, an "entertaining intellect," "a farceur with a philosophical bent."[18] "He smuggles ideas into commercial forms."[19] As satirist and philosopher, he has consistently held the attention of critics, even though called by a few not so enthusiastic, such as Giles Gordon, "a perfectly agreeable boulevarde writer not as serious as people claim."[20]

Frayn was born on 8 September 1933. Sent to Russian language school at Cambridge during his military service, he later returned to Cambridge, influenced by two philosophers on the academic scene during those heady years: the Austrian Ludwig Wittgenstein and the Englishman Bertrand Russell. Frayn's intense interest in things Russian developed, resulting in translations-adaptations of five Russian works, the most ingenious being his reconstruction of Chekhov's *Platonov,* which he titled *Wild Honey*.

In addition to *Wild Honey,* the National Theatre has produced his versions of *The Cherry Orchard* and of Tolstoy's *Fruits of Enlightenment.*

"His ultimate model and inspiration would seem to be Chekhov," and he "always follows the advice of his friend, the playwright Peter Nichols,"[21] an important satirist discussed here in an earlier chapter. He has friends in the Soviet Union and makes frequent visits there. Although consistently opposing cold-war positions, he has, over the years, softened his political stances from Communist and Labourite to Social Democrat.

Even though he has written fewer than a dozen plays apart from his Russian translations/adaptations, Frayn shares a reputation with Ayckbourn as one of England's important post war farceurs. Like Ayckbourn, Frayn has enjoyed commercial success. Breaking the record for long runs at the Savoy Theatre, *Noises Off* (1982) was also a smashing success in its Broadway run (554 performances between 1983 and 1985), its premise being the exposure, to the audience, of the frantic backstage action of a provincial touring company. During its fifth year at the Savoy, *Noises Off* was accompanied by productions of others of Frayn's plays: *Benefactors* and *Wild Honey* simultaneously in New York and London, and the screenplay *Clockwise* in both countries. Frayn's success was not unlike that of Ayckbourn when the latter had five plays running in London simultaneously; in addition, in England and the United States, he is popularly known for only one play—*Noises Off*—as Ayckbourn is for *The Norman Conquests*.

Noises Off is a farce depending on finely manipulated physical slapstick action for its hilarity. In act 1, the audience first sees a provincial touring company of players dress-rehearsing a parody of the plays of Ben Travers. The action shifts to backstage misunderstandings in the personal lives of the company, and the complications result in the offstage actions gradually assuming central importance in the play. The technique of a play within a play—long a staple of British drama—takes still another inventive turn in *Noises Off*, in the dizzyingly fast-paced physical action, in which the technical production details are confused with the personal problems. In *The Norman Conquests*, Ayckbourn utilizes the action of one of the three plays as the offstage action of another, and in Ayckbourne's *Chorus of Disapproval*, the two actions join in a successful onstage scene from *The Threepenny Opera*. In *Noises Off*, however, frontstage and backstage problems alternate, with the former gradually giving way to the latter. The obligatory farce confusion is thus caused by the frantic maneuvering between the two scenes. Nevertheless even this hilarious farce, according to its author, is serious in its concern with "an anxiety everyone has that he may make a fool of himself in public, that he may not be able to maintain his persona, that the chaotic feelings inside may burst out."[22]

Frayn's earlier plays include *After Zounds!* (1957), *The Two of Us* (1970), *The Sandboy* (1971), and *Alphabetical Order* (1975). He enjoyed his first major successes, according to Benedict Nightingale, with *Donkey's Years* (1976), about a college reunion, followed a month later by *Clouds,* about a journalist, a novelist, a college professor, and a guide in Cuba, and then by *Liberty Hall* and *Make and Break* (both in 1980). Frayn's satiric bent has increasingly turned to philosophical reflections in which characters, like clouds, change personal perspectives and the same situation is seen differently by each character.

It is *Benefactors* (1984), however, that pointedly and poignantly deals with Frayn's philosophical, political, and linguistic concerns through two couples who become close friends. Totally opposite the farcical activity of *Noises Off,* the drama concerns four characters: David and Jane, architect and anthropologist, respectively, form a mutual dependency with Colin and Sheila, professional misanthropist and dormouse, respectively. This dependency, simply put, includes the need of one couple to be needed and of the other to be helped. David and Jane serve, in their Good Samaritan roles, as parents, hosts, and chauffeurs to Colin and Sheila and their family, who accept these favors parasitically.

Mental rather than physical action dominates Frayn's comedy of ideas, taking the form of interlocking monologues, sometimes spoken by one character to another, sometimes addressed to the audience. The idealistic David combines philanthropy with his architecture as he envisions a better world, much like, as Mel Gussow has suggested, Ibsen's architect in *The Master Builder.* His problem is a modern one, involving issues like gentrification and public housing. Jane's problem, similarly, is that of being Good Samaritan to the parasitic couple. On philosophical and practical levels, David and Jane eventually are as much victims of themselves as of their dependent "friends." Like Chekhov's characters, each of the four is at times isolated from the others even as all are bound by their individual needs or situations.

As in Frayn's other plays, the sense of constant flux operates in both the actions and the attitudes of the characters, the comedy consisting of the "ironies of existence, the multiple-bottomedness of life, in which every action contains its antithesis and nothing and no one turns out as foreseen, although even opposites are not that different, until both change and sameness lose all meaning except as a joke as in the play's final image of a woman laughing and laughing, though what she is laughing at remains undisclosed."[23] John Simon closes his review with the assertion that "if *Noises Off* was a farce for serious people, *Benefactors* is a drama for people with a sense of humor."[24] It is generally seen as Frayn's dark drama about personal and philosophical matters, as are Ayckbourn's later plays *A Chorus of Disapproval* and *A Small Family Business.*

With his obvious artistic kinship to Chekhov, Frayn has also expressed admiration for the American dramatist David Mamet, in whose plays the virile and poetic energy of language illustrates the Wittgensteinian concern about the relationship between language and the reality beneath that language. Verbal and intellectual constructions, however idealistic, fall prey to pragmatic realities. This battle between language and reality is the essence of Chekhov's dramas, as the by-now standard explorations of his "text and subtext" by actors and scholars alike support. It is also the essence of Pinter's dramas, in which fear of saying what they really mean constantly menaces the characters' sense of security. The comedy of Chekhov, Pinter, Ayckbourn, and Frayn is discomfortingly tinged with reality's constant challenge to appearance, and the given reality of any moment is itself challenged by the unremitting flux inherent in the nature of human relationships.

It is this ultimate contradiction that the reality of history has posed to the idealistic and highly structured thinking of the architect, David, and that the reality of experience has similarly posed to the anthropologist, Jane. In the dismantling of David's arguments for a better world through architecture, ideas are debated. The debates inevitably evoke comparisons of Frayn with Stoppard as a writer of the comedy of ideas. Frayn, however, avoids the pitfall that Stoppard, until *The Real Thing,* fell into: his characters' absence of emotional credibility. Frayn's characters are, above all, intensely human—emotionally as well as socially and intellectually—a totality not realized in most of Stoppard's brilliant comedies of ideas.

CHRISTOPHER HAMPTON

Born on 26 January 1946, Oxford-educated Christopher Hampton has made use of his undergraduate interest in foreign languages, writing more adaptations of other writers than original dramas. Included in these adaptations are Isaac Babel's *Marya* (1967); Chekhov's *Uncle Vanya* (1970); Ibsen's *Hedda Gabler* (1970), *A Doll's House* (1971), *Ghosts* (1978), and *The Wild Duck* (1979); Ōdōm von Horvath's *Tales from the Vienna Woods* (1977) and *Don Juan Comes back from the War* (1978); *The Portage to San Cristobal of A. H.* (1982), from George Steiner's novel; Molière's *Tartuffe* (1983); and *Les Liaisons Dangereuses* (1986), from the only novel written by the eighteenth-century military officer Choderlos de Laclos.

Hampton's first original play, *When Did You Last See My Mother?* (1966), is about two schoolboys whose close relationship, developed in a public school, matures into the adult involvement of one of the boys with the mother of the other. In *Total Eclipse* (1968), Hampton dramatizes the affair between the sixteen-year-old French poet Arthur Rimbaud and another poet, Paul Verlaine, ten years his senior, with the personal involvements here broadening into a discussion of the nature of poetry.

In a parody of Molière's *Misanthrope, The Philanthropist* (1970), Hampton's best-known play, continues the concerns of his first two dramas about academia and art. Here, however, the focus is on the sheltered life of university dons. The play begins in comfortably reassuring university rooms, where dons are discussing the appropriateness of a suicide ending to a play whose author demonstrates, with a faked gunshot, his projected ending. At the end of the act, however, the shooting is real, resulting in the author's actual suicide on stage. The rest of the drama is about the central character, Philip, a philologist who is fascinated by language games and, unlike Molière's Alceste, does not want to hurt people's feelings. "Bullied by the ghastly right-wing novelist he asked to dinner,"[25] Philip engages his guest in witty debate on language and art as one of the many "obstacle courses" (Irving Wardle's phrase) in his life. The nastiness of the suicide in act 1, as well as the news of the murder of the entire government cabinet, seems hardly to affect the academic life, insulated from the violence of outside events. Instead, the group continues playing verbal and sexual games focusing on the deteriorating fortunes of Philip and oiled by the language of "paradox and irony, parallelism and eccentric words in conventional contexts . . . for a long time the gloss on English comedy."[26] The verbal maneuverings combine with Philip's sexual episodes, in an unsettling comedy of academic manners that enjoyed a run of 1114 performances in London.

The play evoked all shades of critical reaction. Peter Lewis of the *Daily Mail* asserts that not even Alec McCowen "can make such a humorless, not to say boring, character worth an evening's attention,"[27] and Nicholas de Jongh of the *Guardian* sees Hampton as "now writing better than Wesker, Osborne or Mercer."[28] Between these two extreme reactions are those of Eric Shorter, who, acknowledging some strains in the play, sees it as a "brilliant third play,"[29] and of Irving Wardle, who appreciated the production and the writing, but felt that even these were no theatrical match for "Philip's stumbling gaucheries and sudden flashes of bleakly pedantic truth."[30]

After two more original dramas (*Savages* in 1973 and *Tales of Hollywood* in 1982), Hampton's *Les Liaisons Dangereuses* (1986 in London and 1987 in New York), a chillingly fascinating tale of sex as power, has called attention once more to Hampton's Oxford education as the currency for his drama. He returns here to his undergraduate interest in the eighteenth century, having questioned, as a student, why "the best prose writers in prerevolutionary France all wrote pornography."[31]

The two totally amoral antagonists are the stock rake with a title and the female aristocrat, who is more than a match for him. Together they plot seductions, he for purely egotistic reasons and she in revenge for the male exploitation of women in her time, saying that she "was born to dominate [his] sex and avenge my own." Hampton describes their maneuvering as "a sex education of the most sophisticated kind" and de Laclos's novel as "*The Tropic of Cancer* of 1782, a best seller stashed, like a Henry Miller novel from the 1930s in the dark corners of bookcases."[32] What Hampton deals with in his original dramas reaches its apogee in *Les Liaisons,* for the dialogue is sharply ironic, paradoxical, and literate, and the scenes are brilliantly paced. Rich describes the "geographically dispersed scenes" as "flowing on the single all-purpose set . . . in a progressively demented choreography, matched with . . . increasingly macabre harpsichord music, which distorts and then strips away the sham minuet of 18th century manners."[33] As in *The Philanthropist,* outside events of the time (in the eighteenth century it was the oncoming revolution) raise questions for the audience. One of the concluding lines—"We're halfway through the 80s"—startles with its clear suggestion of a contemporary parallel.

A resident dramatist at the Royal Court in 1968, Hampton saw his first play produced there in 1966 while he was still an undergraduate at Oxford. His film credits include Graham Greene's *Honorary Consul* (1983) and his versions of *A Doll's House* (1973) and *Tales from the Vienna Woods* (1979). His television work includes *Able's Will,* from Malcolm Bradbury's *History Man,* and his own plays: *Total Eclipse, The Philanthropist, Savages, Treats,* and *Marya.*

Hampton's place in British drama, according to John Russell Taylor, is that of a writer who strives "for a highly literate theatre (without being drily intellectual). Hampton is a civilized voice in the modern theatre we cannot well do without."[34]

JAMES SAUNDERS

In both subject matter and technique, James Saunders, consistently referred to by critics and historians as a liberal humanist, has spanned the gamut of experiments and subject matter of the new British drama, from his early Ionesco-like play, *Alas, Poor Fred!* (1959), to later plays, like *Games* (1971), in which sociopolitical issues such as the My Lai massacre during the Vietnam War are dealt with. Like many contemporaries, Saunders, who was born on 8 January 1925, has been closely associated with small theaters—the Questors in Ealing and the Orange Tree in Richmond. Interested also in live audience participation and the impact of the audience on the play, he is committed "to the perfecting of a finished, and, by recent standards, quite rhetorical text."[35]

Two of his dramas, *Next Time I'll Sing to You* and *Games,* are about real events. In the former, a director and his actors perform—as in

Pirandello's *Six Characters in Search of an Author*—a play about a modern hermit; it is based on Raleigh Trevelyan's *Hermit Disclosed* (a book about Alexander James Mason, who died in 1942). Although the hermit remains central to the action of the play, it is the director's and players' varying concerns and ideas that shape their and the audience's understandings of human experience. Ideas, verbal wit, and game playing look forward to Stoppard's drama, according to Dennis Hatfield. Trevelyan's book on Mason also influenced Bond's *Pope's Wedding* and Livings's television play *Jim All Alone*.

A one-act play, *Games,* like *Next Time I'll Sing to You,* is a play about a play, in which rehearsing actors discuss the actions of Lieutenant William Calley, an American officer in the Vietnam War, and invite the audience to offer suggestions on how to present Calley and his actions.

Bodies (1977) belongs to a twentieth-century genre of plays about two couples, a tradition illustrated quintessentially by Coward's *Private Lives.* Having exchanged partners and then exchanged them again, the two couples reunite after a long separation; this meeting provides a forum for the exploration of different life-styles and values. Their monologues, dialogues, and group conversations progress in a "a rising quasi-Osbornean sequence of jibes and diatribes."[36]

Likened by some to Shaw for using the play as a forum for the discussion of ideas, to Stoppard for his verbal wit, to Osborne for his increasing sense of anger, and to the committed dramatists for using contemporary events as a basis for the discussion of ideas, Saunders is compassionate and literary. His events and ideas are intended ultimately to create self-understanding in the widest range of human experience. His uniqueness lies in the rhetorical stylishness that places him with the so-called traditionalists.

ANTHONY SHAFFER

It has often been said that a writer with published novels is likely to turn to the dramatic form. Such is the case of the Cambridge-educated twin brothers Peter and Anthony Shaffer, born on 15 May 1926. In their case the likelihood is even greater, since their novels contain dialogues that are "the work of playwrights more than of novelists."[37]

Their joint novels include *Withered Murder* (1955), *The Woman in the Wardrobe* (1951), and *How Doth the Little Crocodile?* (1957), the last two published under the pseudonym Peter Anthony.

Peter has continued writing as a profession, whereas Anthony, famous for one detective drama, *Sleuth* (1970), has followed a number of vocations, including law, advertising, and television. With 2,359 performances in London and 122 in New York, *Sleuth* has a record of more performances than the total for all plays by his brother. Writing fewer than a half-dozen plays, Anthony has thus had a sensationally popular one-play career as a dramatist. His first play, *The Savage Parade* (1963), closed after one performance. *Murderer* (1975) and *The Case of the Oily Levantine* (1979) had short runs.

With Laurence Olivier and Michael Caine as the antagonists in the film version of *Sleuth,* Shaffer seems to have staged a contemporary coup de thèâtre in his stunning parody of the classic genre. Its protagonist, Andrew, is a mystery writer who invites his wife's lover to his Agatha Christie–like country manor. The plot begins with a staged crime proposed by Andrew. He lures Milo, his guest, into stealing his (Andrew's) wife's jewels for the insurance money. Each of the men has his reward in mind: Andrew's retrieval of his wife's affections and Milo's reception of the insurance money. Suspense builds as each counterpoints one game with another, creating rising suspicions between them. Cliffhangers, such as a gun pointed at Milo by Andrew after the "theft," provide a teeter-totter action that concludes with the writer's shooting of Milo. It is Milo who wins a questionable victory as the games turn deadly. The early staged gunshot turns real when Andrew is unable to endure Milo's discovery of his (Andrew's) inffectuality with his mistress. Games, a disguise for reality, eventually lose their function, and in a Pirandellian ending, deadly consequences result.

Approached by some as an elegant piece of mystery melodrama of a high order and by others, like Jules Glenn, as a Freudian playing out of relationships between twins—one incomplete without the other, or one shooting the other out of a repressed homosexuality—the play indulges the audience in the much-loved English tradition of gamesmanship, on the level of sheer entertainment. As an "intricate Chinese-box of a thriller . . . full of games, fantasies, shocks and humiliations,"[38] *Sleuth* has provided the postwar era with its most memorable mystery melo-drama, one that spawned many imitations, the most famous being Ira Levin's nearly equally successful drama, *Deathtrap*.

PETER SHAFFER

It is Peter, however, who has earned a place as a serious dramatist, demonstrating in a variety of styles the same high theatricality that characterizes his brother's psychological thriller, *Sleuth*. Warren Syl-vester Smith comments that after *The Royal Hunt of the Sun* (1964), it was apparent that now "[Peter] Shaffer had to be seriously considered as one of that long line of British dramatists who treated the platform with actors on it as a unique form of high art."[39] Shaffer solidly reinforces the critical acclaim of *Royal Hunt* with succeeding plays, especially *Equus* (1973) and *Amadeus* (1979).

In the tradition of drawing-room drama, Peter Shaffer's first work, *Five Finger Exercise* (1958), is about an upper-middle-class English nu-clear family (parents, one son, and one daughter), whose comfortable reliance on the verities of family life is changed by the appearance of a young German tutor. His charm attracts each of the family members for different reasons, making him the catalyst for peeling off the layers of psychological realities underlying the surfaces of family life. Each has her or his self-revelatory monologue, with a haunting mystery remain-ing about Walter, whose chilling yet exotic past includes a father guilty of Nazi concentration-camp atrocities. Like Chekhov's static drama, this one ends ambiguously, with no progression of "clear stages in the dramatic argument; instead the play organizes itself into a series of splendid self-revealing tirades . . . , put together with the aplomb of a Pinero, well-provided with dialogue of remarkable crispness and articulacy."[40] This ambiguity of plot resolution and the absence of a sharp focus on a single protagonist constitute the modernist essence of Shaffer's drama. Yet the language and technical style overall are in the mainstream drawing-room tradition, almost, John Russell Taylor con-cludes, as though "John Osborne and the rest had never lived."[41]

Within ingenious frameworks, Shaffer's short plays—*The Private Ear* and *The Private Eye* (1962), *Black Comedy* (1965), and *White Lies* (1967)—likewise deal with emotional conflicts hidden by appearances.

In *Black Comedy,* a suspicious husband hires a detective to trace the activities of his bored wife, with the detective discovering nothing amiss except her boredom. To convince the skeptical husband of his findings, the two exchange places, with the husband trailing his wife and the detective ensconcing himself in the husband's office.

This inversion, in matter and manner, becomes important in Shaffer's long plays plotted on the grand scale of historical events. With high theatricality, he has created three sensational dramatic spectacles: *The Royal Hunt of the Sun, Equus,* and *Amadeus.*

In *Royal Hunt,* influenced by Jungian psychology with its emphasis on the archetypal and the primitive and on their inevitable collision with civilized values, Shaffer weaves a colorful tapestry of historical events, with Pizzaro and the Incan Sun King, Atahuallpa, at the center of the clash between their cultural and personal visions. By means of masks, mimes, dances, songs and chants, elaborate costumes, repetition, and ritual reenactments of archetypal behavior, Shaffer shows conqueror and king in their personal confrontations to be mirror images of each other.

Shaffer's interest in the collision of primitive impulses and civilized behavior, as well as his theatrical flair, finds its sharpest human focus in *Equus* (1973), with a plot, based on an actual happening, about a seventeen-year-old boy who stabs the eyes of six horses out of fear that they would reveal his sexual molestation which they had witnessed. Again in a highly stylized form—the representation of horses on stage by actors wearing horses' heads made of wire—Shaffer dramatizes the primitive-civilized dance between the boy and the psychiatrist in the reenactment and discussion of the event. The dialogue, as in *Royal Hunt,* seems at times like a ritual incantation. Dreams/nightmares and symbols reinforce words—for example, Alan's riding the horse on a revolving stage as he reenacts his experience. The conclusion of the play, again as in *Royal Hunt,* is ambiguous, the audience being left with the psychiatrist's awareness of the contrast between his own sterile logic and the boy's passionate experiences. Dysart, the psychiatrist, is a variation of Pizarro in the earlier drama.

Equus was followed by still another highly theatrical drama, *Amadeus* (1979). The conflicts of the explorer-adventurer and the psychiatrist in the earlier plays are once again enacted, this time in the unresolved conflict between Mozart and his contemporary Salieri. Shaffer dramatizes the story of the court composer Salieri in his fabled jealousy of Mozart, a story that reaches as far back as Pushkin's lyrical drama *Mozart and Salieri* in the early nineteenth century. Their conflict reaches its climax in "Mozart's recognition of Salieri as a messenger of God and as death beckoning his end as he composes the Requiem."[42] The two composers—one a genius passionate about his music, and the other a mediocrity with the power of his court influence to keep Mozart in his poverty—clash as do Pizzaro and Atahuallpa and the youth and the psychiatrist in the earlier plays.

In *Yonadab* (1985), Shaffer makes still another of his spectacular leaps into history—this time the era of King David, 1000 B.C.—in what Benedict Nightingale calls the most exotic of his locations, "the mind of a wily manipulator" under whose exterior exists a "spiritual buccaneer."[43] In the Book of Samuel, Yonadab is described as a very subtle man, but in Shaffer's play he is sinister as he manipulates the rape of his half sister, Tamar, by David's son Amnon and her seduction by her brother Absalom, her supposed protector. His argument to the two men is that incest "will rapturously transform them into Jewish counterparts of the Egyptian Osiris and Isis."[44]

Yonadab, like Pizarro and the psychiatrist, is an outsider to the "ecstasy" (a term used frequently in regard to Shaffer's Dionysian characters) represented by the Incan chief, the teenage youth, and Mozart. Describing Shaffer as deserving of a medal for his "majestic recklessness," Nightingale criticizes him for too obviously manipulating the plot instead of allowing the characters to develop on their own, as in *Royal Hunt, Equus,* and *Amadeus.* Again dealing with his favorite theme, the clash of visions in which the "coming to any sort of awareness of tragic ambiguity must always be new and painful,"[45] the play did not receive the acclaim of Shaffer's earlier work.

In his dramatization of man's search for God and in his representation of the concomitant experience of ecstasy by one of the protagonists, all within the cultural myths of the time, Shaffer relies on ritual actions and symbols. He talks about being haunted by "apocryphal images: pictures of events which may be real or imaginary, and which either way emit immense power."[46] Using techniques of major dramatic traditions—the rituals of Japanese No drama, some elements of

Brechtian epic and Artaudian cruelty, and even the chorus of Greek and Elizabethan drama in the incantatory dialogues—Shaffer is a re-inventor of established styles, in consort with his modern thematic concerns, particularly the ambiguities of dilemmas that he leaves philosophically unresolved.

JOHN MORTIMER

Since Rumpole of the Bailey is the most famous character in the work of John Mortimer, it seems only natural that any discussion of Mortimer begin with the fact that he is a barrister and the only son of a barrister. He was born on 21 April 1923. Educated at Harrow and Oxford and qualifying for the legal profession in 1948, Mortimer wrote six novels during his first eight years as a lawyer. After his award-winning radio play, *Dock Brief* (1957), about a lawyer and his client, he gave up the novel for the drama, frequently adapting his radio or television plays to the stage, or his stage plays to television. With Chekhov and Dickens as acknowledged influences, Mortimer writes comedy, because "to my mind [it is] the only thing worth writing in this despairing age, provided the comedy is truly on the side of the lonely, the neglected, the unsuccessful and plays its part in the role against established rules and against the imposing of arbitrary codes of behavior upon individual and unpredictable behavior."[47]

The lawyer in *Dock Brief* and the famed Rumpole are prime examples of Mortimer's "failed characters," and his sympathy for middle-class failures was likened early on to that of Terence Rattigan. For example, John Russell Taylor sees *The Wrong Side of the Park* (1960) as "nearer the sort of play which a British dramatist would be writing now if no real challenge to the supremacy of Rattigan had been heard in the theatre than almost any other new play by a writer under forty."[48] Taylor qualifies his comment, however, with a reference to Mortimer's affinity to some linguistic and thematic qualities of the new drama.

John Elsom, on the other hand, sees Mortimer's character studies as a contrast to those of Rattigan, mostly in the acidity of their tone. In their exploration of the failed or unsuccessful, Mortimer's plays have invited rubrics such as George Wellwarth's "the apotheosis of failure."[49] There is also something of Tennessee Williams's concern with failed characters in Mortimer's plays. The heroine of *The Wrong Side of the Park* (1960), about a ménage à trois, has been likened to Blanche du Bois in *A Streetcar Named Desire,* and the narrator-barrister in *A Voyage Round My Father* likened to Tom Wingfield in *The Glass Menagerie.*

Mortimer, like Rattigan, excels in the craft of the short play, and even in his full-length plays he uses a series of sketchlike episodes, gracefully flowing into each other. His settings are "run-down private schools, draughty seaside hotels, nine-to-five offices and the shabbier corners of the courts."[50] And his characters, like Chekhov's, are neither bad nor good, but familiar enough to provide, in his own words, "the shock of recognition."[51]

Dock Brief, a successful one-act play, deals with a failed lawyer who is finally given a charity case at the age of sixty-three. Using his assigned time with his client to fantasize about possible success, he makes a poor case for the client, who is convicted but then pardoned because of the lawyer's incompetence. At the end, the two men leave the prisoner's cell, happy in the outcome, and the lawyer returns to his dreams of success and to the reality of his world, which consists of working out crossword puzzles. Mortimer's Rumpole, like the lawyer in *Dock Brief,* endures failures and a variety of embarrassments, only to return home after a pub stop to his wife, whom he describes as "she who must be obeyed." For rare and brief moments, characters enjoy illusionary fulfillments, in the tradition of the shy lieutenant in Chekhov's "Kiss," who for one unforgettable moment in his dull existence experienced the kiss of a woman in the dark, a kiss obviously intended for someone else.

In his maverick position in the new drama, Mortimer has consistently maintained a foothold in both television and the stage. In fact, in the United States, he is primarily recognized as the author of the acclaimed television series *Rumpole of the Bailey* (also published as stories), *Rumpole's Return, Trials of Rumpole, Rumpole and the Golden Thread, Rumpole for the Defense,* and *A Rumpole Omnibus.* Additional television series include his adaptations of Evelyn Waugh's *Brideshead Revisited,* of Robert Graves's *I Claudius,* and of his own novel, *Paradise Postponed.*

The ambivalence between experiment and tradition, between television and stage, is seen in his traditional style—which Gerald Strauss describes as "clever conception and management of situations, characters that are believable even when they are largely stereotypes, and dialogue that abounds with witticisms"[52]—and in his nontraditional concerns of social conscience, which underlie his humorous explorations of middle-class familial and professional situations. Taylor, acknowledging Mortimer's skill, poses this ambivalence as a trap that the author may have created for himself, a trap that could, however, be "a launching-pad to the discovery of fresh worlds elsewhere."[53]

Ambivalence in Mortimer's work is heightened by the closeness of the author's personal and fictional worlds, illustrated so clearly in *A Voyage Round My Father* (1970), a full-length episodic drama that ranges over twenty years in the lives of his blind barrister father and himself. Adapted for television in 1982, the episodes follow a young boy's sexual initiation, his schoolboy experiences with masters and headmasters, employment with a propaganda film unit during the war, his first marriage and divorce, and his entrance into the legal profession. But the father, recalled in the memory of the narrator, is always present in the play.

Collaborators (1973), like *Voyage Round My Father,* has strong autobiographical references in its main character, a lawyer undergoing changes in his marital and professional states. He becomes involved in writing a script for an American, and his wife joins in the project. The script the trio writes resembles the play the audience is watching, with the artistic and marital complications eventually being resolved when the American leaves and the lawyer's young secretary no longer threatens the marriage. Carrying the scars of the conflict, writer and wife resume their married life, renewed by plans to collaborate on another play. Mortimer has been married twice, in 1949 to Penelope Fletcher (Mortimer), a novelist, and in 1971 to Penelope Gollop, and some autobiographical parallels in the play are clear.

Mortimer's writing for the stage also includes three translations/adaptations of Georges Feydeau's farces: *A Flea in Her Ear* (1966), *Cat among the Pigeons* (1969), and *The Lady from Maxim's* (1977). He has also translated Carl Zuckmayer's *Captain of Kopenick* (1971).

Of all dramatists of the postwar era, Mortimer perhaps comes closest to erasing the lines that separate the modern stage drama from radio/television plays in a time when the latter are increasingly re-garded, not as preparatory for the stage or ancillary to it, but its equal in stature. His dramatization of Waugh's *Brideshead Revisited* superbly illustrates this achievement, even as it brings into sharp focus the darker, heretofore subtler, aspect of what Elsom has described as the acid quality of Mortimer's humor. If his work evokes Chekhov, Ratti-gan, and Williams, it also includes the mordant vision of Waugh, in support of Taylor's view that Mortimer's concern is with the decline of the middle-classes as opposed to the concern of many of the newer dramatists with the ascent of the working classes. [54]

In a *Contemporary Authors* interview, John Mortimer describes his first two plays, *The Dock Brief* and *What Shall We Tell Caroline?* (1958) as surreal in the manner of Ionesco. Mentioning his difference from the socially realistic group of angry writers, "because I wasn't a North Country working-class boy," he admits to becoming angrier as he grows older, just as the "angries" seem to have become less so with age. "They've become conservative old blokes."[55]

JOHN WHITING

"Laconic, darkly tinged with misanthropy . . . aphorisms steeped in vinegar, phrases with tails like scorpions . . . and . . . speeches of the most limpid tenderness to soften the prevalent mood of Swiftian distaste"[56]—this is Kenneth Tynan's description of the language in John Whiting's stage adaptation of Aldous Huxley's novel *The Devils of Loudon.* Tynan goes on to conclude that "language like this has too long been absent from our stage."[57] H. A. L. Craig of the *New Statesman* likens Whiting to John Webster of the seventeenth cen-tury,[58] and Simon Trussler calls Whiting's plays "parables and para-digms of human behavior."[59] *The Devils* (1961), according to Peter Barnes, "influenced the new generation of dramatists in the second half of the 1950s, in particular John Arden and Harold Pinter."[60] Such are the accolades given *The Devils,* the last play of Whiting's pro-duced during his lifetime.

Born the son of an army captain (who later became a lawyer) on 15 November 1917, a conscientious objector who served in the military from 1939 to 1944, and a student at the Royal Academy of Dramatic Art, Whiting utilized his military and acting backgrounds in his plays, described by Audrey Williamson as chilling and riveting.[61] The author of fewer than a dozen plays, Whiting drew mixed notices for early plays such as *Saint's Day* (1951), even as Christopher Fry, Peter Ustinov, and Alec Clunes declared this drama the winner in a competition with nearly a thousand entries. Some critics found *Saint's Day* a "bewildering nightmare,"[62] "a strange, mad, baffling little play,"[63] "incomprehensible."[64] Reactions to Whiting's early plays were contradictory because of their disturbing content and theatrical style.

Two early plays about the military, *A Penny for a Song* (1951) and *Marching Song* (1954), take their titles from the poetry of Yeats. The former was a comedy set in the Napoleonic era, but later underwent revision that involved changing the character of the soldier from that of a "gentle visionary" to one of a "bitter revolutionary."[65]

Both antimilitaristic and misanthropic, *Saint's Day* is about an eighty-three-year-old poet who isolates himself and his family from the rest of the population of a small town but emerges from his isolation to help a mother and her child fleeing from marauding soldiers. Bitter ironies, anticipating those in Arden's *Sergeant Musgrave's Dance* and Rudkin's *Afore Night Come,* pervade this play about a genius whose experiences symbolically retell ancient myths of death and resurrection.

Antimilitarism and moral choices are themes in *Marching Song,* about a general, recently released from prison, who remembers his own "massacre of the innocents," when he was forced to choose between betraying his duty and killing children who were deliberately put in the way of his marching army. Like the poet in *Saint's Day,* the general feels compassion, but only after he has killed the leader of the children. His advance is halted, and forever after he suffers the pangs of treachery to his country. The action of the play consists of the revelation of his past and the inevitable suicide ending. With high theatricality, Whiting presents the contemporary world with an age-old moral dilemma, vivid in its reminder of the 1945 bombings of Dresden and of Hiroshima. Both Whiting and Robert Flemyng, who played the role of the general, served in World War II.

Reversing his early negative judgments on Whiting's work, T. C. Worsley, in his review of *Marching Song,* admits to being among those "too dense to recognize his [Whiting's] talent in the famous Arts Theatre prize play, *Saint's Day.*"[66] He joins Tynan in his admiration of

Whiting's language, commenting on the exciting, taut, and elliptical dialogue. Harold Hobson also notes the "troubled and uneasy poetry whose shadowy tides never wash against the shores of our own land of cricket bats and football pools . . . , another way of saying that the play extends the boundaries of English drama."[67]

The Devils brought Whiting the strongest critical approval of his career. Critics generally called attention to its intellect, language, and compelling theatricality, and its structure as a "marvel of organisation, a mosaic so finely put together that it has the effect of a living picture" and, "in spite of constant changes of character and setting, preserves an absolutely uninterrupted progression from beginning to end."[68]

In addition, the play enjoys historical importance as "the first new play performed by the Shakespeare Memorial Theatre in the eighty-two years of its existence, specially commissioned by Peter Hall from John Whiting, who, despite his critical reputation, was neither an established nor a successful dramatist."[69] In an interview with Richard Findlater, Whiting rhetorically asks, "How many other English playwrights have been given the kind of opportunity Peter Hall gave me?"[70]

Like the poet in *Saint's Day* and the general in *Marching Song,* Father Grandier of *The Devils,* a sensualist-priest (in real life burned at the stake in 1634), finds himself embroiled in paradoxes, as he is accused by a hunchbacked, sexually repressed prioress, Sister Jeanne, of demon possession. Admitting to his lechery but denying possession, the priest, according to Philip Hope-Wallace of the *Guardian,* "becomes a sort of Tennysonian or Wagnerian hero, who seeks to find God through his senses . . . and reconciles himself with that god."[71] Likened by Robert Muller to Arthur Miller's *Crucible,* the play "spares us nothing, the obscene exorcism, the hideous self-intoxication of the nuns, the priest's lusts, and his jailer's instrument of torture." From Aldous Huxley's *Devils of Loudon,* Whiting "has fashioned a powerful dramatic spectacle, a play of depth, force, terror and beauty."[72] Muller concludes that if the drama "represents the type of New Drama we are going to see at this theatre, Mr. Hall's policy will have been triumphantly vindicated."[73] Even Worsley sent Whiting a telegram congratulating him on a masterpiece.

As a contemporary moralist and allegorist, and as a chilling theatricalist in the tradition of England's seventeenth-century dramatists, Whiting established himself with his three major dramas—*Saint's Day, Marching Song,* and *The Devils*—as a dramatist whose plays easily find a place among those of the historical mainstream, as well as those of the politicized new drama. He died on 16 June 1963.

ROBERT BOLT

Among the dramatists since 1950, Robert Bolt, born in Manchester on 15 August 1924, retains a status as one of the most conventional and commercially successful. As a craftsman in the tradition of the well-constructed play middle-class audiences have come to expect, he suffers constant comparisons with other authors, most notably with Terence Rattigan. His drama *The Flowering Cherry* (1960) has frequently been likened to Arthur Miller's *Death of a Salesman*. Bolt's interest in history and ideas has resulted in the highly successful play for which he is most famous, *A Man for All Seasons,* which began as a radio play in 1954, was televised in 1957, staged in the West End in 1960 and on Broadway in 1961, and released in its film version in 1966. Other historical dramas, *Vivat! Vivat! Regina!* (1970) and *State of Revolution* (1977)—about the conflict between Elizabeth I and Mary, Queen of Scots, and about Lenin and the Russian Revolution, respectively—illustrate Bolt's skill in creating historical mosaics of individuals and their ideas in conflict.

In addition to the historical stage pageants, Bolt has written the scripts for famous film epics: *Lawrence of Arabia* (1962) and *Dr. Zhivago* (1965). His version of the film on T. E. Lawrence was chosen over that of Rattigan, who then went on to write his play on Lawrence, *Ross,* for the stage.

In 1957 the *Evening Standard* chose Bolt as the most promising playwright because of *Flowering Cherry,* a play about an unsuccessful insurance salesman who dreams of returning to the orchards and rural life of his boyhood. With its conventional structure and realistic treatment of the subject, ending in the death of Jim Cherry, the play evokes comparison with Miller's Willy Loman in *Death of a Salesman*.

What has haunted the criticism of Bolt's plays can be summed up in Frederick Lumley's description of *A Man for All Seasons*. "[It is] a skillfully constructed play with a genuinely tragic tone; its language is eloquent and its characterisation sure. For all that, it fails to achieve full dramatic power. The reasons may partly be that as a play it is altogether too smooth."[74]

In *A Man for All Seasons*, Bolt skillfully re-creates the personal battle between Sir Thomas More and his king in a series of scenes whose purpose, according to Tynan, was to do for More what Brecht had done for Galileo. Criticizing the play for its oversimplification of the main character and his ideas, Tynan provoked a response from Bolt, who explained his characterization of More as a man who refused to comply with the request from authority to deny himself, as a consequence paying a "frightful price"—his life—just as Brecht's Galileo paid a similarly frightful price for compliance: "the reduction of a man in his own estimation to a status where he has only the right to scratch himself and eat."[75] Tynan continued the debate, insisting that in Bolt's play one never discovers *what* More believes but merely *that* he believes. John Russell Taylor regards Bolt's "discreet adventure into impressionistic staging, half-Brecht, half B.B.C. historical documentary . . . with nothing to put off the most conservative playgoer," as "well-made, reliable entertainment for intelligent people."[76]

In *The Tyger and the Horse* (1960), Bolt ventures into a play about modern concerns—the nuclear disarmament movement, a cause for which he was imprisoned briefly in 1961—but again the conventionality of structure and style seems at odds with the subject and with current stage movements.

Having won Academy Awards in the United States for his screenplays for *Lawrence of Arabia* and *Dr. Zhivago,* and having received plaudits for his films *Ryan's Daughter* and *Lady Caroline Lamb,* Bolt seems established in stage history as a historical dramatist writing highly competent and conventionally structured plays in an age when experiment and new forms, by their very existence, have made second-class citizens of writers engaging in traditional forms.

IRISH DRAMATISTS

Some Irish dramatists have already been discussed as they have participated in the new drama: Brendan Behan and his association with Joan Littlewood; Shelagh Delaney, of Irish descent, also writing for Joan Littlewood's theater; and David Rudkin, born in Ireland but living and working in England.

Traditional in the ways of the earlier Irish Renaissance writers—Yeats, Synge, and O'Casey—several dramatists, writing in Ireland and associated with the famous Abbey and Gate theaters of Dublin, have gained international recognition. The reputation of others has remained within the national confines of Ireland. None can be considered as having particular affinity with the experiments underway in London and environs. Among these, two writers emerge as prominent dramatists: Hugh Leonard (b. 9 November 1926) and Brian Friel (b. 9 January 1929).

Born John Keyes Byrne, Leonard has written a number of adaptations: *The Passion of Peter Ginty* (1961), from Ibsen's *Peer Gynt; Stephen D* (1962), from James Joyce's *Portrait of the Artist as a Young Man;* and *Dublin One,* from Joyce's *Dubliners.*

His early original stage dramas are comedies about suburban life, incorporating satire, farce, and sometimes dark comedy. The best known of his plays in this tradition is *The Patrick Pearse Motel* (1971), about a new business enterprise involving a motel in which each room is named after an Irish national hero, the restaurant is named the Famine Room, and the caretaker is a veteran of the 1916 Easter violence in Dublin. Clearly a burlesque of bourgeois manners and morality in the guise of nationalism, the play, like its predecessor, *The Au Pair Man* (1968), enjoyed some success outside Ireland, in London and New York.

Linked primarily with the Abbey Theatre in Dublin, Leonard also developed associations in the United States: the Vivien Beaumont Theater in New York and a group at Olney, Maryland, where a number of his plays were produced or premiered.

His plays *Da* (1973) and *A Life* (1979), both reaching the New York stage, represent a change in direction from his earlier comedies. Drawn from his intimate past, *Da* is an impressionistic play about a successful, middle-aged writer who returns to his Dublin home for the funeral of his father. Painful and fond memories are dramatized movingly in flashback scenes. The death of his father (his stepfather in Leonard's own case) represents an irreplaceable loss of a love seldom, if ever, expressed during his life. The play won the Tony and Drama Critics Circle awards in New York during the 1977–78 season.

A Life, similarly autobiographical, draws from an early experience involving a civil servant who was influential in helping Leonard get on the land commission. More emotionally intense than the autobiographical *Voyage Round My Father* by John Mortimer, Leonard's backward journeys into the past run the gamut of the bittersweet love–hate relationships of a writer with his past. In the tradition of the new dramatists, Leonard has been active as director of the Dublin Theatre Festival and literary editor at the Abbey Theatre.

Brian Friel's plays have similarly journeyed from Dublin to London and New York. His *Philadelphia, Here I Come!* (1964), *Crystal and Fox* (1968), *The Freedom of the City* (1973), *Aristocrats* (1979), *Faith Healer* (1979), *Translations* (1980), and *The Communication Cord* (1982) reflect the traditional Irish concern with the personal and historical past. *In Philadelphia, Here I Come!,* a man of twenty-seven relives in memory the events up to the time that he is leaving for America, his split character dramatized by two characters in various relationships with relatives and friends he leaves behind. *The Loves of Cass Maguire* (1966) reverses the situation of *Philadelphia, Here I Come,* in its concern with an Americanized Irishwoman returning to her native land after thirty-four years in America. The plays, perhaps at least partly due to uneven productions, have received both positive and negative notices.

Some of Friel's plays, like *The Freedom of the City,* are clearly political, and underneath all of them is the sad and humorous music of the tragedy of Ireland, whether it involves emigration to America or, as in *Translations,* the collision between English and Irish cultures, represented by the imposition of English-language schools in Donegal in 1833.

Another regional dramatist of some importance is John B. Keane (b. 21 July 1928), who has written more than twenty plays, mostly about the remote rural folk life of Ireland, insistently in the peasant tradition of John Millington Synge, yet without Synge's poetry and artistic structure. Popular and populist, Keane, according to D. E. S. Maxwell, has never come "wholly to terms with contemporary Irish life and the erosion, if not the loss, of old customs."[77] A prolific writer of essays and fiction, Keane has been criticized for writing—perhaps as a result of his journalistic background—too much and too fast, his plays lacking the discipline of style or the larger thematic dimensions of Leonard and Friel.

CHAPTER XI

CONCLUSION

Writing the obligatory chapter with conclusions on a history of such recent events is even more treacherous than attempting, as I have done in the preceding chapters, to classify and evaluate British drama since 1950. Some broad reflections, however, are in order.

Referring to the period 1955–68 as the great uprising, Harold Hobson, writing in 1984, remarks that four plays "mark the most brilliant years of modern British drama . . . , set the course of the British theatre for the next quarter of a century, begat a host of inferior imitators, almost destroyed the commercial theatre, stimulated the move towards the establishment of a National Theatre, encouraged the proliferation of fringe theatres, . . . and were the watershed of modern British drama. From them all the great rivers flow."[1] Those plays are Brecht's *Mother Courage and Her Children* (1955), Beckett's *Waiting for Godot* (1955), Osborne's *Look Back in Anger* (1956), and Pinter's *Birthday Party* (1957).

Two years, 1956 and 1968, watershed years in world events, are similarly significant in the revitalization of an era in English drama that had been dominated by polite, middle-class traditions seemingly alien to the social and political realities of postwar Britain. That a single production of a conventionally structured play—*Look Back in Anger*—in 1956 gave impetus to an outpouring of new drama and the emergence of two waves of experimentation in dramatic subjects, styles, and, especially, stage language is a phenomenon that, as Allardyce Nicoll asserts, even those who tend to minimize the importance of that event admit. Furthermore, 1968, the famous year of censorship abolition, when a younger generation of playwrights were at university or were beginning their careers, was a second annus mirabilis and has been asserted by politicized writers like Trevor Griffiths and David Edgar to be the genesis of their careers. This younger generation of dramatists so politicized the stage into a forum for left-wing orthodoxy that even predecessors such as Osborne, Bond, and Arden seemed traditional by contrast.

Significantly for the student of drama history, there developed two streams of the new drama—by dramatists Tynan describes as the "smooth" and the "hairy" writers, the former identified by their detachment from, and the latter by their intense concern for, sociopolitical matters. The feeding of these two streams by their continental sources—the absurdist and epic traditions of Beckett and Brecht, respectively—provides a literary linkage with a larger Western movement, like that forged during the Restoration when the Stuarts returned to England, bringing with them the influences of the French drama.

Now that the first and second waves have settled into history and become in varying degrees part of the mainstream, a time of consolidation seems to have set in. The major British breakers of prevailing stylistic modes—Beckett, Pinter, and Stoppard—continue writing and/or directing, with longer intervals between new plays. Since the middle 1970s, neither Pinter nor Stoppard has written plays that surpass in quality some of his earlier dramas, such as *The Caretaker, The Homecoming, Old Times, Jumpers,* and *Travesties.* Beckett continues writing in increasingly minimalist style, and Brecht's influence in the arena of the political play has remained a constant from the plays of Osborne in the 1950s and 1960s through the more polemical dramatists of the 1970s and 1980s. No new shock waves have been felt since the anger of Jimmy Porter, the linguistic minimalism of Beckett and Pinter, the inventive plagiarism of Stoppard, or the staged violence of Bond's and Arden's plays.

After thirty years, a consolidation that has been quietly taking place manifests itself overtly in an organizational changing of the guard at the two major government-subsidized theaters. The change occurs at an important juncture in their history, when, after decades of planning and the subsequent turbulence in bringing to fruition their plans, they have developed and stabilized, under the leadership of Peter Hall and Trevor Nunn, their identities as keepers of centuries of splendid British dramatic traditions and as encouragers of innovation. In the latter function, they have taken on some of the purpose of the Royal Court Theatre. Now those legacies are to be passed on to the next generation of artistic directors. The proposed change includes the succession of Peter Hall at the National Theatre by Richard Eyre and that of Trevor Nunn at the Royal Shakespeare Company by Terry Hands. In a less noticeable fashion, the consolidation generally under way is illustrated by the presence of dramatists as different as David Hare, a leftist polemicist, and Alan Ayckbourn, a popular traditionalist, at the National Theatre. They have become, in Frank Rich's words, "mainstays of the Hall regime at the National"[2] as both directors and writers.

Rich sees a healthy state, as well, in the West End theaters, where, even though the standard farce and the influence of the American musical are very much in evidence, commercial managers in 1987 still attempt productions of Chekhov's *Three Sisters,* Lorca's *House of Bernarda Alba,* and a new play composed of Eliot's writings, entitled *Let Us Go Then, You and I.* Continuing as well are the transfers to the West End from the more experimental theaters, such as Caryl Churchill's *Serious Money,* which had its premiere, of course, at the Royal Court, which continues to function as antidote to the West End.

Although not as forceful a presence as in the 1950s, 1960s, and 1970s, the Royal Court, true to its experimental function in the stage revolution, became embroiled in January of 1987 in yet another controversy, concerning the production of a drama about Jewish collaboration with the Nazis. The play, entitled *Perdition,* is based on a 1954 libel case about Jewish leaders in Hungary during World War II. With no legal censor to make decisions for the company, the management became its own censor, aborting the production, not because "there are factual inaccuracies in Jim Allen's play or that the play is anti-Semitic," but because "going ahead would cause great distress to sections of the community."[3]

Harold Hobson, of the older generation of critics, in a personal theater memoir, regards drama since 1968, the sequel to the great uprising of 1955, as a period of excessive preoccupations with sex, homosexuality, and the degeneration of language. The causes (Beckett, Osborne, and Pinter) "for which I fought have been won, and there have been several brilliant achievements."[4] Condemning the prevailing contempt for the theater as entertainment, Hobson sees the battles having "to be fought all over again, and the other way round, until it once more becomes possible on the stage for a young man to

CONCLUSION

fall in love with a girl, or speak of his country without contempt, or for an audience once again fully to understand and share . . . tenderness and longing . . . [or] soaring exultation."[5]

Surveying modern British drama in 1968, when the first surge of experimentation seemed to be receding, Allardyce Nicoll divided the movements into five periods: 1) that of Pinero, Henry Jones, and Wilde; 2) that of Galsworthy, the repertory playwrights, and Shaw; 3) that of James Bridie, Priestley, Eliot, and Fry; 4) that of the years 1956–66, beginning with *Look Back in Anger*, ten years that can be compared to the Jacobean decade of 1600–10, the major difference being that in the former "no Shakespeare is to be found"[6]; and 5) that of the current movement, which was as yet in flux but which, "whatever dramatic developments take shape in the immediate future will be largely determined by the nature of the public which the playhouses succeed in attracting during those years."[7] The dilemma remains—of finding "some modern equivalent for the community drama of the Middle Ages," to win back "the audiences which the theatre has been in danger of losing."[8]

Nicoll links the new drama with that of the earlier periods, emphasizing the importance of plays regarded as old-fashioned in the new order of things, plays such as *The Long Sunset* (1955) by R. C. Sherriff, whose major success, *Journey's End,* had appeared several decades earlier. There is also *Ross* (1960) by Terence Rattigan, preceded by *Flare Path* (1942), *The Winslow Boy* (1946), and *The Deep Blue Sea* (1952). And Robert Bolt has his own version of the common man in *A Man for All Seasons,* Bolt, who "knows his Brecht as intimately as any" of the avant-garde new-wave dramatists yet declares that " 'simply to slap your audience in the face satisfies' merely the 'austere and puritanical streak' which runs in many of Brecht's disciples and is 'a dangerous game to play.' " Bolt defines character as "what is common to all of us,"[9] rather than what is exclusively proletarian. Nicoll includes Peter Shaffer's *Private Ear and The Public Eye* (1962) and *The Royal Hunt of the Sun* (1964), Donald Howarth's *Lily in Little India* (1965), and James Saunders's *Next Time I'll Sing to You* (1962) as dramas that will "merit more notice than many 'experimental' efforts in the areas of 'Happenings,' of 'The Theatre of Menace,' and of what has been styled 'The Theatre of Embarrassment.' "[10]

On what he sees as the current division between entertainment and serious drama, Nicoll contrasts the positions represented by Martin Esslin and Noel Coward. For example, in chronicling the absurdist movement, Esslin contends that its purpose is to assert the dignity of man by having him face "reality in all its senselessness; to accept it freely, without fear, without illusions—and to laugh at it." Coward, on the other hand, writes that he knows that "the world was full of hatred, cruelty, vice, unrequited love, despair, destruction and murder." But he defends his being brought up with the now-despised "well-constructed play with a beginning, a middle and an end" and asks, "Since when has laughter been so insignificant?"[11]

Common ground must be found, Nicoll claims, between the absurdist, for whom the theater's purpose is to "teach and strengthen the spectators by a frank presentation of the violence, the brutalities, the enormities of present-day existence"[12] and, indeed, to laugh at these, and the Cowardian position that the purpose of theater is to entertain. Nicoll refers to Shaw as the dramatist who succeeded in achieving this common ground with success, although that success "tended to estrange him somewhat from the school of more serious and embittered playwrights of recent years."[13] Like Hobson, however, Nicoll acknowledges the value of the new drama as having "opened up new vistas and explored territory hitherto almost, if not entirely, neglected."[14]

A modern version of the centuries-old war of the theaters ironically surfaced in 1950, the year of Shaw's death and six years before Osborne's *Look Back in Anger,* in a debate about the drama of ideas carried on in the *New Statesman and Nation.* Begun by Terence Rattigan out of a sense of injury for having been attacked for writing well-made plays lacking ideas, the battle, settling nothing, was fought by James Bridie, Benn Levy, Peter Ustinov, Sean O'Casey, Ted Willis, Christopher Fry, and, finally, Shaw himself. In retrospect, this three-month confrontation, a paper war in contrast with the so-called revolution of 1956, did close one era and serve, perhaps, as a prelude to another.

John Elsom, of the younger generation of scholars and critics, writing in 1979, sees the rapid and profound changes that have occurred over the past thirty years as those that "cannot be assessed simply in terms of individual plays, productions, writers and companies. They are really changes of theatrical 'climate,' " by which he means "something more than a fashion and less than a revolution."[15] With the abolition of the censorship laws, the class-structured theater system was gradually deconstructed, admitting to its traditional precincts not only the proletarian class but a freedom of content— sometimes violence and denunciation of the very values and institutions revered for centuries—and a freedom of language and technique—sometimes obscenity, violence, and nudity. Elsom describes the changes as a "swing against stuffy bourgeois standards" that "resulted, first, in a proletarian fashion, and then steadied into a sort of classless image."[16] The classlessness is especially evident in the dramas of Wesker and Terson, who armed their working-class characters with ideas and articulateness, characters that Shaw could only present in comic terms. Younger, Cambridge-educated dramatists, such as Brenton and Hare, swelled the ranks of the earlier writers, mounting vitriolic attacks on the class structure, particularly on the "old boys" network perpetuated by the public (in America, private) schools and on the past colonialist adventurism of England, going beyond the standard liberal context to one of radical political thinking that Ronald Hayman describes as the politics of hatred.

In assessing the gains and losses realized in the events since 1956, Hayman in 1979 raises a question of language, whether a good playwright can be a bad writer; a question about innovation, whether, in spite of their strengths, the British dramatists can compare with continentals such as Beckett (considered, presumably, French), Ionesco, Genet, or Peter Handke; a third question, about whether sociopolitical didacticism invites a carelessness of "form and phrasing"; and, finally, the question that seems most difficult to answer, about "the new configurations within the play, within the playhouse, and in the relationship between performance and public."[17]

Hayman's evaluations in 1979 are incisive about the past, even as they seem troubled by the present, for at no time since World War II has there been "less occasion for using the words experimental or avant garde."[18] He attributes the state of drama to the loss of the many small experimental theaters, without which the health of drama suffers. Despite the breakdown of the old restrictions, such as the proscenium stage with the audience as the fourth wall, and despite the radical attempt of the anti-illusionistic, Brechtian techniques to challenge passive audiences to reevaluate their own thinking and behavior, the new directions themselves have stopped or at best have become stalemated, so that at present, playwrights are not taking advantage of the possibilities for experimentation. He attributes part of the responsibility to the new openness among actors, directors, and writers, together with the devaluation of the word, the increase in collaborative writing, the augmented importance of the director, and, of course, the mental laziness caused by television. Hayman regrets that traffic with the Americans has been one-way, west to east, despite the fact that some of the major populist experiments have been those of American expatriates like Charles Marowitz (Open Space), Jim Haynes (Traverse), Ed Berman (Inter-Action and a street group, Dogg's Troupe), and Nancy Meckler (Freehold).

Nearly ten years after Hayman's semi-elegiac comments regarding this one-way traffic, Benedict Nightingale described a new direction in English–American affairs of the stage. Having revitalized the theater in Stratford into the Royal Shakespeare Company (including its London company) and successfully engineered the establishment of the National Theatre, Peter Hall retired from the latter on 1 September 1988. Retirement for Hall, however, is not a conventional one. At fifty-nine he planned yet a third theatrical venture, with its tantalizing possibilities of surpassing the successes of his first two enterprises that have already given him an eminent place in stage history. With the playwright Alan Ayckbourn as partner and with producers Duncan Weldon (English) and Jerome Minskoff (American), he initiated an exchange of English and American stage productions that could include classics of both countries. He would "love to hear Shakespeare done by Americans in a full-blooded American accent, while observing the form, observing rhythm. I think American speech is beautiful in itself and, of course, much more like Elizabethan speech than modern English."[19] Hall wants to stage O'Neill's *Mourning Becomes Electra* because the play has been handled too heavily and because the powerful metaphors of O'Neill need to be felt on the stage. In addition, new British plays with their original casts intact could be moved to New York, and American casts in American plays could make the reverse trip.

Complex though the logistics of such a venture are, if there is any one person who can see it through, that person is Peter Hall. There is little contesting Nightingale's description of Hall as "the most influential figure in British theater in the last quarter-century. . . ."[20]

If successful, Hall's enterprising plan could well signal the start of yet another new era on the English-speaking stage, an era in which the effects of the two waves of new drama given impetus by *Look Back in Anger* in 1956 at the Royal Court Theatre would nourish and be nourished by an organized exchange between two major English-speaking cultures. Hayman, thus, may have cause for some consolation regarding the regrettable one-way (east–west) traffic of English and American plays and playwrights. Hall thinks "it's crazy when we share a language that American plays are not done by Americans in England and British plays not done by Britishers over there."[21]

———————

Since beginning this book a little over three years ago, I have changed my perspective on the plays of Alan Ayckbourn. I would, were I beginning this book in 1989, devote a chapter to Ayckbourn, whose mastery of form and ideas has steadily developed. He presents a contrast with other dramatists who may have peaked artistically in their early plays.

Disguised by the laughter of his early conventional farces, his social commentary darkens in later plays such as *A Chorus of Disapproval* (1986) and *A Small Family Business* (1987). In *Henceforward* (1988) Ayckbourn's devastating view of English middle-class life ingeniously fuses technology, family, and neighborhood community. A robot becomes the catalyst for the shaky solution to the personal problems of a composer, who, having made accommodation with the gang that threatens him from the outside, must face his marital, parental, and artistic problems from within. Inner and outer turbulences become the catalyst for his "high-tech" art.

Still entertaining in its wit and situational complications, *Hence-*

forth is a futuristic play, daring and convincing in the interaction of technology with humanity. Having endured a dubious distinction as the British Neil Simon, then, later, as a dramatist of the "theater of embarrassment," Ayckbourn has shed both descriptions in his most recent experiment, as yet unlabeled.

CHRONOLOGY

war; beginning of tensions that dominate second half of twentieth century. United States launches President Harry S Truman's Marshall Plan to rebuild economies of Western Europe.

1948		Israeli state is created. Mahatma Gandhi is assassinated.
1950	George Bernard Shaw dies.	Korean War begins.
1953	Beckett's *En attendant Godot* staged at Thèâtre de Babylone, Paris.	
1955	*Waiting for Godot* staged at Arts Theatre. English Stage Company is formed with George Devine as artistic director and Royal Court Theatre as its home.	Twenty-nine Asian/African nations meet in Bandung, Indonesia, to call for the end of colonialism; beginning of fragmented world power structure. Election of Conservatives and start of their nine years in power in Great Britain (Winston Churchill, Anthony Eden, Harold Macmillan, and Alec Douglas-Home).
1956	Osborne's *Look Back in Anger,* the English Stage Company's third production, staged at Royal Court. Brecht's *Der Kaukasische Kreidekreis* (*The Caucasian Chalk Circle*) and *Mutter Courage* (*Mother Courage and*	Decades of Middle East problems are inaugurated with the Suez Crisis, in which U.S. and Soviet policies coincide and oppose those of Great Britain and France. Soviet Secretary Nikita Khrushchev calls for "peaceful co-

Her Children) staged by the Berlin Ensemble at Palace Theatre. Behan's *Quare Fellow* staged at Littlewood's Stratford East Theatre.

existence"; Soviet army invades Hungary.

1957 Osborne's *Entertainer* staged at Royal Court; Becket's *Fin de Partie* staged at Royal Court.

1958 Pinter's *Birthday Party* staged at Lyric Theatre, Hammersmith; Beckett's *Krapp's Last Tape* (with *Endgame*) staged at Royal Court; Simpson's *Resounding Tinkle* and *The Hole* staged at Royal Court; Delaney's *Taste of Honey* and Behan's *Hostage* staged at Stratford East.

1959 Wesker's *Kitchen* staged at Royal Court; Simpson's *One Way Pendulum* staged at Royal Court; Arden's *Sergeant Musgrave's Dance* staged at Royal Court. The Mermaid opens in London, the city's first new postwar theater.

Cuban revolution brings Fidel Castro to power.

1960 The Aldwych Theatre opens, the London home of the Royal Shakespeare Theatre, under the direction of Peter Hall. Pinter's *Caretaker* staged at the Duchess and

U.S. President Dwight D. Eisenhower aborts trip to Soviet Union as a result of the U.S. U-2 reconnaisance plane shot down over Russia. John F. Kennedy elected

Arts Theatres and his *The Room* and *The Dumb Waiter* staged at Hampstead Theatre Club. Wesker's trilogy *Chicken Soup with Barley, Roots,* and *I'm Talking about Jerusalem* staged at Royal Court. Bolt's *Man for All Seasons* staged at Globe Theatre.

president of the United States.

1961   Queen Elizabeth II rechristens Shakespeare Memorial Theatre as the Royal Shakespeare Company. Whiting's *The Devils* staged at Aldwych.

Former President Eisenhower warns of unwarranted influence by the military-industrial complex.

1962   The Chichester, the first new theater in Britain built with a thrust stage, opens with Laurence Olivier as artistic director. Wesker's *Chips with Everything* staged at Royal Court and Vaudeville; Jellicoe's *Knack* staged at Royal Court; Rudkin's *Afore Night Come* performed at Arts Theatre, the RSC's experimental stage.

Cuban missile crisis.

1963   Littlewood's *Oh, What a Lovely War!* staged at Stratford East. National Theatre at the Old Vic opens with *Hamlet,* directed by Olivier. Traverse Theatre opens in Edinburgh. *Next Time I'll Sing to You* staged at the Arts Theatre.

President Kennedy is assassinated and succeeded by Vice President Lyndon B. Johnson; United States builds up forces in Vietnam.

1964   Osborne's *Inadmissible Evidence* staged at Royal Court; Orton's *Entertaining Mr. Sloane* staged at Arts Theatre; Peter Shaffer's *Royal Hunt of the Sun* staged at Old Vic; Livings's *Eh!* staged at Aldwych; Arden's *Armstrong's Last Goodnight* staged at Glasgow's Citizens' Theatre.

Labour Party (Harold Wilson) elected in Great Britain.

1965   Pinter's *Homecoming* staged at Aldwych; Bond's *Saved* staged at Royal Court; Osborne's *A Patriot for Me* staged at Royal Court; Stoppard's *Rosencrantz and Guildenstern Are Dead* staged at Cranston Street Hall, Edinburgh.

1967   *Rosencrantz and Guildenstern Are Dead* staged at Old Vic; Storey's *Restoration of Arnold Middleton* staged at Royal Court; Nichols's *Day in the Death of Joe Egg* staged at Comedy Theatre; Ayckbourn's *Relatively Speaking* staged at Duke of York Theatre.

Blacks riot in United States; a second Israeli–Palestinian war breaks out and Israel occupies Palestine, intensifying refugee problems.

1968   Trevor Nunn appointed to succeed Peter Hall as RSC director. Open Space Theatre, Arts Lab, Portable Theatre, Inter-Action, Theatre Up-

Great Britain: hated censorship law repealed; France: Anti-de Gaullist student demonstrations; United States: Martin Luther King and Rob-

stairs, Ambiance, and numerous other small fringe theater groups open. Terson's *Apprentices* staged at Jeanetta Cochrane Theatre.

ert F. Kennedy assassinated, Tet offensive escalates war in Vietnam and heightens antiwar demonstrations. Soviet Union invades Czechoslovakia. International mavericks emerge: France's Charles de Gaulle, Rumania's Nicolae Ceausescu, China's Mao Tse Tung. Richard M. Nixon elected U.S. president, using "detente" with the Soviets and People's Republic of China as his slogan.

1969   Nichols's *National Health* staged at Old Vic. Edward Bond season at Royal Court with stagings of *Narrow Road to the Deep North, Early Morning,* and *Saved.* Storey's *In Celebration* and *The Contractor* staged at Royal Court; Barnes's *Ruling Class* staged at Piccadilly Theatre; Orton's *What the Butler Saw* staged at Queen's Theatre.

1970   Storey's *Home* staged at Royal Court; Hampton's *The Philanthropist* staged at Royal Court; Mercer's *After Haggerty* staged at Aldwych; Hare's *Slag* staged at Hampstead.

Conservatives (Edward Heath) elected in Great Britain.

1971   Storey's *Changing Room* staged at Royal Court;

People's Republic of China replaces Taiwan on the

Gray's *Butley* staged at Criterion; *Lay By* staged at Royal Court; Nichols's *Forget-Me-Not-Lane* staged at Greenwich Theatre.

United States Security Council.

1972 Pinter's *Old Times* staged at Aldwych; Stoppard's *Jumpers* staged at Old Vic; Arden's *Island of the Mighty* staged at Aldwych.

United States and Soviets sign SALT I treaty on limitation of nuclear arms. President Nixon reelected.

1973 Ayckbourn's *Norman Conquests* staged at Library Theatre, Scarborough; Griffiths's *Party* and Shaffer's *Equus* staged at Old Vic; *Savages* and Brenton's *Magnificence* staged at Royal Court.

Covent Garden gala marks Britain's European Economic Community entry.

1974 Stoppard's *Travesties* staged at Aldwych; Hare's *Knuckles* staged at Comedy; Rudkin's *Ashes* staged at Open Space.

Labour Party (Harold Wilson and James Callaghan) elected in Great Britain. Nixon resigns as a result of Watergate scandal and is succeeded by Vice President Gerald Ford.

1975 Griffiths's *Comedians* staged at Old Vic; Pinter's *No Man's Land* staged at Old Vic; Hare's *Teeth 'n Smiles* and Barker's *Stripwell* staged at Royal Court.

Margaret Thatcher elected Tory leader with a huge majority. Turkey invades Cyprus. North Vietnamese drive out American forces to bring an end to the U.S. war in Indochina.

1976 Queen Elizabeth II officially opens National Theatre on

Labour Prime Minister Wilson resigns. Jimmy Carter,

London's South Bank where these plays are staged: Beckett's *Happy Days* (with Dame Peggy Ashcroft) at the Lyttleton; Marlowe's *Tamburlaine the Great* (with Albert Finney) at the Olivier; Ken Campbell and Chris Langham's epic show *Illuminatus!* (by the Science Fiction Theatre of Liverpool) at the Cottesloe. Edgar's *Destiny* staged at Other Place; Hare's *Plenty* staged at Lyttleton; Gems's *Dusa, Fish, Stas and Vi* staged at the Hampstead. Brenton's *Weapons of Happiness* is the first new play staged at the Lyttelton.

"human rights" advocate, elected U.S. president.

1977 Nichols's *Privates on Parade* staged at Aldwych.

1978 Hare's *Plenty* staged at Lyttleton; Pinter's *Betrayal* staged at Lyttleton; Stoppard's *Night and Day* staged at Phoenix and his *Every Good Boy Deserves Favour* staged at Festival Hall; Gems's *Piaf* staged at Other Place.

1979 Workers strike at the National Theatre.

Rail strikes in Britain. President Carter promulgates Camp David accords between Israel and Egypt.

Shah of Iran (and Western influence) is overthrown in religious revolution; Americans in Iran are taken hostage, marking the start of hostage-taking as a new means of guerrilla warfare. Soviet troops enter Afghanistan and America offers aid to rebels, creating another East-West confrontation. Conservatives (under Thatcher, Britain's longest serving twentieth-century prime minister) elected: Thatcher initiates industry privatization and begins national financial recovery, which culminates in the "Big Bang" and creates a two-tier society of haves and have-nots. The U.S. Congress fails to ratify Carter's SALT II treaty.

1980   Edgar's *Nicholas Nickleby* adaptation staged at Aldwych.

Ronald Reagan elected U.S. president, ushering in his "Evil Empire" version of the cold war. Reagan spearheads efforts to install American nuclear missiles in Western Europe, prompting antinuclear demonstrations, particularly by women at England's Greenham Common.

1981

Upheaval by Poland's Solidarity union.

1982	London's RSC officially moves from the Aldwych to the new Barbican complex in The City, marking this debut with *Henry IV* (with Joss Ackland as Falstaff).	Britain invades the Falkland Islands. Israel invades Lebanon.
1983		United States invades Grenada. President Reagan proposes Strategic Defense Initiative ("star wars"). Nearly 250 U.S. marines killed in Lebanon bombing. Mikhail Gorbachev assumes secretaryship of the Soviet Communist party. Yearlong miners' strike in Britain fails.
1987	Ayckbourn's *A Small Family Business* staged at the Olivier. Terry Hands replaces Trevor Nunn as RSC director.	Reagan Iran-contra scandal exposed, in which funds from covert arms sales to Iran were diverted to fund the Nicaraguan contras. Wall Street market crashes 19 October.
1988	Richard Eyre replaces Peter Hall as National Theatre director.	United States and Soviet Union sign first nuclear reduction pact. Reagan and Gorbachev meet for the fourth summit, part of an exchange of visits in Washington and Moscow. Gorbachev initiates the period of *glasnost* and *perestroika*.

NOTES

CHAPTER I: INTRODUCTION: NEW FREEDOMS

1. Arnold P. Hinchliffe, *Harold Pinter,* rev. ed. (Boston: Twayne Publishers, 1981), 13.

2. Allardyce Nicoll, *English Drama: A Modern Viewpoint* (New York: Barnes & Noble, 1968), 126.

3. Quoted in Arnold P. Hinchliffe, *British Theatre, 1950–1970* (Totowa, N.J.: Rowman & Littlefield, 1974), 45.

4. Nicoll, *English Drama,* 149.

5. Simon Trussler, ed., *New Theatre Voices of the Seventies* (London: Eyre Methuen, 1981), 158.

6. Ibid., 111.

7. Ibid., 91.

8. Ibid., 130.

9. Ibid., 133.

10. Quoted in Hinchliffe, *British Theatre,* 57.

11. Philip Barnes, *A Companion to Post-War British Theatre* (London: Croom Helm, 1986), 15.

12. Martin Esslin, *The Theatre of the Absurd* (Garden City, N.Y.: Doubleday, 1961), xvi.

13. Tom Stoppard, "Playwrights and Professors," *Times Literary Supplement,* 13 October 1973, 1219.

14. Kenneth Tynan, *A View of the English Stage* (St. Albans, England: Granada, 1976), 178.

15. Kenneth Tynan, "Withdrawing with Style from the Chaos," *Show People: Profiles in Entertainment* (New York: Simon & Schuster, 1979), 47.

16. Hinchliffe, *Harold Pinter,* 23.

17. Stephen Stanton, ed., *Camille and Other Plays* (New York: Hill & Wang, 1960), xii–xiii.

18. Martin Esslin, *Brecht: The Man and His Work* (Garden City, N.Y.: Doubleday, 1981), 227.

19. Martin Esslin, *Antonin Artaud* (Harmondsworth, England: Penguin, 1976), 87.

20. Ronald Hayman, *British Theatre Since 1955: A Reassessment* (Oxford: Oxford University Press, 1979), 76.

CHAPTER II: SAMUEL BECKETT: REDUCTIONIST

1. Deirdre Bair, "Samuel Beckett," in *British Dramatists Since World War II,* ed. Stanley Weintraub (Detroit: Gale Research, 1982), 2: 70.

2. Ibid., 63.

3. Ruby Cohn, *Back to Beckett* (Princeton: Princeton University Press, 1973), 130.

4. Samuel Beckett, *Waiting for Godot,* in *Seven Plays of the Modern Theater* (New York: Grove Press, 1962), 18; hereafter cited in the text as *WG.*

5. Samuel Beckett, *Endgame* (London: Faber, 1958), 12; hereafter cited in the text as *E.*

6. Bair, "Samuel Beckett," 65.

7. John Calder, ed., *Beckett at Sixty* (London: Calder & Boyars, 1967), 60.

8. Harold Pinter, "Beckett," ibid., 86.

9. Fernandel Arrabal, "In Connection with Samuel Beckett," ibid., 88.

10. Alan Schneider, "Waiting for Beckett," ibid., 52.

11. Samuel Beckett, "A Personal Chronicle," ibid., 34.

CHAPTER III: JOHN OSBORNE: AN ANGRY YOUNG MAN

1. Quoted in Anthony Lewis, "A Divided Society," *New York Times,* 5 June 1986, A27.

2. Arthur Athanason, "John Osborne," in *British Dramatists Since World War II,* ed. Weintraub, 2:372.

3. Ibid., 376.

4. John Osborne, *Look Back in Anger* (New York: Bantam, 1971), 119; hereafter cited in the text as *LBA.*

5. Quoted in Athanason, "John Osborne," 380.

6. John Osborne, *The World of Paul Slickey* (New York: Criterion, 1959), 5.

7. Quoted in Athanason, "John Osborne," 385.

8. Quoted in ibid., 388.

9. Quoted in John Russell Taylor, *The Angry Theatre* (New York: Hill and Wang, 1969), 32.

10. Ibid.

11. Ibid.

12. Ibid.

13. Ibid.

14. Ibid.

15. Tynan, *A View of the English Stage,* 176–78.

16. Quoted in John Elsom, *Post-War British Theatre* (London: Routledge and Kegan Paul, 1979), 72.

17. Ibid.

18. Ibid., 80–81.

19. Ibid., 77.

20. Ibid.

CHAPTER IV: HAROLD PINTER: MINIMALIST

1. Arnold Hinchliffe, *Harold Pinter* (Boston: Twayne Publishers, 1967), book jacket.

2. Ibid., preface.

3. Martin Esslin, *Harold Pinter: The Peopled Wound* (Garden City, N.Y.: Doubleday, 1970), 25.

4. Ibid., 50–51.

5. Ibid., 24–25.

6. Andrew Kennedy, *Six Dramatists in Search of a Language* (London: Cambridge University Press, 1975), 168.

7. Program note for *The Room,* Royal Court Theatre, 1960.

8. Harold Pinter, "Between the Lines," *Sunday Times* (London), 4 March 1962.

9. Harold Pinter, *The Birthday Party* and *The Room* (New York: Grove Press, 1961), 98; hereafter cited in the text as *BP* and *R,* respectively.

10. Esslin, *Harold Pinter,* 110.

11. Simon Trussler, *The Plays of Harold Pinter* (London: Gollancz Publishers, 1974), 89.

12. Harold Pinter, *The Caretaker* (New York: Grove Press, 1966), 60.

13. Quoted in Hinchliffe, *Harold Pinter,* rev. ed., 113.

14. Harold Pinter, *The Homecoming* (New York: Grove Press, 1966), 64.

15. Trussler, *Plays of Harold Pinter,* 134.

16. Esslin, *Harold Pinter,* 165–66.

17. Ibid., 165.

18. Harold Pinter, *Old Times* (London: Methuen, 1971), 44.

19. Walter Kerr, *Harold Pinter* (New York: Columbia University Press, 1967), 44.

20. William Baker and Stephen Tabachnick, *Harold Pinter* (Edinburgh: Oliver & Boyd, 1973), 148.

21. Trussler, *Plays of Harold Pinter,* 188.

22. James Hollis, *The Poetics of Silence* (Carbondale: Southern Illinois University Press, 1970), 128–29.

23. Lois Gordon, *Stratagems to Uncover Nakedness* (Columbia: University of Missouri Press, 1969), 62.

24. Hinchliffe, *Harold Pinter,* rev. ed., 158–59.

25. "Yours Truly," *New York Times Book Review,* 10 March 1985, 43.

CHAPTER V: TOM STOPPARD: PARODIC STYLIST

1. Ronald Hayman, *Tom Stoppard* (London: Heineman, 1977), 139.

2. T. E. Kalem, "Dance of Words," *Time,* 10 November, 1975.

3. Richard Ellmann, "The Zealots of Zurich," *Times Literary Supplement,* 12 July 1974, 744.

4. Kenneth Tynan, "Withdrawing with Style from the Chaos," in *Show People: Profiles in Entertainment* (New York: Simon & Schuster, 1979), 102.

5. Clive Barnes, review of *Jumpers,* by Tom Stoppard, *New York Times,* 23 April 1974.

6. Irving Wardle, "Cleverness with Its Back to the Wall," *Times* (London), 18 November 1982.

7. Martin Gottfried, review of *Rosencrantz and Guildenstern Are Dead, Women's Wear Daily,* 17 October 1967.

8. C. W. E. Bigsby, *Tom Stoppard* (London: Longman, 1979), 16.

9. Susan Rusinko, *Tom Stoppard* (Boston: Twayne Publishers, 1986), 1–5.

10. Kenneth Tynan, "Ambushes for the Audience: Towards a High Comedy of Ideas," *Theatre Quarterly,* May–July 1974, 3. Editorial interview with Tom Stoppard.

11. Tynan, "Withdrawing with Style," 64.

12. Tynan, "Ambushes for the Audience," 8.

13. Ibid., 6–7.

14. Tom Stoppard, "Something to Declare," *Sunday Times* (London), 25 February 1968, 47.

15. Tom Stoppard, *Jumpers* (New York: Grove Press, 1972), 28.

16. Tom Stoppard, *Travesties* (New York: Grove Press, 1975), 56; hereafter cited in the text as *T.*

17. See Rusinko, *Tom Stoppard,* 58.

18. Tom Stoppard, *Every Good Boy Deserves Favour* (New York: Grove Press, 1978), 12–13.

19. Dan Sullivan, "Writer's Block Never Stopped Stoppard," *Minneapolis Star and Tribune,* 8 June 1986, 7G.

20. Tom Stoppard, *Hapgood* (London: Faber, 1988), 48.

21. Benedict Nightingale, "The Latest from Stoppard," *New York Times,* 27 March 1988, H5.

22. Ibid.

CHAPTER VI: FANTASISTS: ABSURD, FARCICAL AND PRIMAL

1. Quoted in John Lahr, *Prick Up Your Ears* (New York: Alfred A. Knopf, 1978), 168.

2. Ibid., 169.

3. Ibid.

4. Anthony Curtis, "Professional Man and Boy," *Plays and Players* 25 (February 1978): 23.

5. N. F. Simpson, *The Hole and Other Plays and Sketches* (London: Faber & Faber, 1964), 11–12.

6. N. F. Simpson, *One Way Pendulum* (London: Faber & Faber, 1960), 92.

7. George Wellwarth, *The Theater of Protest and Paradox* (New York: New York University Press, 1967), 212.

8. Ibid., 220.

9. C. D. Zimmerman, "N. F. Simpson," in *British Dramatists Since World War II,* ed. Weintraub, 2:478.

10. Lahr, *Prick Up Your Ears,* 11.

11. Ibid., 172.

12. Quoted in Lahr, *Prick Up Your Ears,* 277.

13. Quoted in ibid.

14. Ibid., 259–60.

15. Ibid., 260.

16. Quoted in ibid., 131.

17. Quoted in ibid., 129.

18. Quoted in ibid., 168.

19. Joe Orton, *Loot* (London: Methuen, 1968), 47.

20. Frank Rich, review of *Loot,* by Joe Orton, *New York Times,* 19 February 1986, C15.

21. John Simon, review of *Loot,* by Joe Orton, *New York Magazine,* 3 March 1986, 135.

22. Ibid.

23. Joe Orton, *The Erpingham Camp* (London: Methuen, 1967), 51.

24. John Russell Taylor, *The Second Wave: British Drama for the Seventies* (London: Methuen, 1971), 136.

25. Ibid., 139.

26. Lahr, *Prick Up Your Ears,* 271.

27. Ibid., 272.

28. Ibid., 261.

29. Joe Orton, *What the Butler Saw* (London: Methuen, 1969), 91; hereafter cited in the text as *WBS*.

30. Frederick Lumley, *New Trends in Twentieth-Century Drama,* rev. ed. (New York: Oxford University Press, 1972), 319.

31. Kenneth Tynan, *Tynan: Right and Left* (New York: Athenaeum, 1968), 115.

32. Ibid.

33. Taylor, *The Angry Theatre,* 306.

34. Tynan, *Tynan: Right and Left,* 115.

35. Tom Milne, review of *Afore Night Come,* by David Rudkin, re-

printed in *New Theatre Voices of the Fifties and Sixties,* ed. Charles Marowitz, Tom Milne, and Owen Hale (London: Eyre Methuen, 1981), 237.

CHAPTER VII: NEW SOCIAL REALISTS

1. Taylor, *The Second Wave,* 21.
2. Ibid., 17.
3. Ibid., 30.
4. Benedict Nightingale, "The Birth and Slow Acceptance of Joe Egg," *New York Times,* 24 March 1985, H4.
5. Ibid.
6. Irving Wardle, review quoted on jacket of *The National Health* (London: Faber & Faber, 1970).
7. Peter Nichols, *The National Health* (London: Faber & Faber, 1970), 35.
8. Peter Nichols, *A Day in the Death of Joe Egg* (London: Faber, 1967), 44; hereinafter cited in text as J.E.
9. Nightingale, "*The Birth,*" 4.
10. Ibid.
11. Ibid., 4, 28.
12. Harold Hobson, review quoted on jacket of *Forget-Me-Not Lane* (London: Faber & Faber: 1971).
13. Frank Marcus, review quoted on jacket of *Forget-Me-Not Lane.*
14. Taylor, *The Second Wave,* 31.
15. Nichols, *Forget-Me-Not-Lane,* 31.
16. Robert Cushman, quoted on cover of *Privates on Parade* (London: Faber & Faber, 1977).
17. Mel Gussow, "Talk with David Storey, Playwright and Novelist," *New York Times Magazine,* 28 August 1977, 29.
18. Ibid.
19. Quoted in Benedict Nightingale, "David Storey: 'The Plays Simply Poured Out,' " *New York Times,* 11 November 1984, H32.
20. Quoted in Nightingale, H32.
21. Quoted in David Storey, *The Contractor* (London: Jonathan Cape, 1970), jacket.
22. Quoted in ibid.
23. Quoted in ibid.
24. Quoted in ibid.
25. Quoted in ibid.
26. Taylor, *The Second Wave,* 153.
27. David Storey, *Home* (London: Jonathan Cape, 1970), jacket.
28. David Storey, *Early Days* (Harmondsworth, England: Penguin, 1980), 52; hereafter cited in the text as *ED.*

29. Simon Gray, *Butley* (London: Methuen, 1971), 55.

30. Nicholas de Jongh, review of *Otherwise Engaged,* by Simon Gray, *Sunday Times* (London), 27 July 1975.

31. Frank Rich, review of *The Common Pursuit,* by Simon Gray, *New York Times,* 2 February 1985, 11.

32. Michiko Kakutani, "A Playwright's Journal," *New York Times,* 22 February 1986.

CHAPTER VIII: LEFTISTS

1. Harold Hobson, *Theatre in Britain: a Personal View* (Oxford: Phaidon Press, 1984), 212.

2. Ibid., 223.

3. Ibid., 200.

4. Trussler, ed., *New Theatre Voices,* 31; hereafter cited in text as *NTV.*

5. Taylor, *The Second Wave,* 91.

6. Quoted in Philip Barnes, *A Companion,* 25.

7. Hobson, *Theatre in Britain,* 214.

8. Barnes, *A Companion,* 264.

9. John Arden, *Sergeant Musgrave's Dance* (New York: Grove, 1960), 90; hereafter cited in the text as *SMD.*

10. Barnes, *A Companion,* 16.

11. Stanley Lourdeaux, "John Arden," in *British Dramatists since World War II,* ed. Weintraub, 1:13.

12. Barnes, *A Companion,* 18.

13. Ibid.

14. Rodelle Weintraub, "Pam Gems," in *British Dramatists since World War II,* ed. Weintraub, 2:194–95.

15. Taylor, *The Angry Theatre,* 78.

16. Ibid., 80.

17. Lumley, *New Trends,* 316.

18. Erica Weintraub, "Caryl Churchill," in *British Dramatists since World War II,* ed. Weintraub, 2:123.

19. Ibid.

CHAPTER IX: WORKING-CLASS WRITERS

1. Quoted in T. F. Evans, "Arnold Wesker," in *British Dramatists since World War II,* ed. Weintraub, 2:549.

2. Arnold Wesker, *The Wesker Trilogy* (London: Penguin, 1967), 76; hereafter cited in the text as *WT.*

3. Tynan, *Tynan: Right and Left,* 35–36.

4. Kenneth Tynan, *A View of the English Stage,* 295.

5. Ibid., 296.

6. Ibid., 299.

7. John Russell Taylor, *Anger and After* (1962; rev. reprint, London: Methuen, 1978), 172.

8. Quoted in Ronald Hayman, "Joan Littlewood," in *British Dramatists since World War II,* ed. Weintraub, 1:301.

9. Quoted in ibid., 300.

10. Ibid., 304.

11. Ibid.

12. Quoted in ibid.

13. David-Pryce Jones, "The Guv and His Gilded Cage," *Times Literary Supplement,* 29 June 1984, 719.

14. Interview, Trussler, ed., *New Theatre Voices,* 51.

15. Taylor, *Anger and After,* 134.

16. Ibid., 136.

17. Ibid., 137.

18. Ibid.

19. Barnes, *A Companion,* 242.

20. Taylor, *The Second Wave,* 114.

21. Taylor, *Anger and After,* 318.

22. Taylor, *The Second Wave,* 41.

23. David Mercer, *Flint* (London: Methuen, 1970), 66.

24. Interview, Trussler, ed., *New Theatre Voices,* 57.

25. Ibid.

26. Allardyce Nicoll, *English Drama: A Modern Viewpoint* (New York: Barnes and Noble, 1968), 138.

27. Quoted in Michael Weimer, "Henry Livings," in *British Dramatists since World War II,* ed. Weintraub, 1:306.

28. Henry Livings, *Stop It, Whoever You Are* (Harmondsworth: Penguin, 1962), 78.

29. Quoted in Weimer, "Henry Livings," 307.

30. Henry Livings, *Eh?* (New York: Hill and Wang, 1965), 30.

31. Henry Livings, *Kelley's Eye* (New York: Hill and Wang, 1964), 61.

32. Barnes, *A Companion,* 142.

CHAPTER X: TRADITIONALISTS

1. Taylor, *The Second Wave,* 161–62.

2. Guido Almansi, "Victims of Circumstance," in *Modern British Dramatists,* ed. John Russell Taylor (Englewood Cliffs, N.J.: Prentice-Hall, 1984), 119.

3. Ibid., 112–13.

4. Frank Rich, "Stage: In London *Fashion, Melon,* and *Family Business,*" *New York Times,* 25 June 1987, C19.

NOTES

5. Albert E. Kalson, "Alan Ayckbourn," in *British Dramatists since World War II,* ed. Weintraub, 1:18.

6. Quoted in ibid.

7. Taylor, *The Second Wave,* 159.

8. Almansi, "Victims of Circumstance," 112.

9. Quoted in Frank Rich, "British Theater's Changing of the Guard," *New York Times,* 12 July 1987, H27.

10. Rich, "Stage: In London," C19.

11. Ibid.

12. Rich, "British Theater's Changing," H27.

13. Kalson, "Alan Ayckbourn," 17.

14. Rich, "British Theater's Changing," H27.

15. Ibid.

16. Quoted in Kalson, "Alan Ayckbourn," 17.

17. Quoted in ibid.

18. Benedict Nightingale, "The Entertaining Intellect," *New York Times Magazine,* 8 December 1985, 67, 125.

19. Ibid., 125.

20. Ibid.

21. Ibid., 128.

22. Ibid.

23. John Simon, "Houses Divided," *New York Magazine,* 8 January 1986, 50.

24. Ibid.

25. Irving Wardle, review of *The Philanthropist,* by Christopher Hampton, in *Post-War British Theatre Criticism,* ed. John Elsom (London: Routledge and Kegan Paul, 1981), 198.

26. Ibid., 197.

27. Peter Lewis, review of *The Philanthropist,* in *Post-War British Theatre Criticism,* ed. Elsom, 199.

28. Nicholas de Jongh, review of *The Philanthropist,* in *Post-War British Theatre Criticism,* ed. Elsom, 200.

29. Eric Shorter, review of *The Philanthropist,* in *Post-War British Theatre Criticism,* ed. Elsom, 201.

30. Wardle, ibid., 198.

31. Quoted in Jeremy Gerard, "A Case of Seduction by the Book," *New York Times,* 26 April 1987, sec. 2, p. 1.

32. Ibid.

33. Frank Rich, "Carnal Abandon in *Liaisons Dangereuses,*" *New York Times,* 1 May 1987, C5.

34. Quoted in Barnes, *A Companion,* 109.

35. Dennis Brown, "James Saunders," in *British Dramatists since World War II,* ed. Weintraub, 2:442.

36. Ibid., 444.

37. Ibid., 447.

38. Taylor, *The Second Wave,* 199–200.

39. Warren Sylvester Smith, "Peter Shaffer," in *British Dramatists Since World War II,* ed. Weintraub, 2:459.

40. Taylor, *The Angry Theatre,* 273–74, 275.

41. Ibid., 274.

42. Barnes, *A Companion,* 226.

43. Benedict Nightingale, "Peter Shaffer Creates Another Outsider," *New York Times,* 22 December 1985, H5.

44. Ibid.

45. Barnes, *A Companion,* 226.

46. Quoted in ibid.

47. John Mortimer, *Three Plays* (London: Methuen, 1958), 10–11.

48. Taylor, *The Angry Theatre,* 258.

49. George Wellwarth, *The Theater of Protest and Paradox* (New York: New York University Press, 1967), 353.

50. Taylor, *The Angry Theatre,* 260.

51. Quoted in ibid., 259.

52. Gerald Strauss, "John Mortimer," in *British Dramatists since World War II,* ed. Weintraub, 2:348.

53. Taylor, *The Angry Theatre,* 272.

54. Ibid., 258.

55. Quoted in Deborah A. Straub, ed., *Contemporary Authors* (Detroit: Gale Research, 1987), 21:318.

56. Tynan, *Tynan: Right and Left,* 73.

57. Ibid.

58. Audrey Williamson, "John Whiting," in *British Dramatists since World War II,* ed. Weintraub, 2:564.

59. Quoted in Barnes, *A Companion,* 260.

60. Ibid.

61. Williamson, "John Whiting," 564.

62. Ibid., 562.

63. Ibid.

64. Ibid.

65. Ibid., 561.

66. T. C. Worsley, review of *Marching Song,* by John Whiting, *New Statesman,* 17 April 1954.

67. Harold Hobson, review of *Marching Song,* by John Whiting, *Sunday Times,* 11 April 1954.

68. Harold Hobson, review of *The Devils,* by John Whiting, *Sunday Times,* 26 February 1961.

69. Elsom, ed., *Post-War British Theatre Criticism,* 103.

70. Quoted in Ibid.

71. Philip Hope-Wallace, review of *The Devils,* by John Whiting, *Guardian,* 22 February 1961.

72. Robert Muller, review of *The Devils,* by John Whiting, *Daily Mail,* 21 February 1961.

73. Ibid.

74. Frederick Lumley, *New Trends,* 304.

75. Tynan, *Tynan: Right and Left,* 29.

76. Taylor, *The Angry Theatre,* 367–68.

77. D. E. S. Maxwell, *A Critical History of Modern Irish Drama, 1891–1980* (Cambridge: Cambridge University Press, 1984), 168.

CHAPTER XI: CONCLUSION

1. Barnes, *A Companion,* 183.

2. Frank Rich, "British Theater's Changing," H27.

3. "London Theater Drops Disputed Play," *New York Times,* 22 January 1987, C21.

4. Hobson, *A Companion,* 235.

5. Ibid., 236.

6. Allardyce Nicoll, *English Drama,* 153.

7. Ibid.

8. Ibid., 159.

9. Quoted in Ibid., 153.

10. Ibid., 154.

11. Quoted in Ibid., 156.

12. Ibid.

13. Ibid., 118.

14. Ibid., 148.

15. John Elsom, ed., *Post-War British Theatre* (London: Routledge & Kegan Paul, 1976; reprinted 1979), 203.

16. Ibid., 207.

17. Ronald Hayman, *British Theatre since 1955,* 129.

18. Ibid.

19. Benedict Nightingale, "This Company Speaks English and American," *New York Times,* 18 September 1988, H18.

20. Ibid., H5.

21. Ibid.

SELECTED BIBLIOGRAPHY

SECONDARY WORKS

REFERENCE GUIDES AND BIBLIOGRAPHIES

Barnes, Philip. *A Companion to Post-War British Theatre*. London: Croom Helm, 1986.

The Complete Guide to Britain's National Theatre. London: Heinemann, 1977.

British Dramatists since World War II. 2 vols. Edited by Stanley Weintraub. Detroit: Gale Research Co., 1982.

Howard, Diana. *Directory of Theatre Research and Information Sources in the UK*. London: Arts Council, 1980.

King, Kimball. *Twenty Modern British Playwrights. A Bibliography, 1956–1976*. New York: Garland, 1977.

Oxford Companion to the Theatre. 4th ed. Edited by Phyllis Hartnoll. Oxford: Oxford University Press, 1983.

SURVEYS AND GENERAL CRITICAL STUDIES

Ansorge, Peter. *Disrupting the Spectacle*. London: Pitman, 1975. A useful source on the development of the fringe theater.

Bigsby, C. W. E., editor. *Stratford-upon-avon Studies, 19: Contemporary English Drama*. London: Edward Arnold, 1981. Critical articles on selected dramatists such as Orton, Osborne, and Stoppard and on later dramatists as well.

Brown, John Russell. *Theatre Language: A Study of Arden, Osborne, Pinter and Wesker*. London: Allen Lane, 1972. An account of their plays on stage.

Elsom, John. *Post-War British Theatre*. London: Routledge & Kegan Paul, rev. 1979. An immense fund of details and trends, intelligently synthesized; valuable for those already familiar with the works and writers mentioned.

———. *Post-War British Theatre Criticism*. London: Routledge & Kegan Paul, 1981. A tastefully designed book (with fascinating drawings by Felix Topolski) of various reviews for each of about fifty important productions; a revealing immediate stage history of the period.

The Encore Reader. Edited by Charles Marowitz, Tom Milne, and Owen Hale. London: Methuen, 1965. Reprints of articles about theatrical activities of the fifties and sixties.

Esslin, Martin. *The Theatre of the Absurd*. Garden City, N.Y.: Doubleday,

1961. Remains the basic source of ideas on one of the two major trends of post–World War II drama, including British, continental, and American writers in this tradition.

——. *Brecht: The Man and His Work*. Garden City, N.Y.: Doubleday, 1961. Like the preceding entry, important for analysis of the second of the major postwar trends, the sociopolitical drama.

Gascoigne, Bamber. *Twentieth Century Drama*. New York: Barnes & Noble, 1962.

Hayman, Ronald. *British Theatre since 1955: A Reassessment*. Oxford: Oxford University Press, 1979. An incisive evaluation of the strengths and weaknesses of the new drama in terms of its style, politics, and current stasis in experimentation.

——. *Theatre and Anti-Theatre: New Movements since Beckett*. New York: Oxford University Press, 1979. A study of multinational writers and their influence (Beckett, Genet, Handke, Albee, and others).

Hinchliffe, Arnold P. *British Theatre: 1950–1970*. Totowa, N.J.: Rowman & Littlefield, 1974.

Hobson, Harold *Theatre in Britain: A Personal View*. Oxford: Phaidon, 1984. A theater memoir, impressionistically mixing favorites from both traditional and avant-garde plays and productions.

Itzin, Catherine. *Stages in the Revolution: Political Theatre in Britain*. London: Eyre Methuen, 1980.

Kennedy, Andrew. *Six Dramatists in Search of a Language*. Cambridge: Cambridge University Press, 1975. An intensive analysis of the language texture of dramas by Shaw, Eliot, Beckett, Pinter, Osborne, and Arden.

Kerensky, Oleg. *The New British Drama: Fourteen Playwrights since Osborne and Pinter*. London: Hamish Hamilton, 1977.

Kitchin, Lawrence. *Drama in the Sixties*. London: Faber, 1966.

——. *Mid-Century Drama*. London: Faber, 1960. A view of the stage in terms of new and old acting traditions and of influences such as American drama, Brecht, Beckett, Ionesco, Chekhov (Moscow Art Theatre), etc.

Lambert, J. W. *Drama in Britain, 1964–1973*. London: Longman, 1974.

Lumley, Frederick. *New Trends in Twentieth Century Drama*. New York: Oxford University Press, 1972. A historian's view of Western drama since Ibsen and Shaw, including Pirandello and Giraudoux. British drama is treated only as it falls into a large pattern of dramatic events.

Marowitz, Charles, and Simon Trussler. *Theatre at Work: Playwrights and Productions in the Modern Theatre*. New York: Hill & Wang, 1967.

Modern British Dramatists. Edited by John Russell Brown. Englewood Cliffs, N.J.: Prentice-Hall, rev. 1984. A collection of incisive analyses of individual dramatists of the First and Second Waves, such as Osborne, Pinter, Hampton, Storey, Arden, Orton, Stoppard, Hare, and Ayckbourn.

New Theatre Voices of the Fifties and Sixties. Edited by Charles Marowitz, Tom

Milne, and Owen Hale. London: Eyre Methuen, 1961. A selection of articles from *Encore* magazine—the voice of the new drama—articles by a wide-ranging group of playwrights, directors, etc.

New Theatre Voices of the Seventies: Sixteen Interviews from Theatre Quarterly—*1970–1980*. Edited by Simon Trussler. London: Eyre Methuen, 1981. A valuable compendium of interviews, mostly from the highly politicized group of Second Wave dramatists.

Nicoll, Allardyce. *English Drama: A Modern Viewpoint*. New York: Barnes & Noble, 1968. A short, yet sweeping and incisive, historical overview from earliest English plays to the "five movements" of modern drama that begin with Tom Robertson and conclude with Bond and Arden.

Peter Hall's Diaries. Edited by John Goodwin. London: Hamish Hamilton, 1983. A revelation of gossipy and sometimes self-serving tidbits from one of the movers of the Royal Shakespeare Company and the National Theatre.

Taylor, John Russell. *Anger and After*. London: Methuen, 1978. (First published in 1962 and retitled *The Angry Theatre* in the 1969 edition.) Remains the basic source for the essential nature of the events of 1956 and thereafter.

———. *The Rise and Fall of the Well-Made Play*. New York: Hill & Wang, 1967. An eminently readable survey of the dramatists of the twilight period of drama, before the First Wave broke in 1956.

———. *The Second Wave: British Dramas for the Seventies*. London: Methuen, 1971. An early survey of the dramatists who form the beginning of the Second Wave in the mid-1960s.

Trewin, John C. *Drama in Britain: 1951–1964*. London: British Council, 1975.

Tynan, Kenneth. *Tynan Right and Left*. New York: Athenaeum, 1967. A collection of wide-ranging articles and reviews of plays from England and the United States covering a ten-year period.

———. *A View of the English Stage*. St. Albans: Granada, 1976. Another collection, mostly from *Observer* reviews between 1944 and 1963.

Wellwarth, George. *The Theatre of Protest and Paradox*. New York: New York University Press, 1964. A study of the mostly European origins of avant-garde movements in the immediate post–World War II era.

Worth, Katherine J. *Revolutions in Modern English Drama*. London: Bell, 1973.

PRIMARY WORKS

JOHN ARDEN

(Asterisks indicate collaboration with his wife, Margaretta D'Arcy.)
Armstrong's Last Goodnight. London: Methuen, 1965.

The Island of the Mighty. London: Eyre Methuen, 1974.
The Non-Stop Connolly Show. London: Pluto Press, 1978.
Sergeant Musgrave's Dance. London: Methuen, 1960.
Three Plays (*The Waters of Babylon, Live Like Pigs,* and *The Happy Haven*).
    Harmondsworth: Penguin, 1964.
The Workhouse Donkey. London: Methuen, 1964; New York: Grove, 1967.

ALAN AYCKBOURN

A Chorus of Disapproval. London: Faber, 1986.
The Norman Conquests. London: Chatto & Windus, 1975.
Relatively Speaking. London: Evans, 1968; New York: French, 1968.
Sisterly Feelings and *Taking Steps*. London: Chatto & Windus, 1981.
A Small Family Business. London: Methuen, 1987.
Three Plays (*Absurd Person Singular, Absent Friends,* and *Bedroom Farce*). London: Chatto & Windus, 1977; New York: Grove, 1979.

HOWARD BARKER

Stripwell and *Claw*. London: Calder & Boyars, 1977.
Two Plays for the Right (*The Loud Boys' Life* and *Birth on a Hard Shoulder*.
    London: Calder & Boyars, 1981.

PETER BARNES

Collected Plays. London: Heinemann, 1981.
The Ruling Class. London: Heinemann, 1969.

SAMUEL BECKETT

Breath and Other Shorts (*Come and Go, Act Without Words I: A Mime for One
    Player, Act Without Words II: A Mime for Two Players,* and *From an Abandoned Work*. London: Faber, 1971.
Collected Works Of. 19 vols. New York: Grove, 1971—.
Come and Go. London: Calder & Boyars, 1967.
Endgame. London: Faber, 1958. (Originally published as *Fin de Partie*. Paris:
    Editions de Minuit, 1958.)
Footfalls. London: Faber, 1976.
Happy Days. New York: Grove, 1961; London: Faber, 1962.
Krapp's Last Tape and *Embers*. London: Faber, 1959.
Not I. London: Faber, 1973.
Play and Two Short Pieces for Radio. London: Faber, 1964.
Rockabye and Other Short Pieces. (Includes *Ohio Impromptu, All Strange Away,*
    and *A Piece of Monologue*.) New York: Grove, 1981.

Waiting for Godot. New York: Grove, 1954; London: Faber, 1956. (Originally published as *En attendant Godot*. Paris: Editions de Minuit, 1952.)

BRENDAN BEHAN

The Quare Fellow. London: Methuen, 1956; New York: Grove, 1957.
The Hostage. London: Methuen, 1956; New York: Grove, 1957.

ROBERT BOLT

Flowering Cherry. London: Heinemann, 1958.
A Man for All Seasons. London: Heinemann, 1961; New York: Random House, 1962.
State of Revolution. London: Heinemann, 1977; New York: French, 1977.

EDWARD BOND

Plays: One (*Saved, Early Morning, The Pope's Wedding*). London: Methuen, 1977.
Plays: Two (*Lear, The Sea, Narrow Road to the Deep North*). London: Methuen, 1978.

HOWARD BRENTON

Brassneck (with David Hare). London: Eyre Methuen, 1974.
The Churchill Play. London: Eyre Methuen, 1974.
Lay by (with Brian Clark, Griffiths, David Hare, Poliakoff, Hugh Stoddart, Snoo Wilson). London: Calder & Boyars, 1972.
Magnificence. London: Eyre Methuen, 1973.
Plays for the Poor (*The Saliva Milkshake, Christie in Love, Heads, The Education of Skinny Spew,* and *Gum and Goo*). London: Eyre Methuen, 1980.
Pravda (with David Hare). London: Methuen, 1985.
The Romans in Britain. London: Eyre Methuen, 1981.
Weapons of Happiness. London: Eyre Methuen, 1976.

CARYL CHURCHILL

Cloud Nine. London: Pluto Press, 1979.
Serious Money. London: Methuen, 1987.
Top Girls. London: Methuen, 1984.

SHELAGH DELANEY

A Taste of Honey. London: Methuen, 1959; New York: Grove, 1959.

SELECTED BIBLIOGRAPHY

DAVID EDGAR

Destiny. London: Eyre Methuen, 1976.
The Jail Diary of Albie Sachs. London: Collings, 1978.
Nicholas Nickleby. New York: Dramatists Play Servive, 1982.

MICHAEL FRAYN

Alphabetical Order and *Donkey's Years*. London: Eyre Methuen, 1977.
Make and Break. London: Eyre Methuen, 1980.
Benefactors. London: Methuen, 1984.
Noises Off. London: Methuen, 1982.
Wild Honey. London: Methuen, 1984.

BRIAN FRIEL

Philadelphia, Here I Come! London: Faber, 1966; New York: Farrar, Straus & Giroux, 1966.
Translations. London: Faber, 1981.

PAM GEMS

Dusa, Fish, Stas and VI. New York: Dramatists Play Service, 1977; London: French, 1978.

SIMON GRAY

Butley. London: Methuen, 1971; New York: Viking, 1972.
Close of Play and *Pig in a Poke*. London: Eyre Methuen, 1979.
The Common Pursuit. London: Methuen, 1984.
Dutch Uncle. London: Faber, 1969.
Otherwise Engaged and Other Plays. (Includes *Two Sundays* and *Plaintiffs and Defendants*.) London: Eyre Methuen; New York: Viking, 1976.
Quartermaine's Terms. London: Eyre Methuen, 1981.
Wise Child. London: Faber, 1968; New York: French, 1974.

TREVOR GRIFFITHS

The Comedians. London: Faber, 1976; New York: Grove, 1976; rev. Faber, 1979.
Lay By. (See Brenton.)
Occupations and *The Big House*. London: Calder & Boyars, 1972; London: Faber, rev. 1980 as *Occupations*.
Oi for England. London: Faber, 1982.
The Party. London: Faber, 1974.

CHRISTOPHER HAMPTON

Les Liaisons Dangereuses. London: Faber, 1976.
The Philanthropist. London: Faber, 1970; New York: French, 1971.

DAVID HARE

The Asian Plays: Fanshen, Saigon, A Map of the World. London: Faber, 1986.
The History Plays: Plenty, Knuckle, Licking Hitler. London: Faber, 1986.
Lay By. (See Brenton.)
Pravda. (See Brenton.)
Slag. London: Faber, 1971.
Teeth 'n Smiles. London: Faber, 1976.

ANN JELLICOE

The Knack. London: Encore; New York: French, 1962.
The Sport of My Mad Mother. London: Faber, rev. 1964.

HUGH LEONARD

The Au Pair Man. New York: French, 1974.
Da. Newark, Del.: Proscenium Press, 1975; rev., London: French, 1978.
The Patrick Pearse Motel. London: French, 1971.

HENRY LIVINGS

Eh? London: Methuen, 1965; New York: Hill & Wang, 1967.

DAVID MERCER

After Haggerty. London: Eyre Methuen, 1970.
Flint. London: Eyre Methuen, 1970.

JOHN MORTIMER

Collaborators. London: Eyre Methuen, 1973.
Three Plays (The Dock Brief, What Shall I Tell Caroline, I Spy). London: Elek,
    1958: New York: Grove, 1962.
Rumpole of the Bailey. Harmondsworth: Penguin, 1978.
A Voyage Round My Father. London: Methuen, 1971.

PETER NICHOLS

Born in the Gardens. London: Faber, 1980.
A Day in the Death of Joe Egg. London: Faber; New York: Grove, 1967.
Forget-Me-Not Lane. London: Faber, 1971; New York: French, 1972.
The National Health. London: Faber, 1970; New York: Grove, 1975.

Passion Play. London: Eyre Methuen, 1981.
Privates on Parade. London: Faber, 1977.

JOE ORTON

The Complete Plays (*Entertaining Mr. Sloane, Loot, What the Butler Saw,* among others). London: Eyre Methuen, 1976; New York: Grove, 1977.

JOHN OSBORNE

The Entertainer. London: Faber, 1957: New York: Criterion, 1958.
Epitaph for George Dillon. London: Faber, 1958; New York: Criterion, 1958.
Inadmissible Evidence. London: Faber, 1965; New York: Grove, 1965.
Look Back in Anger. London: Faber, 1957; New York: Criterion, 1957.
Luther. London: Faber, 1961; New York: Criterion, 1962.
A Patriot for Me. London: Faber, 1966; New York: Random House, 1970.
Plays for England: The Blood of the Bambergs and Under Plain Cover. London: Faber, 1963; New York: Criterion, 1964.
Time Present and *The Hotel in Amsterdam*. London: Faber, 1968.
Watch It Come Down. London: Faber, 1975.
West of Suez. London: Faber, 1971.
The World of Paul Slickey. London: Faber, 1959; New York: Criterion, 1961.

HAROLD PINTER

The Birthday Party and Other Plays. (Includes *The Room* and *The Dumb Waiter*.) London: Methuen, 1960; New York: Grove, 1961.
Betrayal. London: Eyre Methuen, 1978; New York: Grove, 1979.
The Caretaker. London: Methuen, 1960; New York: Grove, 1961 (with *The Dumb Waiter*).
The Collection and *The Lover*. London: Methuen, 1963.
Complete Works. 4 vols. New York: Grove, 1972, vols. 1 & 2; 1978, vol. 3; 1981, vol. 4.
Family Voices. New York: Grove, 1981.
The Homecoming. London: Methuen, 1965; New York: Grove, 1967.
Landscape and *Silence*. London: Methuen, 1969; New York: Grove, 1970.
No Man's Land. London: Eyre Methuen, 1975.
Old Times. London: Methuen, 1971; New York: Grove, 1973.
Tea Party and Other Plays. (Includes *The Basement* and *Night School*.) London: Methuen, 1967.

STEPHEN POLIAKOFF

American Days. London: Eyre Methuen, 1975.
Breaking the Silence. London: Methuen, 1985.

Lay-By. (See Brenton.)
Strawberry Fields. London: Eyre Methuen, 1977.

DAVID RUDKIN

Afore Night Come. New York: Grove, 1963.
Ashes. London: French, 1977.

ANTHONY SHAFFER

Absolution. London: Severn House, 1970.
Murderer. London: Calder & Boyars, 1976.
Sleuth. New York: Dodd, Mead, 1970; London Calder & Boyars, 1971.

PETER SHAFFER

Amadeus. London: Deutsch, 1980.
Black Comedy (includes *White Lies*). New York: Stein & Day, 1967.
The Collected Plays of Peter Shaffer. New York: Crown, 1982.
Equus. London: Deutsch, 1973.
Equus and Shrivings. New York: Athenaeum, 1974.
Five Finger Exercise. London: Hamish Hamilton, 1958; New York: Harcourt Brace, 1959.
The Private Ear and the Public Eye. London: Hamish Hamilton, 1962. New York: Stein & Day, 1964.
The Royal Hunt of the Sun. London: Hamish Hamilton, 1964; New York: Stein & Day, 1965.
The White Liars, Black Comedy. London: Hamish Hamilton, 1968.

N. F. SIMPSON

The Cresta Run. Faber & Faber, 1966; New York: Grove, 1967.
The Hole and Other Plays and Sketches (*A Resounding Tinkle, The Form, One Blast and Have Done* and *Oh*). Faber & Faber, 1964.
One Way Pendulum. London: Faber & Faber, 1960; New York: Grove, 1961.
A Resounding Tinkle. London: Faber & Faber, 1958.
Some Tall Tinkles (*We're Due in Eastbourne in Ten Minutes, The Best I Can Do by Way of a Gate-leg Table Is a Hundredweight of Coal,* and *At Least It's a Precaution against Fire*). London: Faber & Faber, 1968.

TOM STOPPARD

After Magritte. London: Faber, 1971; New York: Grove, 1972.
Albert's Bridge and *If You're Glad, I'll Be Frank.* London: Faber, 1969.
Dirty Linen and *New-Found-Land.* London: Faber, 1976; New York: Grove, 1976.

Dogg's Hamlet, Cahoot's Macbeth. London: Faber, 1979.

Enter a Free Man. London: Faber, 1968; New York: Grove, 1969.

Every Good Boy Deserves Favour and *Professional Foul*. London: Faber, 1978.

Jumpers. London: Faber, 1972; New York: Grove, 1972.

Hapgood. London: Faber, 1988.

Night and Day. London: Faber, 1978, rev. 1979.

The Real Inspector Hound. London: Faber, 1968; New York: Grove, 1969.

The Real Thing. London: Faber, 1982.

Rosencrantz and Guildenstern Are Dead. London: Faber, 1967; New York: Grove, 1967.

Travesties. London: Faber, 1975; New York: Grove, 1975.

DAVID STOREY

The Changing Room. London: Jonathan Cape, 1972; New York: Random House, 1972.

The Contractor. London: Jonathan Cape, 1970; New York: Random House, 1970.

Cromwell, London: Jonathan Cape, 1973.

The Farm. London: Jonathan Cape, 1973; New York: French, 1974.

Home. London: Jonathan Cape, 1970; New York: Random House, 1971.

In Celebration. London: Jonathan Cape, 1969; New York: Grove, 1975.

The Restoration of Arnold Middleton. London: Jonathan Cape, 1967; New York: French, 1968.

C. P. TAYLOR

And a Nightingale Sang. London: Methuen, 1981.

Good. London: Methuen, 1983.

PETER TERSON

The Apprentices. Harmondsworth: Penguin, 1970.

Zigger-Zagger and *Mooney and His Caravans*. Harmondsworth: Penguin, 1970.

ARNOLD WESKER

The Plays of Arnold Wesker. 2 vols. (Includes *Chicken Soup with Barley, Roots, I'm Talking about Jerusalem, Chips with Everything, The Four Seasons,* and others.) New York: Harper & Row, 1976.

JOHN WHITING

The Collected Plays Of John Whiting. Edited by Ronald Hayman. 2 vols. London: Heinemann, 1969; New York: Theatre Arts Books, 1969.

REFERENCE GUIDE FOR MAJOR DRAMATISTS

JOHN ARDEN

Arden on File. Compiled by Malcolm Page and Simon Trussler. London: Methuen, 1985.

Grey, Francis. *John Arden*. New York: Grove, 1982.

Hayman, Ronald. *John Arden*. London: Heinemann, 1968.

Hunt, Albert. *Arden: A Study of His Plays*. London: Eyre Methuen, 1974.

Kennedy, Andrew. *Six Dramatists in Search of a Language*. Cambridge: Cambridge University Press, 1975, 213–29.

Leeming, Glenda. *John Arden*. Edited by Ian Scott-Kilvert. Harlow, England: Longman, 1974.

ALAN AYCKBOURN

Billington, Michael. *Alan Ayckbourn*. New York: Grove, 1984.

———. "Ayckbourn is a Left-Wing Writer Using a Right-Wing Form." *Guardian*, 14 August 1974, 11.

Coveney, Michael. "Scarborough Fare," *Plays and Players*, September 1975, 15–19.

Ian Watson. *Alan Ayckbourn: Bibliography, Biography, Playography*. Theatre Checklist, no. 21. London: T. Q. Publications, 1980.

———. *Conversations with Ayckbourn*. London: Macdonald Futura, 1981.

White, Sidney Howard. *Alan Ayckbourn*. Boston: Twayne, 1984.

HOWARD BARKER

Itzin, Catherine. *Stages in the Revolution: Political Theatre in Britain since 1968*. London: Eyre Methuen, 1980, 249–58.

PETER BARNES

Dukore, Bernard F. *The Theatre of Peter Barnes*. London: Heinemann, 1981.

"Liberating Laughter" (interview). *Plays and Players*, no. 25, March 1978, 14–17.

SAMUEL BECKETT

As No Other Dare Fail: Festschrift for Samuel Beckett. Edited by John Calder. New York: Riverrun, 1986.

Bair, Deirdre. *Samuel Beckett: A Biography*. New York: Harcourt Brace Jovanovich, 1978.

Beckett at Eighty: Beckett in Context. Edited by Enoch Brater. Oxford: Oxford University Press, 1986.

SELECTED BIBLIOGRAPHY

Beckett at Sixty. Introduction by John Calder. London: Calder & Boyars, 1967.
Cohn, Ruby. *Back to Beckett.* Princeton: Princeton University Press, 1973.
Davis, Robin. *Samuel Beckett: Checklist and Index of His Published Works.* Stirling, Scotland: privately published, 1979.
Fletcher, Beryl, and others. *A Student's Guide to the Plays of Samuel Beckett.* London: Faber, 1978.
Fletcher, John. *Samuel Beckett's Art.* London: Chatto & Windus, 1967.
————and John Spurling. *Beckett: A Study of His Plays.* New York: Hill & Wang, 1972.
Kenner, Hugh. *Samuel Beckett: A Critical Study.* London: Calder & Boyars, 1962.
————. *A Reader's Guide to Samuel Beckett.* London: Thames & Hudson, 1973.
Tindall, William York. *Samuel Beckett.* New York: Columbia University Press, 1964.

BRENDAN BEHAN

Boyle, Ted. *Brendan Behan.* New York: Twayne, 1969.
Kearney, Colbert. *The Writings of Brendan Behan.* New York: St. Martin's, 1977.
Mikhail, E. H. *Brendan Behan: An Annotated Bibliography of Criticism.* Totowa: N.J.: Barnes & Noble, 1980.
McCann, Sean, editor. *The World of Brendan Behan.* New York: Twayne, 1966.

ROBERT BOLT

"English Theatre Today: The Importance of Shape." *International Theatre Annual,* vol. 3. Edited by Harold Hobson. London: Calder & Boyars, 1958, 140–45.
Emerson, Sally. "Playing the Game: Robert Bolt and William Douglas Home." *Plays and Players* 24 (June 1977): 10–15.
Hayman, Ronald. *Robert Bolt.* London: Heinemann, 1969.
Pree, Barry. "Robert Bolt." In *Behind the Scenes: Theater and Film Interviews, Transatlantic Review.* New York: Holt, Rinehart & Winston, 1971, 199–204.

EDWARD BOND

Bond on File. Compiled by Philip Roberts and Simon Trussler. London: Methuen, 1985.
Coult, Tony. *The Plays of Edward Bond.* London: Methuen, 1977.
"Edward Bond: An Interview by Giles Gordon." *Transatlantic Review* 22 (Autumn 1966): 7–15.

Calder, John, Harold Hobson, Jane Howell, and Irving Wardle. "A Discussion with Edward Bond. *Gambit* 5, no. 17 (1970): 5–38.
Hay, Malcolm, and Philip Roberts. *Bond: A Study of His Plays*. London: Methuen, 1980.
Trussler, Simon. *Edward Bond*. Harlow, England: Longman, 1976.

HOWARD BRENTON

Bond, Edward. "The Romans and the Establishment's Fig Leaf." *Theater* 12 (Spring 1981): 39–42.
Kerensky, Oleg. *The New British Drama*. New York: Taplinger, 1977, 206–25.
Merchant, Paul. "The Theatre Poems of Bertholt Brecht, Edward Bond and Howard Brenton." *Theatre Quarterly* 9 (Summer 1979): 49–51.
Itzin, Catherine, and Simon Trussler. "Petrol Bombs Through the Proscenium Arch" (interview). *Theatre Quarterly* 5 (March 1975): 4–20.

SHELAGH DELANEY

Armstrong, W. A., editor. *Experimental Drama*. London: Faber & Faber, 1960, 186–203.
Taylor, John Russell. *Anger and After*. London: Methuen, 1962, 109–18.
Wellwarth, George. *The Theatre of Protest and Paradox*. New York: New York University Press, 1964, 250–53.

DAVID EDGAR

"A Drama of Dynamic Ambiguities" (interview). *New Theatre Voices of the Seventies*. Edited by Simon Trussler. London: Eyre Methuen, 1981, 156–71.
Hayman, Ronald. *British Theatre since 1955*. Oxford: Oxford University Press, 1979, 107–13.
Itzin, Catherine. *Stages in the Revolution: Political Theatre in Britain since 1968*. London: Eyre Methuen, 1980.
New Theatre Voices of the Seventies. Edited by Simon Trussler. Introduction by Martin Esslin. London: Eyre Methuen, 1981, 157–72,

MICHAEL FRAYN

Jack, Ian. "Frayn, Philosopher of the Suburbs." *Sunday Times,* 13 April 1975, 43.
"Playwrights on Parade." *Sunday Times Magazine,* 26 November 1978, 71.

BRIAN FRIEL

Hogan, Robert. *After the Irish Renaissance: A Critical History of the Irish Drama since "The Plough and the Stars."* Minneapolis: University of Minnesota Press, 1967, 195–97.

Maxwell, D. E. S. *Brian Friel*. Lewisburg, Pa.: Bucknell University Press, 1973.
————. *A Critical History of Modern Irish Drama, 1891–1980*. Cambridge: Cambridge University Press, 1984, 200–12.

PAM GEMS

Itzin, Catherine. *Stages in the Revolution: Political Theatre in Britain since 1968*. London: Eyre Methuen, 1980.
Peters, Pauline. "Pam Gems, Piaf and Domesticity" (interview). *Sunday Times,* 3 February 1980, 36.
Garson, Barbara, "Piaf—Her Own Best Impersonator." *MS* 9 (May 1981): 72–74.

SIMON GRAY

Gussow, Mel. "Teaching Is My Bloody Life." *New York Times,* 9 February 1977, C12.
Kerensky, Oleg. "Laughter in Court: Alan Ayckbourn, Simon Gray, Tom Stoppard." *The New British Drama*. London: Hamish Hamilton, 1977, 132–44.
Taylor, John Russell. "Three Farceurs." *The Second Wave*. London: Methuen, 1971, 169–71.

TREVOR GRIFFITHS

Ansorge, Peter. *Disrupting the Spectacle*. London: Pitman, 1975, 63–66.
Hay, Malcolm. "Theatre Checklist No. 9: Trevor Griffiths." *Theatrefacts* 3, no. 1 (1976): 2–8, 36.
Hunt, Albert. "A Theatre of Ideas." *New Society,* 16 January 1975, 138–40.
Itzin, Catherine, and Simon Trussler. "Transforming the Husk of Capitalism" (interview). *Theatre Quarterly* 6 (Summer 1976): 25–46.

CHRISTOPHER HAMPTON

"Hampton on His Early Plays" (interview). *Theatre Quarterly* 3 (October–December 1973): 62–67.
Hennessy, Brendan. "Christopher Hampton Interviewed by Brendan Hennessy." *Transatlantic Review* 31 (Winter 1968–1969): 90–96.

DAVID HARE

Ansorge, Peter. "Underground Explorations No. 1: Portable Playwrights." *Plays and Players* 19 February 1972.
Trussler, Simon, editor. "David Hare" (interview). *New Theatre Voices of the Seventies*. London: Eyre Methuen, 1981, 110–20.

Itzin, Catherine. *Stages in the Revolution*. London: Eyre Methuen, 1980.
Peter, John. "Meet the Wild Bunch." *Sunday Times,* 11 July 1976, 31.

ANN JELLICOE

Findlater, Richard, editor. *At The Royal Court: 25 Years of the English Stage Company*. New York: Grove, 1982.
Rubens, Robert. "Ann Jellicoe" (interview). *Transatlantic Review* 12 (Spring 1963): 27–34.
Taylor, John Russell. *The Angry Theatre*. New York: Hill & Wang, 1962, 64–71.

JOHN KEANE

Feehan, John M., editor. *Fifty Years Young: A Tribute to John B. Keane*. Dublin: Mercier Press, 1979.
Maxwell, D. E. S. *A Critical History of Modern Irish Drama, 1890–1980*. Cambridge: Cambridge University Press, 1984, 168–70.

BERNARD KOPS

Cohn, Ruby. *Modern Shakespeare Offshoots*. Princeton: Princeton University Press, 1975, 190–94.

HUGH LEONARD

Maxwell, D. E. S. *A Critical History of Modern Irish Drama, 1890–1980*. Cambridge: Cambridge University Press, 1984, 175–78.
Taylor, John Russell. *The Angry Theatre* (rev). New York: Hill & Wang, 1969, 119–23.

HENRY LIVINGS

Giannetti, Louis D. "Henry Livings: A Neglected Voice in the New Drama." *Modern Drama* 12 (1969): 38–48.
Taylor, John Russell. *The Angry Theatre*. New York: Hill & Wang, 1969, 286–300.
Thomson, Peter. "Henry Livings and the Accessible Theatre." *Western Popular Theatre*. Edited by David Mayer and Kenneth Richards. London: Methuen, 1977, 187–202.

DAVID MERCER

"Birth of a Playwrighting Man" (interview). *Theatre Quarterly* 3 (January-March 1973): 43–57.

SELECTED BIBLIOGRAPHY

Jarman, Francis, editor. *The Quality of Mercer: Bibliography of Writings by and about the Playwright Mercer.* Brighton: Smoothie Publications, 1974.

Taylor, John Russell. *The Second Wave.* New York: Hill & Wang, 1971, 36–58.

JOHN MORTIMER

Hayman, Ronald. *British Theatre since 1955: A Reassessment.* Oxford: Oxford University Press, 1979.

Morley, Sheridan. "Brisk Business at the Bar." London *Times,* 4 January 1982.

Strauss, Gerald. 'John Mortimer." In *British Dramatists since World War II,* vol. 1, pt. 2, 341–50. Detroit: Gale Research, 1982.

PETER NICHOLS

Barnes, Philip. *A Companion to Post-War British Theatre,* 165–67. Breckenham, England: Croom Helm, 1986.

Brater, Enoch. "Peter Nichols." In *British Dramatists since World War II,* vol. 13, pt. 2, 354–64. Detroit: Gale Research, 1982.

Kerensky, Oleg. *The New British Drama,* 59–77. London: Hamish Hamilton, 1977.

Taylor, John Russell. "Peter Nichols." In *The Second Wave: British Drama for the Seventies,* 16–35. London: Methuen, 1971.

JOE ORTON

Lahr, John. *Prick up Your Ears: The Biography of Joe Orton.* London: Allen Lane, 1978.

Gordon, Giles. "Joe Orton" (interview). *Transatlantic Review* 24 (Spring 1967): 93–100.

JOHN OSBORNE

Banham, Martin. *Osborne.* Edinburgh and London: Oliver & Boyd, 1969.

Carter, Alan. *John Osborne.* Edinburgh and London: Oliver & Boyd, 1969.

Hayman, Ronald. *John Osborne.* London: Heinemann, 1968.

Hinchliffe, Arnold. *John Osborne.* Boston: Twayne, 1984.

John Osborne Reference Guide. Boston: G.K. Hall, 1977.

Trussler, Simon. *The Plays of John Osborne: An Assessment.* London: Gollancz, 1969.

HAROLD PINTER

Baker, Ely, and Stephen Tabachnick. *Harold Pinter.* New York: Harper & Row, 1973.

Diamond, Elin. *Pinter's Comic Play.* Lewisburg, Pa.: Bucknell University Press, 1985.

Dukore, Bernard. *Harold Pinter*. New York: Macmillan, 1982.
Esslin, Martin. *The Peopled Wound: The Plays of Harold Pinter*. London: Methuen, 1970; rev. in 1973 as *Pinter: A Study of His Plays*.
Hayman, Ronald. *Harold Pinter*. London: Heinemann, 1969.
Hinchliffe, Arnold. *Harold Pinter*. New York: Twayne, 1967; rev. 1981.
Imhof, Roger. "Pinter: A Bibliography." *Theatre Quarterly*, 1975; rev. 1976.
Quigley, Austin. *The Pinter Problem*. Princeton: Princeton University Press, 1975.
Trussler, Simon. *The Plays of Harold Pinter: An Assessment*. London: Gollancz, 1973.

STEPHEN POLIAKOFF

Hayman, Ronald. *British Theatre since 1955*. Oxford: Oxford University Press, 1979, 118–25.
Kerensky, Oleg. *The New British Drama*. London: Hamish Hamilton, 1977, 245–68.

DAVID RUDKIN

Milne, Tom. Review of *Afore Night Come*. Reprinted in *New Theatre Voices of the Fifties and Sixties*. Edited by Charles Marowitz, Tom Milne, and Owen Hale. London: Eyre Methuen, 1981, 237.
Salmon, Eric. "David Rudkin." *British Dramatists since World War II*. Vol. 13, no. 2. Edited by Stanley Weintraub. Detroit: Gale Research, 1982, 433–39.

JAMES SAUNDERS

Brown, Dennis. "James Saunders." *British Dramatists since World War II*. Vol. 13, no. 2. Edited by Stanley Weintraub. Detroit: Gale Research 1982, 440–44.

ANTHONY SHAFFER

Glenn, Jules. "Anthony and Peter Shaffer's Plays: The Influence of Twinship on Creativity." *American Image* 31 (Fall 1974): 270–92.

PETER SHAFFER

Kerr, Walter. "Waiting for an Ingenious Twist That Never Comes" (review of *Amadeus*). *New York Times*, 4 January 1981, sec. 2, p. 3.
Lawson, Wayne. *The Dramatic Hunt: A Critical Evaluation of Peter Shaffer's Plays*. Ph.D. dissertation, Ohio State University, 1974.
Taylor, John Russell. *Anger and After*. London: Eyre Methuen, 1962, 227–30.

SELECTED BIBLIOGRAPHY

N. F. SIMPSON

Dennis, Nigel. *Dramatic Essays.* London: Weidenfeld & Nicolson, 1962, 23–31.

Lumley, Frederick. *New Trends in Twentieth Century Drama.* Oxford: Oxford University Press, 1972, 305–8

Taylor, John Russell. *The Angry Theatre.* New York: Hill & Wang, 1969, 66–73.

Trussler, Simon. Interview. *Plays and Players,* November 1965, 11–12.

Wellwarth, George. *The Theatre of Protest and Paradox.* New York: New York University Press, 1964, 212–20.

Worth, Katherine. "Avant Garde at the Royal Court Theatre: John Arden and N. F. Simpson." *Experimental Drama.* Edited by W. A. Armstrong. Bell, 1963, 204–23.

TOM STOPPARD

Bigsby, C. W. E. *Tom Stoppard.* Harlow, England: Longman, 1976.

Billington, Michael. *Stoppard: The Playwright.* London: Methuen, 1987.

Brassell, Tim. *Tom Stoppard: An Assessment.* New York: St. Martin's, 1985.

Corballis, Richard. *Stoppard: The Mystery and the Clockwork.* London: Methuen, 1985.

Dean, Joan Fitzpatrick. *Tom Stoppard: Comedy as a Moral Matrix.* Columbia: University of Missouri Press, 1981.

Hayman, Ronald. *Tom Stoppard.* London: Heinemann, 1977.

Hunter, Jim. *Tom Stoppard's Plays.* New York: Grove, 1982.

Jenkins, Anthony. *The Story of Tom Stoppard.* Cambridge: Cambridge University Press, 1987.

———. *The Theatre of Tom Stoppard.* Cambridge: Cambridge University Press, forthcoming.

Londre, Felicia. *Tom Stoppard.* New York: Ungar, 1981.

Rusinko, Susan. *Tom Stoppard.* Boston: Twayne, 1986.

Sammells, Neil. *Tom Stoppard: The Artist as Critic.* New York: St. Martin's, 1987.

Whitaker, Thomas. *Tom Stoppard.* New York: Grove, 1983.

DAVID STOREY

Free, William. "The Ironic Anger of David Storey." *Modern Drama* 16 (December 1973): 307–16.

Kalson, Albert. "Insanity and the Rational Man in the Plays of David Storey." *Modern Drama* 19 (June 1976): 111–28.

Taylor, John Russell. *David Storey.* Harlow, England: Longman, 1974.

———. *The Second Wave.* London: Methuen, 1971, 108–25.

PETER TERSON

Taylor, John Russell. *The Second Wave*. London: Methuen, 1971, 108–25.

ARNOLD WESKER

Hayman, Ronald. *Arnold Wesker*. London: Heinemann, 1970.
Leeming, Gloria, and Simon Tressler. *The Plays of Arnold Wesker: An Assessment*. London: Gollancz, 1971.
Leeming, Gloria. *Wesker: The Playwright*. London: Methuen, 1982.
Ribalow, Harold. *Arnold Wesker*. New York: Twayne, 1966.

JOHN WHITING

Hayman, Ronald. *John Whiting*. London: Heinemann, 1969.
Milne, Tom. "The Hidden Face of Violence." *New Theatre Voices of the Fifties and Sixties*. Edited by Charles Marowitz, Milne, and Owen Hale. London: Eyre Methuen, 1971, 115–24.
Salmon, Eric. *The Dark Journey: John Whiting as Dramatist*. Barrie & Jenkins, 1979.
Trussler, Simon. *The Plays of John Whiting: An Assessment*. London: Gollancz, 1972.

INDEX

ABOUT THE AUTHOR

The author of books on Terence Rattigan and Tom Stoppard in Twayne's English Author Series, Susan Rusinko has published reviews and articles, particularly on modern British drama, in *Modern Drama, The Shaw Review, World Literature Today, British Dramatists since World War II, Critical Surveys,* and other reference works by Salem Press. As Professor of English at Bloomsburg University, she specializes in modern drama and conducts theater study trips to London.